Trauma, Shame,
and the Power *of* Love

TRAUMA, SHAME, *and the* POWER *of* LOVE

The Fall and Rise of a Physician Who Heals Himself

CHRISTOPHER E. PELLOSKI, MD

Author's Note
Some of the names have been changed or omitted for the sake
of confidentiality. Also, for the sake of brevity, some
conversations have been combined or condensed.

ISBN-13: 978-1-5007-5553-9

Printed in the United States

9 8 7 6 5 4 3 2 1

To my wife, for her unwavering courage,
and to my children—may their lives see more peace than mine.

I would like to thank B.V. and E.H. for believing in the story and making this book happen, the right way.

And thank you to all who unconditionally loved and supported me in my darkest hours. You kept me breathing, one breath at a time.

"Emotion, which is suffering, ceases to be suffering as soon as we form a clear and precise picture of it."

——Viktor Frankl in *Man's Search for Meaning*, quoting Benedictus de Spinoza's *Ethics*

Chapter One

IT WAS TUESDAY, JULY 16, 2013. I was away at a scientific conference at the University of Colorado, in Boulder. I had just returned
from a poster viewing session where I talked with fellow scientists and
had a few cold beers. My family was back in Columbus, preparing to
fly out to meet me the next day, after the conference wrapped up. I
was just about to sit down at my spartan dorm room's desk and edit a
manuscript I had been working on, which showcased my lab's recent
discoveries, but needed to run to the restroom first to get rid of the
excess volume that beer brings to its consumer. When I returned, I saw
that my mobile phone had some unusual texts on it. There were a few
from neighbors back home.

"Dude, what in the hell is going on at your house?"

"Is everything OK?"

And then the big one: "This is Detective Starr from the Franklin
County Police Department. Please call me as soon as possible."

I had a hunch about what this text meant. But it really couldn't be
possible. I'd barely done *that*. The people I'd read about in the news
were people with stockpiles of this shit, or they were part of far more
devious activities—part of some underground organization. I doubted
I would ever be a blip on anyone's radar. I just wasn't "that guy." This
wasn't a hobby or recreation for me, and besides, it was right there,
open and free. It *couldn't* be that.

I was already bargaining with myself.

There were no texts from my wife.

So I called the number.

"Dr. Pelloski. This is Detective Starr. Thank you for promptly calling back. Right now, we have your wife and children who are sitting on

your couch—they are OK—and our team is searching your house for all computers and digital equipment. These will be confiscated. Can you tell me why you are involved with child pornography?"

My body felt as if its entire blood volume had been instantly replaced with ice water. I had never sobered up in a fraction of a second before. My liver must have given off a heat plume that could be viewed from a spy satellite, as it metabolized all the ethanol floating around in me in an instant. I could barely speak, and neither could he. I am sure the adrenaline of a bust gets the better of even the most experienced law enforcement officers.

It was an awkward conversation, with pressured speech on one side and reluctant, soft incoherence on the other. I could not believe this was happening. My wife and kids were in the house, and had been for an hour or so, while agents looked though drawers and closets and dismantled digital cameras and external hard drives in front of them. My wife had been questioned about my activities and predilections as she was handed affidavits and search warrants and a pile of paperwork inches thick.

They had been watching me.

"The preliminary results of the scans of one of your computers, the desktop in that back room? Yeah, we were able to pull some disturbing images from them. Any reason why we are finding these on your computer?"

I couldn't even muster an excuse that sounded plausible to myself. "It was … a mistake."

"Mistake? Really? We have watched you going on there multiple times in the last six to nine months, Chris. One time—maybe that's a mistake. But c'mon, man, this is no mistake." Jesus. "We saw that you watched a video of a six-year-old girl performing oral sex on a grown man a few weeks ago."

I stammered, "I was just looking for … teen stuff… I …" I thought I could hide behind one of the most common search terms used on the Internet. An excuse that was both lame and creepy in its own right. But neither the detective nor I believed my words.

"We know what search terms you used. You were *not* looking for that. Not on that peer-to-peer network you would download—and then delete so we couldn't catch you."

"Oh no ... Oh no." I started repeating that, stuck, signaling what might be the end of constructive conversation. My head was reeling. My face was tight and numb. Suddenly, I remembered what it was like to helplessly watch everything you've worked for disappear. On a wet high school football field, I'd once watched my right foot slide away from me at an angle perpendicular to how a knee is supposed to bend, a split second before a pile of players landed on my knee, crushing it. All the hours of training and the hopes of Division I sports vanished. My adolescent world had been destroyed back then, and now that feeling was back. Only this time, it was not high school sports—it was real life. It wasn't the destruction of a dream but a nightmare of losing everything. It was not a knee but my career and family that were about to be gruesomely, excruciatingly twisted and crushed.

I could only make sounds with my vocal cords. They had no structure or meaning.

"Yes. This is a big thing. You and your wife have a lot of talking to do. She will be calling you soon, I would imagine." Another horrible call awaited. "Chris, just let me know, am I going to see any pictures of your kids involved in this or any kids that you know?"

"God, no."

"Are you sure? We found a picture of your daughter with a temporary tattoo on her belly and she is completely naked."

"I have no idea about that picture." My kids loved those tattoos. It could have been from any day they got a bath. My mind was still reeling and grasping at anything stable.

"You are sure you have never touched her? Have you ever touched any child in a sexual way?"

"Jesus, no!" These last few questions snapped me back into the moment. "God, no. I would never do that. Ever."

"OK. Did we get all of your computers?"

"No, I have my OSU work laptop here."

"OK, stay right where you are. Give me your location, and someone from the Boulder Police Department will take it from you. Do not

3

turn it on, do not delete anything, and do not modify anything. We will know if you did, and that will be considered an obstruction of justice. Do you understand?"

It took less than fifteen minutes before the officer arrived and I surrendered my laptop, something that had been connected to me for the last three and a half years.

My wife, Susan, called. I could barely hit the talk button to accept the call, and she could barely speak. Her voice was clogged and weak from crying.

"What happened? Is all of this true?"

It felt like hours before I could answer. "Yes."

"Why? Do you like this shit? Did you get off on this? Are you some God damned pervy-perve? Do you like kids like that?"

"No."

"Then why?" she started sobbing again. "Why did you do this?"

"Remember I told you a long time ago I think someone molested me or did something weird? And I mentioned something about a pool and a man?"

There was a long pause. "Yes."

"Well, I was right. And there was a whole lot more that happened. A lot. And not just the guy from the pool. Other people. Other things. And I looked at that stuff. It made me remember. The police are correct. They are right about everything."

"Why didn't you tell me?"

"I couldn't. I couldn't tell anyone. I am so sorry."

"I already talked to my dad." My wife's father is six foot four. I pissed him off twice in my lifetime, and each time I had the fear of God in my soul when he showed his anger. A man that big defending his daughter is a scary image. It matches the fury of a soldier defending his homeland. This would be the ultimate. I could not muster the words.

"What did he say?"

"He said we need to give Chris our love and support and get him through this. He needs our help."

It was like a fever breaking, when I heard that.

"I told him you once told me you thought you were molested, when he asked me if something happened to you. But you never elaborated after that.

"I will stand by you, too. But please, tell me. Be honest. Have you ever done anything to our kids? Are you aroused by kids? Tell me now. If you tell me what I want to hear and then I find out later that you lied, God help you, I will be the end of you."

"No. Good God, no."

"Then I am with you. I love you and we will fight through this."

I have been given Ritalin for suspected attention deficit disorder and Effexor for suspected generalized anxiety disorder. I have taken Motrin for fevers and arthritis. I have taken Ambien for insomnia and Flexeril for muscle spasms. I have taken all kinds of drugs for many ailments. But no drug had ever worked so quickly and expansively to reduce my symptoms as this phone call did. It was a watershed moment. The very biochemistry of my brain would be forever changed with just those words. The one-hit alteration powers of heroine or crystal meth had nothing on my wife's words.

I had finally told someone who loved me that I was abused, badly, and that I had viewed child pornography—and she still loved me afterwards. Both of the first two people to learn the full truth were going to be there for me. A massive burden was lifted. I could breathe again. And even though I faced a massive legal and public battle, I knew I was going to make it. I'd survived for over thirty years with secrets that were unknown even to me for most of that time, but had gnawed away at me, constantly, in every moment and with every breath. After that, I could surely endure whatever life was going to hand me next.

My wife returned me to the moment with more practical questions. "What are we going to do with the kids? Should we still do our vacation? Or should you come home? The kids will be devastated if we cancel the vacation. It is all they have been talking about for weeks." The plan was for my family was to fly to Denver the next day and we were to start our ten-day vacation.

Our marriage seemed always immersed in some kind of crisis. Susan's mother had died a month before our wedding, we had endless family drama on both sides, obstetrical emergencies, medical school and law school, massive debt, inhumanely long work hours. We called our relationship Winston Churchill, as he was an excellent prime minister during wartime, but terrible during the peace. Overachievers, we thrived on turmoil. This was a massive crisis, so we immediately began planning, inside our interpersonal comfort zone.

"Let me call the detective back and ask what we should do," I said. "I think we should just go ahead with it. I am sure the kids are freaked out their home was raided. We don't need to compound it and freak them out more by canceling the vacation."

"Yeah, that's what I'm thinking."

There was a pause, and then practicality returned to despair. "Chris, it was horrible. They kept saying all this sexual stuff in front of the kids, when they were asking questions and telling me stuff. I had to keep telling them to keep their voices down and to not rip things apart in front of the kids. They wouldn't let them go to the neighbors. They made them sit on the couch for two and a half hours! They are five! Neighbors kept circling the block. The police cars were everywhere—and they wouldn't leave—even when they knew it was just me and the kids here. Were they expecting a shootout? And he kept talking so loudly on his damn phone with you. Pacing up and down so everyone could hear." She was sobbing again.

"I will call him," I said in an effort to calm her.

"OK." She settled down a bit.

When I called the detective back to make sure our family could still have its vacation, it completely took him by surprise. He was a bit shocked that my wife would still want to see me and bring our children around me. I think he was also baffled by my tone. It was part shock and part the calm talking with my wife had lent me, but I might have been asking to borrow his car to run to the grocery store. He answered that these computer forensic investigations take seven to ten days to complete and that as long as I kept in contact with him or an attorney it should be OK. (Oh, yeah. I needed to find a lawyer.)

He then switched back into investigative mode: "Chris, do you masturbate to these prepubescent children getting molested?" This was the second time I'd been asked this question in fifteen minutes, and it was a harbinger of questions to come. In fact, it may have been the most popular question I was asked throughout my case.

"No. God, no. It was … gross … Like looking at a car wreck more than anything." It was strange, but it was somewhat of a relief to talk about this, even with a complete stranger who also happened to be coming after me. "You know … I have been abused like that. Before. When I was a kid." It was already getting slightly easier to say that. Slightly.

"Chris, that is unfortunately something I hear quite often, and I am sorry to hear that happened to you." His tone softened.

Our family vacation was still on.

I did a cursory search using my phone and found a criminal defense attorney online who appeared to specialize in this kind of crime: "Sexual Offenses" appeared in big bold print on his website. This was not the kind of research I was used to conducting. I left a message on his voicemail to call me in the morning (it was already around 10 p.m. in Columbus).

Then it was just me, sitting in my University of Colorado dorm room, alone with my thoughts. A few colleagues from the meeting texted me to meet for drinks, but the words appeared to me as if in a dream, as if I were reading a scroll from a whole lifetime ago, meaningless. Since my internship year, when I would sometimes stay awake for thirty-six to forty-eight hours straight (my year was the last before the eighty-hour workweek limit was established for medical residents), I'd been able to fall asleep instantly, whenever and wherever. I had never stayed awake just lying in bed. If I was up all night it was because I was pulling an all-nighter to get a report done or was on call for the surgical team or was admitting patients to the floor from the ER. Or occasionally because a night of revelry and heavy drinking gave way to the morning. But this night, I lay fully awake. My eyes remained wide open, and I felt as if I were floating, completely surrounded by the palpable pitch black of the night. There was no visual input, but my mind was racing. I was going through a list of all the many people who would be disappointed, angry, confused, and afraid. I was figuring out how I would explain myself, and which relationships would be lost.

Then there were the projects and tasks awaiting me when I returned. My research team had finally gotten the funding to get us through another year, but the October cycle of the R01 submissions was on the horizon, and preliminary data needed to be generated. The revised manuscript of my latest paper was due in mid-August; I was adding the final touches on this trip. I had six letters of recommendation for undergrads and medical students to write; they were applying for the next phases of their careers and needed those letters badly. There was my sixteen-year-old patient with a pituitary adenoma that I needed to treat with Gamma Knife radiosurgery. Another patient had a nasty loco-regional recurrence of a malignant peripheral nerve sheath tumor that required an IMRT plan that needed to be precisely matched against the previously irradiated neck to minimize the overlap and toxicity. I needed to initiate the paperwork for taking on three more residents in the upcoming match season—meaning that once again I had to coordinate with the ACGME, NMRP, our GME Office, and The James Financial Group. I was in the middle of negotiating for more lab space. I was forced to grovel, despite the millions of dollars I brought into the medical center every year from my clinical productivity…

The list went on. How was all of this going to get done? So many people were relying on me.

It was around 5 a.m. when I realized how completely warped my priorities had been—just how far my head had been lodged up my own ass. Everything had revolved around my work. *Everything*. And it had been that way since I entered college. My grandparents had died. I'd missed countless weddings, births of nieces and nephews, dinner invites with friends, and multiple serious family crises—but none of these things had ever really had the chance to sink in when they happened. I never really felt them, couldn't afford to, I was too worried they would throw me off schedule. All that was ever before me was the to-do list of the day, week, month, and year. I reasoned—either consciously or subconsciously—that if I took this kind of personal break I would never get back in the race. Invited to watch a football game on a random Sunday night I would give it the same split-second consideration I would have a high-risk long-term mission to establish a colony on Mars: No thanks!

So finally, after worrying about my work and career all night, I started seeing things differently. Perhaps the lack of sleep slowed my mind enough for clarity. Twelve hours previously, Susan and her father learned that I had viewed child pornography, after my family was subjected to a two-and-a-half-hour police raid by many men in Kevlar jackets, during which our house was ransacked while neighbors looked on, puzzled and scared. And after all that, their conclusion was to support and love me, when most would have left me in an instant. And I am worried about an *R01 grant submission*? How in the hell did I evolve into this person? How was I that disconnected?

The questions that should have instantly flooded my mind were *What are we going to do if the neighborhood turns against us and the kids start kindergarten in a month? How will bills get paid, once I lose my job? How quickly do we need to sell the house? Should we even start the kids in school? What if I go to prison or can never be a doctor again? What am I supposed to do now?*

It took me those twelve hours to surgically remove my head from my lower digestive tract. It had been there so long that a collateral cranio-rectal circulation had been established between the blood vessels of my head and ass. Those were the last twelve hours of my previously pathetic existence. My by-then-pointless perseverations about work were evidence of its last throes. Never again would I make my family second or third priority in the grand scheme of my life. At the front end of this twelve-hour patch, I cast off the burden of secrecy about my sexual abuse and my deplorable activity. At its conclusion, I liberated myself from the bondage of the all-consuming career I had shackled myself with. A significant repair and renovation happened within an instant (relative to the timescale of my life), and it came just at the right moment. Much fine-tuning remained, though.

I finally got ahold of the attorney, Benjamin Newton. It was 6:30 a.m. for me, mountain time, and 8:30 eastern back in Columbus, I was wide awake, nearing twenty-four hours of being wide awake, still in yesterday's clothes. It was a grim discussion. His voice was extremely low, and I could hear his mind start prepping for what was coming.

"I will start asking around. I know the detectives in your raid." I could hear him taking notes. I wondered how much business those detectives generated for him. "Do not talk to them anymore, by the way," he quickly advised me. "The first thing I need to do is find out if this is going to be a federal or state case. This is important; they are two *very* different ballgames. And, if it goes federal, you need someone with federal experience, which I have. Not as many criminal defense attorneys have federal experience. With your permission and pledge of retainer, I could get to work for you. Just so you know, for starters we are talking around $30,000, but it can get to be two to three times that before it's all said and done. And, I hate to say it, but you are going to be looking at some serious prison time, most likely. They are very serious about this kind of stuff these days."

"Jesus …" I took a deep breath, "Yes, you can get started." What he'd said took a while to soak in. "My family is flying out to see me today. That is the plan for now at least. The detective said it was OK to go through with it. Should we even bother?"

"If they are giving you clearance and your family still wants to see you," he seemed a bit surprised by this, "then by all means do that. Spend time with them. I will make sure that you can stay out there, but when I need you to come back, you need to move fast, cut it short, and get to Columbus. This is going to take a long time. It is going to be a freaking meat grinder, and your life will never be the same again afterwards."

My mom was next on the notification list. The conversation was gut-wrenching. At first she thought I was in trouble for *legal* porn on a work computer. "No, Mom. It was kids, young kids. It was bad, and I am in deep, serious, massive trouble."

"Jesus."

When these discussions eventually ended, I just stared at my smartphone, wondering if some hacker had installed an app on it that, once activated, made it spew forth nothing but horrible, shitty personal news.

Despite the catastrophic developments in my life, when I finally stepped outside on July 17, the morning after the raid, the sun was still low in the east, just peeking over the Rocky Mountains, and the day was absolutely beautiful. I felt very different. I had not seen my share of sunrises. I'd spent my adult life getting to work when it was still dark, or sleeping in until noon when I could, to catch up on missed sleep.

Not just the light, but everything seemed more vivid that morning. The sounds of birds singing were so clear and distinct I could almost translate their chirps into English. I smelled pine, flowers, and soil in the air. The sky was pure azure and gold. The conifer needles and deciduous leaves, all of whose taxonomy I had at one time memorized for a premed biology exam, now appeared to me as living and breathing things with the sharpest of detail in the light and a story to tell. It all reminded me of driving home from the optometrist in fifth grade in brand-new glasses and seeing for the first time that lawns were actually composed of innumerable and individual blades of green grass.

It was my third morning in Boulder, and I knew it was identical to the first two, but I'd noticed none of these things before. The beautiful scenery had been outside of the mental tunnel I walked within to and from dorm room, lecture halls, cafeteria, and beer. No doubt I was still in shock, given all that had just happened, but with shock sensations are typically blunted. What I experienced was the opposite. I felt alive, experiencing for once real-time, full sensory input from a benign environment. I was present in the moment. Merely existing and breathing actually felt kind of good. The clouds of impending doom, heavy secrets, deadlines, and nearly impossible tasks had evaporated during the night, and my eyes were beginning to adjust to the blinding light of a golden sun.

I checked out of the dorm early, and no one mentioned the visit from the police the night before. It was all smiles and thank you for staying with us. There was no drama. I could leave quietly. Good.

On my drive from Boulder to Denver, my father-in-law called me. He said I had nothing to explain and that he loved me.

Chapter Two

WITH MY FAMILY EN ROUTE to Colorado, I searched frantically for an open hotel, driving all over the Denver area and running through multiple toll roads whose cameras snapped my license plate and later billed me. The plan was to stay near the airport on the first night, but nearly all of them were full. The ones with vacancies looked like they charged by the hour or would have been a great place to score some smack. I already envisioned the rest of my life spent wearing only a burlap man-diaper and smashing rocks into pebbles under the scorching sun. I was not ready to join the World of the Condemned just yet.

The other type of hotel with available rooms was on the opposite end of the spectrum: a Four Seasons right in downtown for a king's ransom per night. What better place for my wife and me to have our first excruciating face-to-face talk than in the lap of a luxury, when we would soon be parting ways. Still, this wasn't the best start to our mandatory cost-cutting program.

When I first saw my family at the airport passenger pickup, my heart completely melted. I had never been so happy to see my wife and children. It was if their lives had been threatened but then at the very last minute they were spared, and I was given a second chance to see them again. Susan looked like a wilted flower, still beautiful, but completely drained by tears and travel. In the last twenty-four hours, she'd spent two and a half sitting through the raid, having been told her husband was a child pornography aficionado, then stayed up all night dealing with our daughter, who had lost consciousness after face-planting while running and slipping on our dining room floor. Then she spent most of the next day dragging exhausted five-year-old twins through two flights and three airports.

I remember seeing my children for the first time without the fog of anxiety and career preoccupation, and again, I was stunned at how much detail I had been missing. My son's eyes were huge as he scanned this new scene with wonder and some apprehension, looking for Daddy. His mop of red hair rotated with his gaze. My daughter looked studious in her glasses and buttoned-up sweater and was much more methodical in finding me among the pack. The poor thing had a bruise the size and shape of a hen's egg on her forehead that I could see from the car, thirty yards away. When they saw me, huge smiles lit up their faces and they pointed me out to my wife. They were probably the only two people in the entire world who would have been excited to see me at that moment. The raid had not turned them against me. They did not distrust me or harbor any anger. And they were no longer blurs of noise and distraction, armed with entropy, who would undermine my nightly attempts to carry my workday home with me. They were little, adorable creatures with tiny features I could finally notice. They had big thoughts and dreams, but still needed to hold their mother's hand for warmth, security, and assurance.

That night, my wife completely amazed me again. I was prepared to stifle or hush any yelling or crying to avoid waking the kids, but we had a talk, not a shouting match. She was not about to further traumatize our children. And so we set the tone; this is how we were going to handle the situation, to keep the kids as psychologically safe as possible. Of course, there were tears, but mostly we worked to figure out what in the hell we were going to do … about *everything*. We talked for almost three hours.

Susan was furious with me for what I did (I still await a promised massive face-punch), yet her heart was broken as I shared more details of what had happened to me as a kid. My wife's mother had had a harrowing childhood, so she was quite familiar with post-abuse psychology. She has a law degree, is brilliant (I rarely win an argument against her), and understands that issues are never black and white. These are the reasons she didn't bolt immediately, as most wives would, understandably, have done immediately after the house was tossed by the police for something I did.

She wanted to stand by me at least as a friend and the father of her children, since she viewed my presence in their lives as important to them. She didn't want her anger with me to trump the needs of our kids. She said one of the conditions of her staying was that I repair my relationships with our children, so that when I went to prison they would be able remember the good in me.

With the revelations of my childhood abuse, she finally understood why I had been so difficult to be with for significant portions of our sixteen-year marriage, despite seeing a shrink and taking meds. She understood why I had become such a powder keg lately. Her previously not knowing *all* of what had happened to me was like having the first few chapters of the Chris Pelloski instruction manual ripped out and tossed into the shredder. My increasing anger at home, drinking, and hours away at work had worn thin over the last several years. Divorce, or at least separation, had been on the horizon. But now, any changes to our marriage and relationship were going to be tabled for the moment, a discussion for later, after *this* catastrophe had some semblance of resolution.

She also told me she'd thought I wasn't going to live much longer, given the amount of work and stress I'd been dealing with. She said she'd spoken to our financial advisor about getting more life insurance on me, because she was convinced that I was going to drop dead before I turned fifty.

My next round of phone conversations was equally painful and tear-filled. The calls ran together, like one continuous, surreal nightmare. I needed to tell one of the top officials at the Ohio State University Medical Center, someone with whom I'd developed a great professional relationship, what I'd done. He'd already received a message from the authorities that I was under criminal investigation, that my laptop had been seized. IT had already locked me out of the OSU server, the morning after the raid. My chairman was devastated when I told him what happened and why. I'd been his first recruit and was helping him build great programs for the department. I asked that the people in my lab be looked after and suggested a few replacements for the residency program director.

"Chris, do not worry about *any* of this. You need to worry about you. Are you with your family?" He is someone who is normally an excellent poker player when it comes to talking—absolutely no tells. But I could feel how shaken and concerned he was, through my cell phone, from over a thousand miles away.

"Yes."

"Good. You have a lot to live for, Chris. Please do not hurt yourself. You have beautiful children to live for, and you will. I will take care of everyone here. Don't worry about your people. You have my assurances." Within hours of these discussions, I started to receive texts and phone messages from my concerned coworkers, asking why the locks were being changed on my office door and police tape strung across it. Word was spreading quickly among the top brass, as well.

The psychiatrist I'd been seeing since 2010, at the same medical center where I worked, was blindsided, too. I had always just showed up to get my Ritalin and Effexor, and told him everything was fine so that I could get the hell out of there before I was discovered in a psychiatrist's office (we can't have crazy docs running around) or before my pager went off and I was needed to see a patient or put out some other fire in our department. I always concealed my visits, even from my assistant, telling her I had a research meeting. Hospital policy dictated that my psychiatric record be kept separate from my electronic medical record, in a loose-leaf folder, locked in a file cabinet, so no one would know there was a doctor who needed to see a shrink. The message that *You are bad and defective—and no one can know about it* was certainly one of the implied messages. It was so cloak-and-dagger there was no way I was going to open up in that environment. And I certainly wasn't going to get bogged down in long discussions. There weren't enough hours in the day for my work as it was. I'd let a tooth rot away for two years after a Jolly Rancher candy ripped its crown off, and never had time to go see a dentist. I wasn't going to make time for lengthy "talk" therapy.

"Why didn't you tell me? Any of this?" his voice came through exasperated over the phone.

"I couldn't. I had so much shit I had to take care of. I didn't want to stop all of it. If the medical board caught wind that I was drinking a lot or that a pediatric radiation oncology director was looking at child pornography, it would have been over. I would have been in the same trouble I'm in now. So I kept it in. Why would I tell anyone?"

"I am your psychiatrist. You can tell me things."

"Not those things. How would I know if you would or would not tell the board? About the drinking—any of it. I just didn't want to address it, anyway. I thought it all would go away, like it did before."

"Ugh … Good God. I am so sorry, Chris. I will do what I can for you. This is a horrible sickness. You are a good person. Don't forget that. I have seen this before. You are not a bad guy. But you need to be ready. This is going to be the fight of your life."

My psychiatrist came from a family of lawyers and had been an expert witness in child pornography cases before, so he had some insight into the legal system. As soon as I told him that I blacked out sometimes when I drank, he instantly connected me with a rehab center, saying that courts are more lenient toward people with alcohol problems and that this would *help* me.

He also insisted that I call someone he felt was the best criminal attorney in town, Edward Dickins, who had thirty-plus years of experience. So I did. Dickins wanted to wait until after I was charged to meet with him, though. He had great things to say about my current attorney, Newton, so I was encouraged I was in good hands already.

Despite all the breaks for difficult phone conversations to address my impending catastrophe, I had the best vacation I'd ever had with my family. In many ways, it felt like I met them all for the first time. Previous family excursions were characterized by frequent interruptions while I pecked away at my laptop; it was always within arm's reach. This time, no laptop.

We checked out of the Four Seasons and spent the rest of our nights in Glenwood Springs, a place that historically drew those seeking the healing powers of its hot springs, including Doc Holliday. After all the hiking, crossing rivers over fallen trees, bathing in the salty hot springs, laughing, learning, teaching, exploring caves, rafting down the Colorado River, and going down the Alpine roller coaster over and over, as a whole, happy, undistracted family unit, I can vouch for the area's recuperative powers. The Ute people were definitely onto something with this special place. These were a magical five days, full of big mountains, bright sun, and so many things to discover. Sorting rocks, naming states, looking for animals, and making sure we had popcorn for family movie nights at the hotel—that was the order of the day.

I got to see how gentle my son's spirit is. He thinks of others before he thinks of himself. He always wants to include people when playing, so that no one is left out. He is so open and earnest. He will approach anyone and say, "Hey, do you want to play cars or chase?" He loves making friends.

My daughter is both fearless and scared at the same time. Ever since she was a baby, she could not wait to grow up. She is exceptionally bright, can remember everything, and can tie together very abstract concepts. She is tuned in to people's emotions and expressions. Just as I could as a child, she sensed when her parents were talking about something stressful, and would get in between Susan and me to draw our attention to her, instead. It was as if she was throwing herself on a stress grenade to spare us the anguish of whatever we were talking about. The raid, the change in our vacation plans (I was told to be back to Ohio by Monday at the latest), and our hushed conversations let her know that something was up. Nothing got by her.

Going into the weekend, I finally heard back from Newton. My case was going to be a federal one. As the web crosses state lines, most Internet crimes are federal, while most hands-on contact sexual crimes are handled by the states. A prosecutor had already picked up the case, and Newton had been in contact with her. They knew each other, and he gave her assurances that I would be compliant. I was allowed to return home and was to be charged on Wednesday, July 24. Monday night was the latest I could be away from Columbus—otherwise, federal marshals would come get me. A self-surrender had been negotiated, and he was working on having me remain on house arrest, as opposed to sitting in a county jail while my case transpired.

So once again, we were confronted with the decision of what to do with our vacation. I had driven to Colorado for the conference, and the original plan was for us all to drive back, camping along the way. Obviously that option was off the table. Fortunately, my father-in-law was able to fly out and be with my family on Sunday and help Susan with the kids on the drive back from Colorado. My children were excited about the idea of camping under the stars. So my wife kept that promise, visiting relatives in Colorado and setting up tents along a circuitous route home instead of just heading straight back to Columbus. It was another instance where we abandoned being pragmatic and financially conservative to maintain stability for our children and shield them from the nightmare. I also didn't want them around when the news broke.

I was the same age as my children when a lot of the traumas that shaped me occurred. We were not about to let that happen to them. I would return Monday night and my family would return on Thursday, the day after my charge went public. The kids would still get about three-quarters of the planned trip; the second part would just be with Grandpa, not Dad. They were going to be OK with this. We also arranged that our parents would keep the kids for a week, until we felt safe enough in our home for their return.

It was difficult saying goodbye to my family that Monday morning. Even though my early departure cut the planned vacation short, the previous five days had been a utopian existence. Life cruelly gave me a glimpse of what I could have had for my home life, right before it would be impossible to ever have it that way again. When I kissed my children on the forehead, I knew they were seeing me for the last time as the person they knew, their "doctor dad," and that when (and if) they saw me next, I would have an entirely new and sinister public image, and their lives would never be the same. My father-in-law gave me a bear hug and told me it was all going to get better—family was all that mattered.

Susan drove me to the nearest shuttle stop with the numbness of driving to a funeral, a perfect contrast to yet another bright and shiny day. I faced a four-hour shuttle ride to the Denver airport, but I was comforted knowing that a few more fun days awaited my children. Our goodbye was brief. It had to be. We would have lost our composure, and then the kids would have asked my wife what was wrong a hundred times when she returned to them. I also had to stay sharp for the trip back.

On the ride to Denver, my phone kept buzzing with texts. Residents, nurses, my assistant, the people in my lab—all were concerned and scared for me. I was being systematically removed from the Ohio State University Medical Center, as if I'd never been there, with a rapidity and efficiency that would have made any dictatorship jealous. My name was taken off of clinical trials, removed from the department's website, and erased from the office plaque. Patients on treatment were reassigned to other physicians. I told everyone it was all OK, a misunderstanding, and that things would sort themselves out.

I even posted a family picture of us hiking on Facebook to allay their fears. I was told to do this, by my attorneys, to avoid a huge wave of fear and rumors. Though, of course, on the day I was formally charged, the wave broke anyway. My mind vacillated between the terror of what was to come and the amazing moments that I'd spent with my family. They were what I needed to live for, I reminded myself, to survive and endure. Having a criminal dad who loves them is better than having no dad at all. I needed to stay strong. My family had flown from Ohio to Colorado to meet me, just a day after my actions subjected them to a raid on our home. I owed it to them to stay strong.

As usual, the giant Ohio State Comprehensive Cancer Center sign greeted me as I glided down the escalator of the Columbus airport. To my relief, no one had climbed this sign with a brush and bucket of paint to announce my arrival and the shame that I would bring to the institution. Only our immediate neighbors were privy to the two-hour police raid on my home. Since there were no police or search dogs waiting to bite my genitals off at the airport, I was convinced of the promise made by the attorneys that I would not be ambushed and taken into custody that night.

By design, I arrived in Columbus at midnight, to use the cover of summer darkness to return home. But I was certain that the neighbors were taking turns manning a tall, hastily constructed twenty-four-hour lookout tower situated above the tree line. My arrival would be signaled by the ringing of bells and an elaborate relay of bonfires that would ignite from block to block for a radius of two miles. I needed to somehow slip past the perimeter, under everyone's watchful eyes, to get back home.

Since my family had the car, I had to take a cab, which was perfect for my planned surreptitious return. My car would have been spotted on sight, or would have snagged a tripwire laid across my driveway, bringing down a pile of empty cans with a crash that would have heralded my arrival.

My driver was a very pleasant middle-aged Somali man. I had just my duffle bag and almost empty laptop case. I missed my laptop; it had attained virtual organ status for me, and now I knew it was surrounded by strangers and undergoing all kinds of invasive probes and forensic scans. I held onto my luggage and crawled into the backseat. When I told the driver my destination, he gave me an extra glance. I had dressed as inconspicuously as possible. Maybe too much so: baseball cap, T-shirt, shorts, stubble, and the look of fatigue a twelve-hour trip without eating or drinking provides. I did not have that burnished shine my neighborhood warranted, and was being called on it. "I'm visiting a friend. I've been traveling all day from Colorado."

This seemed to calm the driver's curiosity. We proceeded with taxi small talk. Columbus already felt and looked different to me, even though I had taken this path so many times. I told him that I just had the best family vacation of my life. I said the lack of email and work-related phone calls allowed me to finally just be with my family. I omitted the whole search-and-seizure and forced-paid-administrative-leave part of it, of course. "You cannot put a price on the time spent with your children. They do not stay little forever." This universal observation, brought to my attention by the driver, had been foreign to me as recently as six days before.

As we came off the freeway, I asked to be dropped off on the main road, several blocks away from my home, the destination I'd clumsily divulged at the onset. I would be a terrible spy, conducting my business so carelessly like that. Again, hesitation and a look of uncertainty appeared on the driver's face. "Are you sure? It is no problem for me to drop you off at your friend's house," he offered, as if trying to prevent a crime from happening. I explained that I liked to walk a bit before visiting, hoping he would buy it. I could tell he didn't as I caught his glance in the rearview mirror. He eyed my duffle bag as if I were clutching my tools for breaking and entering. I gave him a $10 tip on a $30 fare to buy his silence and fend off skepticism. Still, it took a while before he drove off, keeping an eye on me as I crossed the street.

It was 12:25 a.m. Perfect. I was definitely back in the Ohio River Valley and not the thin, arid Colorado atmosphere anymore. The humidity collected in an uncomfortable condensation on my clothing, which had been blasted to an unnatural chill by the cab's air conditioner. It was a nearly silent Monday night, or rather Tuesday morning. I started down the avenue. The oaks, ashes, and maples of a mature and stately neighborhood created a canopy and made the street seem like a tunnel. It looked more like a three-mile gauntlet than the three-block walk it really was. I took a deep breath and crossed into my neighborhood.

I trod the sidewalk as if hunting woodland creatures by stealth, hoping my sandals would maintain their moccasin-like silence. My computer bag was slung over my shoulder and I carried my duffle at my side. I kept my line of sight downward, with the bill of my cap concealing my eyes. I dared not look toward the windows of homes, sparing myself the sight of disappointed and furious neighbors peeking from behind the curtains, wishing that I had never come and brought this mess with me. I felt as if thousands of eyes were following my shameful progress down the street.

As I made the left turn onto my street, those reflections evaporated and my heart crawled into my mouth to beat against my gums. I started walking like an Olympic power walker. I had two more houses on each side of the street, and then I would be home. Once under the cover of our driveway tree, which shaded me from the moonlight and streetlamps, I bolted from view, hit the latch of the side gate, and almost laughed in triumph that I had made it home unscathed.

I found myself standing in the middle of our backyard patio in a moonlight that cast an eerie glow on the brick, house, and furniture, as if all were coated with a smooth layer of phosphorescent paint. The giddiness left me in an instant when, after scanning the yard, my gaze caught on the kids' play structures, silhouetted against the background of trees and shrubs. I saw their scattered toys and the plastic picnic table nestled up next to the adult-size wrought-metal table, as if trying to hold its hand. The strongest pang of guilt, shame, remorse, and sadness up to that point overtook me then. Everything was real now. My children loved their yard. They loved making up games and crushing sidewalk chalk into a fine powder, mixing it with water and creating a preschooler's version of war paint. The sparklers, the inflatable pool, kicking the soccer ball around, lying in the soft cool grass. All of this was going to be gone soon. Because of me. And their lives would never be the same. Their dad was going to be a child pornography felon. They would have to leave the neighborhood they loved. How could I ever explain this to them—now or even when they were old enough to know? I had never felt a more profound sense of failure. My eyes welled with tears, warping my vision of an otherwise serene setting. My throat felt like Clorox was clinging to its sides.

I snapped out of it before completely becoming unglued. Soon the angry mob, wielding pitchforks and torches, would come for the monster. I wiped my eyes and darted into the screened porch. I would not allow myself even to make eye contact with the porch furniture, where once upon a time I'd sat and talked and drank wine with Susan, where we'd had family dinners while it rained. I could not mourn that loss on top of the rest. I kept my face forward, on task, as I fumbled with the keys in the dark to get the house door open. Finally, with the catch and turn of the key, I was in, and let the door close quietly behind me. I took off my shoes, stood, and looked over my moonlit living room. I had just snuck into my own house for the first time since I was in high school. Only this time, I was thirty-nine years old, and my home was completely empty.

Chapter Three

WITH THE TRAVEL AND ANTICIPATORY STRESS, I was exhausted, and actually slept very well. I set my alarm so that I could finally meet Newton. Up until then, it had been a series of grim phone calls a thousand miles apart. The meeting was at 9:30 a.m., so again, the time of day was on my side for keeping my cover. The neighbors would be well into their day, with only landscapers bustling about, manicuring lawns and not giving a damn about me.

I was not ready to see anyone yet. Despite the pervasive calm I'd developed, my brain was still not impervious to the exterior world. When it came to my insides, I was at peace. When it came to the outside, I was still in shock. I miserably failed to pull quietly out of my garage and driveway. I nearly ripped off the side mirror along the edge of the garage door, scraped the bottom of my car going over the curb instead of the center of the driveway, and squealed the tires as I backed into my turn. So much for a clandestine exit. I prepared for eye contact with any neighbors drawn to all the noise I was making, which would have obliged me to respond with a sheepish wave. But my good fortune persisted and I was spared this humiliation.

At this point, I had told my full story to my wife, in-laws, parents, the department chairman and OSU medical director, and my psychiatrist. Each time got a little easier, but there were still plenty of tears left in the tank. So, of course, I lost my composure when telling my story to my attorney. Newton was a good guy, very sympathetic to my story. I could see in his face that he was used to this, in much the way I had become accustomed cancer patients and/or their family members crying and asking *Why me?* as we discussed their bleak prognoses and difficult treatment courses. Turns out he had heard all this before.

It was at this point that he explained there were two types of Internet sex offenders. The first were the more talked about "creeps," about whom what everyone assumes is correct. He had recently defended a man who not only had an extensive child pornography collection but had also offered up his nine-year-old daughter to one of his deviant online colleagues.

However, a not insignificant minority were people like me, he went on: people who were otherwise good and caring, but because of past abuses, went to dark places to look for answers. He said it was almost like therapy for these kinds of offenders. This was the first time I'd heard this perspective, but it would not be the last. This theme would be repeated by other professionals involved in my case. But even at that point the comparison felt accurate to me.

He gave me my first insight into current statutes as well. Prosecutors and defense attorneys alike were struggling with these cases, where the law dictates that this second type of offender, who are already suffering, have their pain further compounded by the severe punishments that the law prescribes. The majority of the federal judges across the country didn't follow the tough sentencing guidelines for possession-only cases, giving these offenders much shorter prison terms. "It's a treadmill that many want to get off of. But they can't. The political liability of looking soft on sex offenders would cost legislators votes, and so their offices," Newton explained.

"This is all very reminiscent of the early War on Drugs era, when instead of getting some help and counseling after being found with a miniscule amount of cocaine or marijuana, people were sent off to prison for five to twenty-five years, effectively ruining their lives and conscripting them into a life of crime to make ends meet. It's a common problem in our country. People tend to vote for what sounds like the right thing to do, without thinking it through and considering societal norms." As a result, the United States accounts for 25 percent of the world's prison population but only 5 percent of the total world population.

I would learn that my case was further complicated by the fact that the very same Internet task force that detected me had identified some very sick and dangerous individuals and removed them from society, thus protecting children. The task force, formed in 2009 and run at the local county and city level, apprehended rapists, molesters, people who were planning to meet underage victims for sex, and those who were producing child pornography. Currently, however, those who fit my profile and reasons for committing this sex offense—and are nonviolent, have no sexual contact with children, and are not involved in producing pornography—are lumped together with the dangerous offenders. So it was going to be assumed that I was a predator/monster from the start, tarred by association.

Newton warned me this was what was going to happen. He said, "it would be like lumping someone in a bar fight with a serial killer if we substituted the spectrum of sex offenses with violent crimes. But most people don't look at it that way." He said some new laws are being drafted that reflect my demographic, since it has become recognized among researchers of this crime. But these statutes were not on the books yet, and might not be for a while due to their political riskiness. It took around ten years between when changes to the laws on crack cocaine versus powder cocaine were proposed and when they began to be enacted—despite the racial bias underlying the difference in sentencing rules. The changes to the Internet sex offender laws were not going to happen soon enough to help me any.

"You will surrender yourself at the federal building tomorrow at 1 p.m. Your charge will be given at 3:30. I have negotiated house arrest for you, and we have a very reasonable judge. We know you are not a physical danger, so this shouldn't be an issue." This was the point where I learned how the randomly assigned judges could have a profound impact on the evolution and outcome of a case. "They will process you, do a background check, and take your passport. Bring your CV with you tomorrow." As our meeting concluded, after about an hour and a half in his office, he warned me that the media was already sniffing around for the story and to expect a big blowup. "The public loves going after overpaid doctors who are also perverts," he said, elbowing me with a cynical yet sympathetic grin. The fact that I treated children with cancer made the headlines practically write themselves. He warned me to not watch the news afterwards. Advice that I would soon wished I'd followed.

I had one more order of business that night: how to part ways with OSU. I had to tell my friend and high-ranking official that charges were coming—the next day. And so yet another painful conversation ensued. There were really just two options. Do nothing, receive my charges, and then be terminated for cause, which would forfeit all potential for continuing for health insurance coverage through COBRA for eighteen months. Or I could resign without eligibility for rehire. If I resigned, I would automatically forfeit my bonus, which would have been around $70,000. That's a lot of money, though not so much relative to my annual technical and clinical billing for the medical center—around $10 million, plus another $500,000 I was bringing in through research grants and contracts. It was a lot of money for *me* though, and it could have covered the bulk of my upcoming legal fees. If I decided to hang on and see what happened, though, what would happen was that I would still not get my bonus (or health insurance for my family). So I was to resign the next morning. I could not go against this option. The institution was going to wall me off like an abscess. No individual was bigger than the institution. I'd seen that firsthand.

During the time I was at OSU, a popular football coach who won a national championship and beat the University of Michigan every year was fired/forced to resign because he tried to protect players who traded their OSU memorabilia for free tattoos. This despite the fact that, in Columbus, the energy that goes into beating the Michigan Wolverines is akin to the domestic war effort in the early 1940s. This singular purpose permeates the area during Michigan Week. The whole place shuts down for "The Game," which is the symbolic continuation of 19th-century Ohio-Michigan border dispute known as the Toledo War.

The university also let go of its president, who raised probably a billion dollars for the school during his tenure, because his "aw-shucks" sense of humor wasn't appreciated. He poked fun at Catholics at Notre Dame and the academic standards of Southeastern

Conference schools. (I thought it was great tongue-in-cheek humor.) So I knew there was no way in hell the university was going to stand by a director of pediatric radiation oncology who'd had child pornography charges leveled at him. I couldn't hold that against them; it would be bad for business to support me.

Again, despite the heavy options I had to weigh and the knowledge that my career was about to evaporate before me, I was thinking rationally and clearly. I was so rational I was concerned by how calm I was. I should have been a wreck. Again, it was difficult to decipher if I was in shock or still in the early phases of what life feels like when you are mentally healthy despite being submerged in massive live stressors. I had been more emotional when I wasn't able to find my car keys in the morning than during this conversation. The serenity felt so foreign—my world was caving in, yet this was the best I had ever felt inside my own skin.

My itinerary for July 24 was one of the simpler ones in recent memory:

7:30 a.m.	Wake up and email my resignation from The James Cancer Center and Nationwide Children's Hospital, the dream job I had worked almost twenty years to attain.
1:00 p.m.	Surrender myself at the J.P. Kinneary Federal Courthouse and get processed.
3:30 p.m.	Appear before the magistrate judge to be charged.
4:30 (or so)	Return home before getting ambushed by the media (assuming I was to be released; I had assurances that I would).

The resignation was easy. After the conversation the night before, I crafted emails to my chairman and the appropriate administrators. I woke up (per itinerary), clicked and sent, and went back to sleep.

It is with the deepest regret that I am writing this letter.

Effective today, July 24, 2013:

I hereby resign from my faculty appointment, medical staff appointment, physician employment agreement, and any other administrative or academic appointments and responsibilities that I currently have at The James Cancer Hospital, The Ohio State University Medical Center, and Nationwide Children's Hospital.

Please let this email serve as my official resignation letter. Please verify this electronic transmission has been received.

Thank you for the opportunity you have given me.

Sincerely,
Christopher E. Pelloski

Eventually, I showered and shaved and put in my contact lenses. I decided to look how doctors are supposed to look when not in the clinic: blue polo shirt, khakis, and brown dress shoes. I looked like I was ready to go golfing. I didn't golf, but I could at least look the part. I printed out my twenty-page CV, grabbed my passport, and was just into my garage when Wednesday's noon tornado siren test went off. Its air-raid-inspired ballad seemed to beckon me to the federal building, such that I would mindlessly move toward it, enter, and then have my limbs ripped apart as I was devoured alive by the Morlocks who burrowed there.

Of course, in my complete calmness, I forgot to eat or take my Ritalin and Effexor. Missing my Effexor meant my head would feel like a helium balloon bobbing on a string by the end of the day. Not taking Ritalin meant I would not absorb all the details that would be thrown at me that day. I was going into battle unarmed. I was almost to the courthouse when I realized how vulnerable I'd left myself. I could not go back; it was probably not good practice to show up late for your surrender. The feds wouldn't appreciate that much, and being the over-achiever I had always been, I did not want to screw up my very first self-surrender and criminal processing.

At the federal building, the bailiff who processed me was young, a nice guy, and very professional. There was no judgment or shortness in his voice. He was tall, broad-shouldered, with dark hair cropped military close. The processing room was not much bigger than ten by ten. With all the gadgetry and devices on metal shelves and cabinets, it reminded me of my old laboratory—complete with the smell of rubbing alcohol and other solvents. Only *I* was the experiment. The mug shot, then digital and ink fingerprinting, just like in the movies. And a DNA swab from inside my cheek (with me worrying that I might have the same sequences in my genetic code as some serial killer whose blood had been found on a pile of dead bodies). When going through my belongings, the guy chuckled and turned to me. "I have been doing this for six years. I have never had anyone bring their CV *or* health insurance card to processing ... and you brought both!" At that point, I relaxed a bit. There was empathy in his voice, and his smile was warm.

All was going well until he reached into a metal bin and pulled out the four-point shackles. The set was intimidating even in a heap on the shelf or dangling innocuously in his hand, unengaged. Two wrist and two ankle cuffs, bound by a chain, all made from the same alloy and chromed, as if forged at the same time from the same fiery chasm. Shackles are the most intimate and physical symbol of custody. Just seeing them made me feel defenseless. I must have looked terrified and turned as white as alabaster. "This doesn't mean we are going to keep you," he said very quickly, seeing that I was obviously shaken. "I think you are being discharged. This is protocol. We always restrain defendants when they are charged." I was going numb again. Sweat trickled down my back. As in my moment of clarity on the back porch a few nights before, there were times when reality would check in with my mind and keep it abreast of my life's current events. This was one of those moments.

As each limb was shackled—first my wrists, then my ankles—I could feel the blood receding from the distal end, as if the metal restraint repelled the hemoglobin the way the magnetic poles with the same polarity repel each other. Each restraint point seemed to reach through my skin and flesh and anchor itself directly to the bone beneath. When the chains connecting the cuffs were joined into a single unit, I became the undead, and my hunched posture reflected this new physiologic state. I felt nauseated, and momentarily forgot how to breathe. As I shamefully peered down at my new accessories, I realized how ridiculous I looked in my golfing attire. I assumed the courtroom would burst into laughter at the absurdity of my fashion statement, as if I were the butt of a demented practical joke.

I was led away toward a holding cell to wait. The bailiff was accompanied by a portly, gregarious partner, who in between jokes and self-induced laughter reminded me to stay to the right side of the halls and to face the back of the elevator. "Jesus H. Christ, Doc! This is a big fucking CV. You have been busy," he said, fingering through my packet while I stared at the blank wall of the rear elevator. "Man, I even added some extra pages of bullshit to my CV, and OSU never called me back for anything. Fucking bastards."

"Well," I felt comfortable enough then to talk with these two. I always feel an instant kinship for those who swear, especially when they barely know me and drop F-bombs without reservation for any occasion. "If it's any consolation to you, I don't think I will be adding too many pages to that for a long time." I kept my face turned to the back of the elevator, following protocol, but my voice held the edge of the gallows humor I'd developed to deal with the significant portion of my cancer patients who died within a year of our meeting.

The partner first laughed out loud, but then chuckled in a more subdued and serious manner. "I know, Doc. Hang in there."

In addition to my country club gear, the shackles, and my hunched posture, the limited slack of the restraints reduced me to a shuffling, Parkinson's-like gait, complete with a rhythmic head bob. I could not have looked more pathetic, confusing, and harmless to the two men in the cells adjacent to the one I spent the next forty-five minutes in. It was pristine, cold, and lifeless. The polished steel of the toilet, sink, and bed made the cell seem suitable for ten-hour liver transplant—there wouldn't be the slightest concern about post-operative infections.

The cells were constructed such that a wall of cinderblocks prevented any contact between detainees. But they did not prevent conversation, and I had arrived in the middle of one. The quintessential criminal comparison of notes resumed as soon as my escort left.

"Have you been in fed before?"

"Nope, you?"

"Yeah, I did three years at …" The name meant nothing to me. "For drugs. Selling."

"Damn, and you back again?"

"Yeah, and they's pissed as hell at me, too. Ten to fifteen years."

"Damn."

"Whatchyu in here for?"

"I thought I was talking to a fourteen-year-old girl on email and was going to meet her, but it turns out was the cops the whole time." There was a pause. I could sense the drug dealer shared my discomfort with this remark.

"Well, uh … good luck with that," the dealer mumbled. Then it became clear to me. I remembered hearing how other criminals treat pedophiles. This was a conversation killer, even for a veteran drug dealer looking at up to fifteen years in federal prison. Jesus, how did my life come to this? Ten days before, I was mingling with some of the world's top scientists in pharmaceutical development, plotting collaborations while coordinating my lab and clinic remotely from my laptop. I had plans for a grant submission and a set of challenging radiation treatment cases awaiting my return. Now, I was sitting next to a repeat felon and a guest star on *To Catch a Predator*. A few days before, I was rafting in the Colorado River with my family, quizzing my son on the states that begin with the letter *A*.

Then a much worse thought seeped into my mind: I was going to be lumped together with that monster in the next cell, and then, already convicted, I'd be judged again by murderers, robbers, rapists (of adults only, of course), and drug dealers.

The cell felt crushingly heavy around me, as if I were thousands of feet underground and behind the bricks and ceiling were millions of tons of earth pressing down. The forty-five minutes I waited felt like weeks, frozen and stunned as I was. The roar of the air circulators, bringing in air from some undisclosed opening, miles away, was deafening, but the only connection I felt with the outside world. Only my memories and this air duct, whose blades sliced and pushed the stale air into my lungs, were keeping my body alive. I had to keep telling myself that I was married, had kids who loved me, had gone to medical school, could still snap a curveball on a full count, and was the product of a live birth from my mother. I was still me. I had to keep reminding myself of that or my systems would shut down. My heart would refuse to beat and my kidneys would stop filtering my blood if they thought my head was gone. Multiorgan failure. Death.

Finally, my name was called, and it was time to shuffle out in my chains. Another walk, staying to the right side of the hallway and facing the back of elevators, to get to the courtroom.

When the tall, stately double doors opened, I was pulled into a sea of fluorescent-lit wood, chairs, and navy blue carpet that dampened sound. Only the tables for the prosecution and the defense, which face the judge's bench, seemed to be real and not part of the background. My attorney was at the defense table. His was the first face I had recognized all day. He quietly implored me to take a seat and asked under his breath how I was holding up. At the table to our left was the prosecutor and someone who looked like an intern or law student. In the gallery were about ten people, all of whom seemed to smirk as I hobbled in. I would later learn that they were all reporters—the feared Morlocks—and their thirst for my flesh and blood would not be satiated near enough on that day. One of them, I would later read (once enough time had passed) fell hook, line, and sinker for my selection of clothing. He took it upon himself to mention my blue polo shirt and khakis in his article, faithfully painting the picture of the casual doctor I wanted to convey. However, I did take issue with his description of the ankle restraints as "scrunching" the pant legs of my khakis.

The judge was not in yet. My attorney and the prosecutor talked in hushed tones about my case and others they were working on in opposition to each other, I imagined. I had seen defense lawyers and prosecutors talk like this before, when I was on jury duty years before. They reminded me of two chess players who meet in the park every Sunday afternoon, having a nice conversation while trying to outwit and defeat each other on the board.

There was a stapled set of papers in front of me. It was my charge, the complaint, the affidavit. Like medicine, law has three or four different names for the same thing. It said "The United States of America v. Christopher Pelloski." The whole damned country was against me, the most powerful nation on the planet, and this was the document to prove it.

I used my shaking left hand to leaf through it, with my right hand clumsily in tow due to their mutual bondage. All the salacious details and graphic descriptions of the horror I'd watched online were there. Words like *forced oral sex, prepubescent,* and *insertion* leapt off the pages, past my bound hands, and burned themselves into my retinas. People would soon know what I'd seen. They were going to think I was a monster. How could I have explained myself to anyone reading this for the first time without having had a chance to explain first? Even the people with whom I *had* talked to first were going to be—rightly—disgusted by this. The parents of my patients were going to think I had gotten some base and despicable gratification from their suffering children. My heart ruptured within my chest. It was going to be my word versus that of a nation's.

Then I saw my home address included in the report. This was going to be the public document. It would be released after the hearing. People were going to know where to throw their rocks and Molotov cocktails. Was some vigilante, hoping to rid the earth of pedophiles, going to mistakenly shoot my wife in the head through the window, in front of my children, because from his vantage point on the street, he thought the silhouette on the curtain was me?

Then I saw the phrase "including defendant's own minor children in various states of undress ..."

Another massive wave of powerlessness was about to overtake me when the pretrial services clerk came by with house arrest papers for me to sign. I was not going to sleep in that holding cell or be carted off to jail. I was being released. But then she asked a question I didn't understand: Where would I live once my children returned from Colorado? "What do you mean?" I asked.

My attorney broke from his conversation with the prosecutor. "He is being released for house arrest," he said.

"Yes, but there were concerns about his own children in the affidavit. He is not to be in the same house that they will be due to concerns for their safety."

"I have never, *ever* …" My mind was starting to go numb, my voice quavering and my pulse screaming and whispering at the same time. My lawyer quickly cut me off, placing his hand on my arm.

"Let me handle this." He then summoned the prosecutor and pretrial services officer for an impromptu meeting just outside the door. The room fell completely silent as the reporters and I tried to hear the sharp dialogue muffled by the doors. I sank back into my state of shock, sitting by myself at the defense table and feeling the weight of the audience behind me. I felt completely sick to my stomach. Why did they mention my children? In various states of undress? People have tons of pictures of their children coming out of baths or pools in which they are unclothed. Mentioning that in the complaint was only going to raise suspicions or allegations that I was abusing my own children. They should have thrown in that there may be fifty dead bodies buried under my basement floor, for good measure. Jesus. There was nothing delicate about the wording. It left a huge vacuum for interpretation, and only the worst assumptions were going to be made.

My attorney returned looking tense and sat down again. "It is all taken care of. You can go home and be with your family. Don't worry. I don't know why in the hell they put that in about your kids. Cheap shot." Then he calmed down a bit to deliver more information. "All of those people behind us are media. So try to find a way out of here if you can. I will hold them off with comments."

When the judge walked in we all rose. As the prosecutor read my charge, the judge scolded me with her eyes. She did not even have to say anything. The anger and disappointment poured over her reading glasses as if I had borrowed her car in the middle of the night, without permission, and totaled it while drinking with the boys. I was an incorrigible teenager and was going to be dressed down, in front of others. The humiliation continued as the judge began to speak. I was told how serious my crime was against children, that I was not to have any contact with children, except my own with the supervision of their mother or another responsible adult who was aware of my charge. I was not to have any pornographic media in my home. I was not to possess or use any device that could access the Internet. My crime fell under the Adam Walsh Act, a law designed to protect children from serious harm. These declarations were like swords being run through my abdomen and limbs, avoiding critical organs and arteries so that I would not die but had to stand and take all the unbearable pain that was being inflicted upon me.

I had spent the last three and a half years of my life, working non-stop at the expense of my family, mental health, and own life expectancy to revolutionize the discipline of radiobiology in childhood cancers and to build a pediatric radiation oncology program unlike any other in the world. Before turning forty years old, I had already given thousands of years of increased life expectancy to the cancer patients I treated and gained great insights with my laboratory work. From this point on, however, I would be branded a monster and remembered only for this. A threat to children. A harmer of children. A deviant and a pariah. A predator.

When the court was adjourned, it didn't register. I simply stood there with swords jutting from my upright body.

I was soon returned to the processing room, and the bailiff and his partner, whom I'd mentally dubbed "Good Buddy." As they undid the shackles, the latter shot me a glance, as if saying, I told you we weren't going to keep you. I asked them if there was an alternate exit from the building, so I could avoid the pack of Morlocks gathered at the building's main entrance with their cameras and microphones primed. They looked at each other as if silently asking themselves, *Should we tell this guy?* The bailiff nodded.

"OK," Good Buddy started, after symbolically looking over his shoulder, eager to partake in this covert and somewhat rebellious operation, "when you go down that main elevator, don't go left. Make a buttonhook to the right and go down a long hall. There will be steps down to a door. That will get you out at the rear exit, right on the river." He handed me my belongings. "Good luck, Doc." I didn't know if this was on old prank played on defendants, to walk them right into a media trap, but I knew if I went out the front, I was a sitting duck. I had no choice but to try their way.

On my way out I looked no one in the eye and acted like I had been in the building a thousand times. The bailiff and Good Buddy did not betray me. When I opened the door, I was greeted by the warmest of sunlight on my face. The air was fresh. The weight of the shackles finally fell away, and the stale air from miles underground finally cleared out of my lungs. The river was a dark navy blue with gray ripples from a light breeze. The surface sparkled where the sunlight struck it just so. People in groups or talking on cell phones walked past me, engaged in their conversations and never casting a glance on me. It was my last few minutes of anonymity.

I emerged about a block and a half down the street, right across from the parking garage, and out of the corner of my eye, I could see the horde gathered on the federal building's steps. The street had a bend to it, so I could remain concealed as I crossed. I looked forward and tried to walk quickly, with purpose, and without movements suggesting flight. I kept waiting to hear the words *There he is! Get 'im!!* and imagined looking over my shoulder as a mob of reporters came stampeding down the street in their ties and suit dresses, loafers and high heels, dragging cameras and microphones dangling on cords and creating sparks on the pavement. They would scream and chase me down the road like rabid fans in a scene from *A Hard Day's Night*. But that scream was never uttered. I made it back to my car and stroked it like you would a dog that comes panting to your chair for a greeting after it's been outside. I hadn't been sure if I was going to see it again that day, so it was a reassuring sight. My keys still worked.

I stopped at a gas station to collect my thoughts and grab a few Gatorades and protein bars. I still hadn't eaten and was in acute Effexor withdrawal besides. I planned to hole up, barricading myself in the house. It was around 5 p.m. I texted a neighbor I'd given a heads up about what was going to happen that day: "Are there any news people around the house?" after a minute or so, he responded, "No. All clear." I texted again, "Any news on TV yet?" and there was a much quicker response:

"It has already started." Shit. I drove home, quickly.

I had prepared for hurricanes before. Preparing for this storm was going to be easier. All curtains shut. All lights off. All paths by windows clear of debris. All essentials kept in a sheltered part of the house to minimize moving about. That was pretty much it. No need to board up windows or make sure there was enough food and water to last a few weeks. The master bedroom was the base of my operations. All the windows there had blackout shades on them.

The first knock came around 5:30. I dropped below window level and crawled up the stairs to get a view from the upstairs windows. The horizontal blinds on that window were obscured by the canopy of a tree. I could see and be unseen from here. So far, it was just one news van. A sharply dressed woman and a huge beast of a man in jeans were looking around, figuring out which would be the best camera angle to capture the all-important location shot that always instantly added validity to any story. The big guy worked on his tripod while the woman rehearsed her lines. Since they'd got there first, they had the best and most expansive mobile stage. Then two more news vans arrived. One of them brought its own generator and a massive antenna that looked capable of detecting the background cosmic microwaves that provide evidence of the Big Bang (or was my story being broadcast across the universe, to warn intelligent life to avoid this planet of monsters?). All the tech crews and their corresponding on-air talent scurried around trying to avoid getting in each other's shots. Channel 4 would definitely not want to give Channel 10 free advertising.

Another knock at the door. I saw this one coming. A morbidly obese man who looked two pounds away from needing a Rascal power scooter lumbered up my sidewalk. His movements contrasted with those of the others, who now numbered around a dozen. The rest maintained an insectlike coordination, the way a legion of army ants skeletonize a fallen mammal on the jungle floor. He tried a second knock at my door and then, disappointed, returned to his van.

Soon it was four vans, four crew-reporter sets from four different ant colonies, jockeying for position and access to the carrion inside the home. The generators from each van tried to out-hum the others, too. The antennae looked ready to clash against each other like sabers, but instead took to silently shouting over each other with their electromagnetic transmissions. What a mess. A week before the street had swarmed with police cars as agents pulled computers out of our house. Neighbors looked on and went on second and third "dog walks" around our block, texting and talking on their cell phones. Now there was another spectacle for them to endure. Another shock to the peace and tranquility of the neighborhood that initially attracted Susan and me. And again, the invaders were here because of me. I could feel the shame and humiliation seep from our home's stately white planks. I looked across the neighborhood and realized how powerless I was to prevent this vapor of disappointment from oozing down the streets and into the homes of my friends and neighbors.

Then the texts started:

"I am praying for you and your family," from a friend from my men's baseball league.

"What the fuck, man?" from a friend I'd left in the dark about what was happening.

"Are you OK?" from my mom.

"Are you home with the kids?" from one of the neighbors.

Then one from my wife: "My phone is blowing up. Not sure what to do or say." She did not want to talk in front of the kids in the car.

So it had begun. I walked slowly away from the window, into the bedroom, and just laid back on our bed, staring at the ceiling. My phone was firing texts every ten seconds or so. Again I asked myself, *How did it come to this?* Then my phone rang. Susan. She'd made her dad pull over, off the freeway, in Kansas, so she could get out.

"You better call your fucking attorney! They are saying the kids involved were known to you! People are asking me if their kids are OK, if you hurt our kids or your pediatric patients. You need to call them. This is inexcusable! This is exactly what I was afraid was going to happen." Her voice was trembling from crying. I was so glad that she was on the road somewhere in Kansas with the kids and her dad and not here, in the middle of this hornet's nest. But she felt powerless, too. "Just got another text saying Channel 6 is saying that you confessed to doing all of these things, to kids you know. You better call the attorneys and tell them they need to make some fucking calls and tell the news to back off." Then she hung up.

Within seconds I called my attorney and told him what the news was saying. "They do this shit all the time," he told me. "They are misconstruing the affidavit and focusing on your kids and making it sound like you produced this stuff with them or kids you know. Let me get on the phone and straighten it out." This was bad. Very bad.

Of course, being the masochist I had always been, I just had to catch a glimpse of my own assassination on TV. So I went down to the basement and immediately tuned the TV to Channel 6. Sure enough, there were live shots of my home—even my children's play structures in our backyard were captured by the cameras, zoomed in on to provide a metaphor for the innocence and pure evil that dwelt there. The address and 2009 purchase price of the home were given. Then there was the stock footage of me from previous interviews and speaking bits on research or human interest stories about my patients. Only this time, the footage was in slow motion and set to menacing music. A slow zoom into my face, and then a freeze frame where I had blinked and moved my mouth so that I looked deranged or deformed. Bright graphics across it read "OSU Pediatric Oncologist Charged with Child Pornography." It was like something out of a *Colbert Report* local news spoof—only it was real and it was me. I got to be Goldstein in my very own version of *Nineteen Eighty-Four*'s Two Minutes Hate!

Then they cut back to my children's play structures again, and the parts of the affidavit that concerned my five-year-old twins were highlighted, again to emphasize the danger. At this point, I could feel myself leaving my body, like my soul was tearing through my skin, peeling it off like Velcro to get out of my body. *Surreal* does not fully encompass what I was feeling, or not feeling.

I snapped back when I felt the house's wood frame rattling. Helicopter. Air support? Not for this. At first, I assumed it was a traffic helicopter and would go away. It drifted, but then returned as I ran back up the stairs. Then it came again, too quickly for the typical holding pattern of choppers. There were two helicopters—*two* huge wasps hovering over my home, rattling the slate roof tiles. What were they hoping to see? Dead bodies pulled out from my basement? A standoff where I ended up putting a bullet through my brain? I looked out the upstairs window again. The news crews armed with big superbright lights to compensate for the darkening skies, the sound of helicopters overhead, and my phone firing nonstop texts—these were the backdrop for the knowledge that each of the local news networks was implying I was a monster who exploited not only his own children but children with *cancer*.

I stepped back from the window and laughed. What else could I do? How much worse could it get?

Then I started giggling. I needed to, to save my life from my own hands. I dropped to the floor and crawled on my stomach from window to window like a soldier at boot camp during live-round exercises, and popped up at each new vantage point to laugh and curse the people on my lawn, praying for a rogue asteroid to strike them. I was giddy.

Some people at work had started calling me an absent-minded professor because I always had so many things going on at once in my head that I forgot things. But I had gone full Mad Scientist now, and completely broke with reality. The news crews stayed for hours, even after helicopters left. What more was there to show and talk about? Would a location shot at night make it scarier? I wondered if this was how it was going to be all the time.

Eventually I came to. I found myself lying on my bed staring at the ceiling. I wasn't sure how I'd got there. I had been sleeping. It was around 10 p.m. I think the day, not eating, completely losing it, and the lack of meds had caught up with me, and I just passed out. Simply to see if it was all a bad dream, I peeked out of my primary viewing window. Sure enough, two vans and crews remained. They were just kind of sitting there, listless and texting on their mobile phones. Damn. Not a dream. I thought of how many friends, family members, and colleagues were reading about me right at that moment. For most, this would be the first time they heard about what was going on with me. It was going to be a massacre. The darkest of assumptions were going to be made. Articles with questions in the form of statements were going to rule the day: *Did Pediatric Cancer Doctor Molest his Patients?* Other media-speak would be used, where the pretense *allegedly* is followed by the worst possible scenario. My mind shut down and forced me to fall back asleep.

I woke up again around midnight and checked outside. There was only one holdout crew, there on orders most likely, and bored out of their skulls. By 2 a.m. everyone was gone. It was silent, peaceful, and windless. Not a single blade of grass would have betrayed what had happened earlier.

Chapter Four

RELATIVE TO MY THEN STATION in life, I had been in this kind of serious trouble before. As soon as I started preschool, it was obvious I was not like other children. I was wild, constantly moving. I wasn't a mean kid; I just could never stop. Mine was beyond the typical high activity of toddlers and preschoolers. I was "wired"—and wired differently. My maternal grandfather once gravely told my dad, after I'd popped the screen out of his front door as a final straw in a camel-load of other acts of destruction I'd waged against his house, "There is something wrong with that boy."

I was kicked out of two preschools for bad behavior. *Two*. Who in the hell is so unmanageable between the ages of two and four that they get expelled from preschools? *I* was. Getting expelled from preschool was a pretty uncommon occurrence in the seventies, unlike today. So there were multiple third parties attesting to my difference—and in fairly harsh ways. This behavior pattern followed me to elementary school. I left my seat and wandered around the classroom, couldn't maintain focus, didn't complete tasks or follow directions. I was smart, so I blurted out answers without raising my hand, much less waiting to be called on—the concept was foreign to me. The writing on the wall was that I had ADD or ADHD. I needed an evaluation.

But this presented my mother with a difficult decision. As a nurse, educated in the healthcare system, she knew such a diagnosis meant a prescription for Ritalin (it was just coming into vogue in the early eighties), and she had reservations about giving a kid amphetamines. Not much was known about the long-term effects then. She worried about how it would affect my growth and kidney function.

She also feared having me labeled ADD and made to enroll in my school's special education program. She didn't want me to have to endure the stigma of being a "Special Ed" kid, nor being marginalized by the school district. At least some of these were legitimate concerns, and all were appropriate for a mother at that time. The Special Ed kids were made fun of all the time by the "normal" students, and it was especially difficult for the "'tweeners"—those who went to the special education room for a portion of the day and returned to the traditional classroom for the rest. It was a painfully slow, shameful walk for them to enter the door of the regular classroom and make their way to their seats, especially when it was quiet and all attention focused on them. Everyone in the room knew where they were coming from.

So my mother refused to have me evaluated, so that I could not be diagnosed. She made this decision with my best interests at heart. And, based on her knowledge at the time, she made the *right* decision. I highly doubt that I would have made it to medical school or became a physician if she hadn't insisted on my inclusion in the standard and, later, honors classes—despite phone calls from the principal's office, teacher's notes sent home, and other headaches that resulted from my behavior. None of the children enrolled in the special education program ever appeared in the honors classrooms in high school. In my district, once you were Special Ed, you were pigeonholed—it was a life sentence, pretty much literally. At my high school, if you didn't get into honors classes your likelihood of completing a four-year college program was abysmal. And, without college, medical school would have been an impossibility.

Being spared the stigma of being a Special Ed kid made a huge difference in another way as well. Having to endure the derision of my peers on a daily basis would have chipped away at my nearly nonexistent self-esteem. So Mom did right for her little boy.

However, it came at a price. From kindergarten through junior high, I was constantly assailed for my behavior and lack of self-control. I was called immature, incorrigible, irresponsible, wild, disrespectful, impulsive, hyper, uncontrollable, loud, etc. There were stretches when I was sent home with a note about my disruptive classroom behavior every week or two. My parents had no idea what to do with me or how to make me change, and their fear of child psychologists and the stigmatizing conclusions they would reach didn't help with the situation. I was wedged between two immovable realities—upset school officials and my exasperated parents—and bearing the brunt of the inevitable anger and frustration on both sides. I just wanted to figure out how to make everyone stop being mad at me and saying I was a bad kid. That dilemma was my academic start.

I was a problem child up until eighth grade. Then I suddenly became an overachieving athlete, hell-bent on perfection in everything I did. For a long time, I attributed it to hitting puberty early, being the biggest kid in my junior high, and just growing out of my hyperactivity. But it was far more complex than that. Ironically, I discovered the root cause for this pivotal point in my young life when I began addressing my addictions.

At the outset of my case, my psychiatrist and legal team were "encouraged" by the fact that I had drunk to blackout several times over the year leading to my arrest. Statistics show that when alcohol is involved in offenses sentencing is more lenient. I had multiple issues with this diagnosis, though. Ever since the night of the home raid, I had lost all desire to get drunk. Sure, I'd had a beer or two since, Coors Light, which was like a rehydrating sports drink for me compared to the hoppy, thick stuff I had been anesthetizing myself with: double IPAs and imperial IPAs that were around 10 percent alcohol. If I was truly addicted to alcohol, given that I was facing federal child pornography charges, with career and financial ruin just around the corner, wouldn't my desire for alcohol shoot through the roof—not disappear entirely?

The addiction psychiatrist who screened me explained that someone drinking to blackout is a "slam dunk" for alcohol abuse, and I would be required to enter a twenty-eight-day inpatient substance abuse program before I could even think about getting my medical license again. It turns out that when the blood alcohol content exceeds around 0.20 percent, which is pretty stinking drunk, the hippocampus cannot form new memories. A normal person is unconscious at this level, but if you are up walking and talking (probably annoyingly so, as I had become), then you had developed a pathologic tolerance to the sauce and were, thus, abusing alcohol. I agreed with that. I *was* abusing alcohol. I knew a lot of other people who would fit this bill, too—but I wasn't sure they needed a month in rehab either. Yes, I was using beer like an inhalational anesthetic, but once my reasons for it disappeared, so did this kind of heavy usage.

This didn't matter to anyone, though. From that point on, I was to be an "alcoholic," who attended Alcoholics Anonymous meetings, who would ultimately need to do a stint in rehab, and who could never be allowed to touch alcohol again, because that would lead to a relapse, because an alcoholic is incapable of just having one drink or one sip. In short, adding the "drunk doctor" label to "child porn doctor" was (supposedly) a good move. But, on top of probably being inaccurate, the label and diagnosis would create a new set of problems for me in the long run.

It only took me one or two AA meetings before I realized I was *not* an alcoholic. I would listen to people recall their very first and last drink as if they were talking about the days they got married or their kids were born. Even people who had not had a drop of alcohol in twenty years had photographic recall of these milestone days and devoted an enormous amount of psychological energy daily toward preventing that first sip. One sip, and the cravings would overtake them and a vicious cycle ensue. Every day they woke up, they needed to figure out a way to not drink for the next twenty-four hours. Prayer, meditation, and calling a sponsor were common strategies. My heart ached for them.

Nonetheless, it was through AA that I learned what my true addiction was. It was why I stopped being a wild child in eighth grade. By the time I went to my first meeting, I had not had a drink in almost two months and thought nothing of it. But I listened to the stories of how alcohol crept into people's lives and slowly began to take it over. The first step of the twelve-step program is "We admitted we were powerless over alcohol—that our lives had become unmanageable." I heard how at first alcohol felt good, but then after a while didn't, so people would drink more and more to try to get that good feeling back. I heard how people felt like alcohol robbed them of their lives because they were never present to experience and feel the life before them, because one foot was stuck in the past and the other was set in the future. They straddled the present, but were never really in it. I heard how they thought about alcohol all the time, and the intricate and ingenious things they did to maintain their habit and hide it from others. They lamented how they initially looked to alcohol to give them a false sense of worth and confidence.

Much of what I heard was familiar—but for me it wasn't attached to alcohol. I was a successoholic. Work and success were my drug of choice—my deepest and purist addiction. After a few AA meetings, I had my own version of Step One. I admitted that I had become powerless over my work/career/success—that my life had become unmanageable.

It all started innocently—with eighth-grade algebra. The first hit was intoxicating: 98 percent on our first algebra quiz. It felt so good. Wow. I was on top of the world. People liked me and were impressed when this happened. I stopped being reprimanded and told I was uncontrollable and not good enough for anything. I got praised. I learned I could show people they were wrong about me, too.

Interestingly, my junior high's administration did not want me to continue in the honors math program, mainly because I'd behaved like such a little bastard toward the pre-algebra teacher. My mother insisted that I remain in the program, and I set the curve in that class. But algebra just was a gateway drug. To keep my high going, I had to start excelling at everything I did. My parents were happy, and teachers actually started considering me one of the smart kids. If I had been found shooting smack into my arm on the playground, there would have been a massive uproar, expulsion, and intervention. But with work and its success providing my high, it was as if all the authority figures in my life, who'd previously written me off as trouble and constantly punished me, were scoring me great shit—with clean needles to boot. I was hooked, and it transformed my life. It defined me and gave me an exaggerated sense of worth and confidence. I was going to show everyone just how wrong they were about me. And like all good drugs, at first it felt great, but after a while, it stopped being fun and just created more problems.

Success became my identity. From eighth grade through high school, I got one B, in typing. The rest were A's. That was good, but it was just high school. College was next. In the first semester of college, I got 4.0 GPA, after being advised not to take chemistry and biology at the same time in my first term, and ignoring that advice. That was great, too, but fleeting.

The real fix was the MCAT: 11-13-11-R? Not bad. But getting into a kick-ass medical school would be where I'd really make my mark and reach that nirvana of achievement—the ultimate high. But, no. That wasn't it either. OK, the USMLE Step I: rocking a 251 opened a lot of doors within the competitive specialty of radiation oncology. The University of Texas MD Anderson Cancer Center? Yes, it's the best cancer center in the country. I will go there. I worked there, in the Radiation Oncology department, for two months as a visiting medical student, living in a roach-infested student hovel, and delivered a presentation on my research that blew their socks off and secured me a residency there.

But slowly the success stopped giving me the high it once had. I was building up a tolerance and getting less pleasure per unit of work-success achieved. The personal, marginal gain was dwindling, yet the real-world merits of my achievements were growing exponentially. I was accomplishing things that a kid from my neighborhood and college were not supposed to accomplish.

The first existential crises of my adult life occurred in college—the anxiety over whether I would get into a medical school, how to pay for it, what classes to take to preserve my GPA, and so on. So to escape the worry, I lived at two extremes. I was the guy who could study in the library for hours and then by the end of the night drink so much that he would fall through closet doors. My drinking was legendary. I once drank a whole fifth of gin before noon on pledge day, broke planks of ice over my head that were six inches thick, and scared the hell out of guys twice my size in my lunatic's rage. I had to be taken to the emergency room for punching open a wire-reinforced window because I thought I failed a calculus exam (it turned out I had set the curve for my class). There were a few times when the words on a page that I was studying appeared as gray blurs; I couldn't read them and would go into a full-blown panic attack, convinced that I'd forgotten how to read. My chest would hurt, my hands tingle and cramp, and I would have trouble breathing. I was still that crazy hyper kid. I'd just shape-shifted into the form of a highly organized and ambitious overachiever. It fooled everyone, including myself.

It was in college psychology my sophomore year that I first met Susan. She was tall, thin, and beyond cute, and had this long black hair that was always wet from showering after her swimming class right before. She intrigued me. When she smiled, her whole face did. It was the kind of a smile that meant she knew something about you that no one else did, yourself included. And unlike me, she was quiet, but so confident.

As she got to know me, she saw through the façade of the driven overachiever and understood that I was just a scared kid who needed help and a *lot* of guidance. She liked my humor, random pop culture recitations, self-deprecation, and concern for others. She liked that I was "handsome" (her words) and knew all the answers to the questions posed by our psychology professor, while everyone else remained silent. She liked me. She liked *who* I was, not *what* I was. She appeared to be the first person to ever like me this way, at least from my perspective. It was refreshing. She didn't treat me as if I were a commodity or possession, unlike most of the girls at my college, who demanded exclusivity if you so much as looked their way. She was pure, cool confidence. She admired my drive and dedication to everything.

She tempered me, though. Her unconditional love and slower pace toward life took some of the edge off. She would make me stop studying and hang out—assuring me it would not prevent me from becoming a doctor one day. She made me take spontaneous three-hour road trips into Windsor, Canada, in the middle of the school week. We would go bar-hopping and dancing all night, and then drive back to campus early morning. I stopped drinking so heavily because I didn't need to escape myself anymore.

We got married in 1997, right before I started medical school and she started law school. I'd actually been accepted into Johns Hopkins

School of Medicine (my ultimate goal since the start of college) to start in 1996, but I wanted to defer a year. My future mother-in-law had recurrent, metastatic breast cancer, and I wanted to be closer to Lansing, Michigan, for her and my wife. So I chose Northwestern in Chicago, instead, which let me take that year off. The choice also meant Susan had more law schools to choose from within a reasonable distance. Of course, this was the first and last time I made a career decision where I considered my loved ones' needs ahead of my own ambition.

Still, at the age of twenty-three, my short, explosive temper remained, and it was problematic. I couldn't shake that part of me. I went to anger-management counseling before I got married and started medical school. My wife's family insisted on it, after hearing about how much of a wreck I'd been in college. I had about ten sessions with a psychologist. I related how I'd struggled in elementary school and the way I'd had to study in high school and college to do well (in the middle of the night, with massive amounts of caffeine and complete isolation), which led to the diagnosis of ADD my mother had feared. I kept it hidden from my parents until years later. I was so worried I would let them down, especially after my mom had battled so hard for me against it.

Ritalin was prescribed. Wow. That stuff really worked on me. It was hard to argue against the ADD diagnosis when it had been suspected since I was a small child, and the way the world finally slowed down once I took Ritalin was the capper. As I look back, I think I know why Ritalin worked for me when I really needed to focus. My mind had been telling my brain to be on high alert for years. It never really explained to my brain why, but it demanded that the brain be ready for some catastrophe just around the corner. That is why I was a hyper kid and needed complete sensory isolation to study in high school and college. What the Ritalin would do is placate the part of the brain that was dealing with these imaginary crises. By stimulating my brain, it tricked it into thinking the imaginary crisis was being handled. And by keeping that part of my mind busy doing *something*, I could focus on the less exciting tasks that lay before me.

Ritalin was a godsend for medical school. I could not have memorized the origin and insertion sites of the nearly 650 skeletal muscles of the human body while my brain chemistry was better geared toward bracing myself for an F5 tornado. Ritalin kept my brain busy, so that it would stop interfering with what I needed to do. It worked very well.

I kept my diagnosis secret during medical school, worried the ADD label could compromise my ability to secure a competitive residency position. I paid out-of-pocket for my drug-maintenance appointments with a psychiatrist and name-brand Ritalin prescriptions, so it wouldn't show up on my student health insurance. I didn't dare to ask for any special testing considerations, like untimed exams, not wanting to stand out as having a learning disability among my medical classmates.

Fortunately, I did very well in medical school. In our mock awards ceremony, my classmates voted me Most Academic and Most Likely to Win a Nobel Prize. Although these awards were in jest, and included other categories such as Who Looked the Hottest After Being on Call and Who Looked Like They Were on Call Without Actually Having Been on Call, they were a tip of the hat from my classmates toward my research insights and teaching abilities. They remained entirely unaware of the neuropsychiatric gymnastics it took to accomplish what I did.

Finding it necessary to hide my assumed learning disability and mental health issues, though, was just part of the indoctrination into the culture of stoicism and infallibility that is the medical profession. You don't disclose your weaknesses to *anyone,* mental or physical. You certainly don't call in sick—that creates extra work for your colleagues, who are already a few hours behind in their own daily mess. A study in 2007 revealed that 40 percent of executive directors of state medical boards felt that just a *diagnosis* of a mental illness was sufficient to sanction a physician—even if there was no evidence that the illness affected their ability to care for patients and they were fully compliant with their treatment program. Just the label was enough. Another study that came out in 2009 found that many physicians who actually did seek help of their own volition—being responsible and doing the *right thing*—reported losing their medical careers or being less able to find work, and experiencing financial hardship as a result.

Why it is critical to regulate an otherwise excellent obstetrician or pathologist with a ten-year history of well-controlled bipolar disorder—while also *publicly* broadcasting it in medical board periodicals and on websites—is beyond me. In some states, the physician's address and contact information is provided along with his or her diagnosis. How in God's name does that help *anyone*? And what message does that send to the public about mental illness? Can't all this be addressed behind closed doors, and if there is no problem with job performance or patient safety, then just let doctors practice in peace? My job performance certainly didn't suffer from whatever it was that I had. I was a rising star in the field. I was among the best.

We spend so much time and effort abiding by our patients' HIPAA rights, which protect the privacy of individually identifiable health information. Yet when it comes to our own privacy, these rights are trampled upon. Medicine's own governing bodies reinforce the misguided culture of martyrdom. So apparently I was doing the *smart thing:* keeping quiet, hoping things would pass on my own, and avoiding any labels that could have undermined my future.

Behind all of these emotional issues, though, something else was eating away at me. It was during the very last session of my anger management counseling, before our marriage, before my "illustrious" medical career started, that something other than ADD came up. It was something that Ritalin would not be able to fix for the long haul.

I had my first recollection that something sexually inappropriate had happened to me as a child. I couldn't remember any details then; I only remembered my mother and grandmother arguing about me going to the pool of an adult my mother didn't know. That was it. I suspected there was more to the story, but thanks to the Ritalin I thought my problems were solved anyway. And so did my therapist. We both minimized the vague recollection. He probably saw this good-looking, athletic guy with a beautiful new wife and medical school ahead of him and thought I would be fine. I had everything going for me.

I didn't have the archetypal characteristics of someone bogged down and consumed by a troubled childhood. I was never a Goth or burnout. I played three sports until I destroyed my knee, then stuck with baseball and starred in high school musicals. I was on our homecoming court, voted most likely to succeed and to host *Saturday Night Live*. In college, I won numerous academic awards, was on the dean's list every semester, was my fraternity's vice-president, and I was marrying a tall, beautiful woman, who was heading to law school herself. The world was my oyster.

Me, at 23 years old, right before marrying a beautiful woman and beginning medical school at Northwestern.

Once I made it to MD Anderson, though, I started making unilateral decisions about where we were going to live, based solely upon my own work and success, uprooting us a year early so I could participate in an enhanced internship program, and thus preventing Susan from obtaining her LLM in health law. I also began thinking about work and success all the time, though I would hide it. Sometimes I would have to check a few emails or run one more analysis on SPSS Statistics software under the guise of going to the bathroom, when I really should have been spending time with my wife or watching the exciting game on TV. I couldn't control myself. I tore through my residency program and rode a wave of research success, winding up with an unprecedented numbers of publications in some fairly strong biomedical journals. Ritalin, of course, was no longer sufficient, as my temper and anxiety had returned. An additional diagnosis of generalized anxiety disorder (GAD) was given, and Effexor was added to the mix, to counter the rage that came with my fluctuating Ritalin levels and inevitable crashes.

Chapter Five

IT WAS TOWARD THE END of my residency, when I was about thirty-two years old, that I came across my first glimpse of child pornography. I thought I'd downloaded a movie from the "golden age" of adult movies, the 1970s. Peer-to-peer programs (similar to Napster) were the only places that had these older movies back then. Most video rental stores didn't carry those titles anymore, and those that might were always a bit seedy. I also wasn't about to drop my credit card number for online "vintage porn" only to have it taken in an identity theft scheme that relies on embarrassment to ensure the duped victims' silence. However, a problem with peer-to-peer, I would soon discover, is that the files are not always correctly labeled.

So when I clicked on the movie, expecting a scene featuring a few of the "legends of porn," what filled my computer monitor was a man entering a bathroom, clad only in a dark robe, with a fully erect penis, and approaching a girl about six or seven years old. As if trained already, she began performing fellatio on him. The revulsion I felt was so extreme it was as if a hand had reached out from the monitor and began crushing my larynx with sinewy fingers that wrapped around my neck. It was hard to breathe, my heart raced, and I could feel my internal organs move uncomfortably of their own accord, in disgust.

I wish that was the only reaction I had. I would have ripped the computer from my desk, taken it outside and smashed it. But, the robe, the man, the erection, the small hands of the child and large hand of the man on her shoulder, in a bathroom—I realized at that moment that this had happened to me, when I was about that girl's age. The memory was so clear. It appeared from nowhere. It was there for the first time, yet somehow I knew about it all along. The musty smell of old-man penis, the sun shining behind the curtains of that small bath-room window, the sounds of other kids playing in the pool, laughing and splashing, returned to me as well. The leathery hand reaching out to my shoulder to bring me in and the massive glans approaching my then-small face. I felt locked in, as if there were a monitor in front of my eyes and another behind them, in my mind, with their contents in sync, mirroring each other.

Almost ten years had passed since that last anger management session in which I'd had a vague recollection that something sexual had happened in my childhood, but I couldn't remember anything significant. Watching the video, however, I knew *exactly* what had happened in that past moment of my young life. "The Pool Man" was my first clear memory, and it was invoked by seeing another child being sexually abused in the same manner, by technically committing a felony.

A psychological trap had been set. I was like a moth to the child pornography flame: I couldn't *not* look. And it was very easy to retrace my steps to get back there, too. When I was low enough to want to learn more, to deal with the pain from my past or test whether my memories were true, I knew how to trigger my mind to reveal its hidden secrets. Wherever my mind had gone during those moments in my childhood, viewing children being sexually abused brought me right back to that place. A sick and damaging form of "therapy" had been established. There were patches of my life that were lost or forgotten, and I became obsessed with getting those pieces back, regardless of the legal, moral, or ethical considerations. I didn't care.

I did this multiple times for a year or so. I was reeling from the revelation that something terrible had happened to me. Something physical. Something I couldn't tell anyone about. There was too much going on in my life at that time, and the new knowledge add shame and confusion to the mix.

This realization could not have come at a worse time. In addition to my addiction to success and the medications that could not contain my anxiety, Susan and I had staggering debts: loans for medical and law school (over $250,000), which was accruing interest during my residency, and credit card debt topping the $60,000 mark (we bought a starter-home money pit based on the promise of Susan being employed upon our arrival in Houston—a promise that eventually proved hollow).

I was also embroiled in a conflict with an influential and powerful faculty member at MD Anderson, which had the potential to affect my future employment prospects. My credibility and future were being undermined by this figure because, heaven forbid, I'd had the temerity to raise my voice to her when it became apparent that I would not be permitted a three-day leave from my (medically unnecessary) post to say goodbye to my grandfather on his death bed. (I never did.) Before this incident I could do no wrong in her eyes, clinically or academically. An international leader in the field who goes out his/her way to hamstring a trainee is about as bush league as it gets. However, when ambition, career, and prestige replace humanity, behavior such as this becomes not uncommon in the academic medical field.

Additionally, my wife and I were having trouble conceiving, and on top of that, I felt a profound reluctance and fear about having children, as I associated childhood with unhappiness. I couldn't relate to children, and always feared for their safety and felt uneasy around them. I was petrified at the thought of becoming a father.

I was in the midst of yet another existential crisis. Being low already, I consciously or subconsciously told myself, *Well, if it is this shitty, let's just see how shitty it can get.* It was a form of self-torture for me. I was driven by the compulsion to remember what happened to me, but to also inflict pain and punishment on myself. I knew there was more to what had happened. I started noticing subtle differences in my flashbacks about The Pool Man that made me wonder if what I was remembering happened on different occasions—that things had happened more than once with this man. And there were more flashes of sights, sounds, and sensations that these images evoked in me.

Then, like storm clouds suddenly parting, good things began to happen for me. I had worked my way into a laboratory and was invited to stay on faculty as a physician-scientist at MD Anderson after graduating from my residency training. One would think I finally reached the pinnacle of academic achievement and would be content. And I was. I even had the audacity to take my foot off the gas pedal for a moment. This was primarily brought on by the birth of my twin children, a beautiful boy and girl. I was enjoying my life. I still worked hard, but my maniacal approach had waned, for the betterment of my health. And I closed the door on that early part of my life. It was like that part of me went dormant, like a fever broke. For the next four to five years, I didn't want to learn any more about what had happened, so I never went back to that dark well of online child pornography. (Even the forensic evidence, the vestiges of files on our old desktop computer, confirmed that they had not been accessed recently and were deleted more than five years prior to the raid.)

I started playing baseball, started pitching, again. With maturity (no longer the head case I was in college), some commitment to training, and my Ritalin-Effexor cocktail to help keep me calm on the mound when I started getting hit hard by batters, I was very good, actually. I faced a lot of former college and professional players, who regarded me as one of the top pitchers in our men's amateur league. The highpoint came when I was thirty-four. On a dare, I tried out for a local independent minor league team. My two-seam fastball clocked between 84 and 86 mph, I threw a good curve and a forkball with a decent slider that day, and I got a callback. My arm didn't even hurt the next day. It was awesome.

I could still bring it: This is me pitching a mid-80 mph fastball in my mid-30s.

Over the several years after my children were born and I graduated from MD Anderson, things only got better. My children were thriving with me as their father. As they got older, I made them breakfast before I left for work and came home at a decent hour to be with them. I could see that a normal childhood was possible, despite not having any example of this throughout my life. I started making money, and the debt from medical school and residency started dwindling. Life was good. I knew there was more to my childhood traumas, other memories had yet to come to light—but, at that point, I didn't want to deal with it, and I had enough energy to keep those memories far away. I didn't want to view that stuff ever again. I finally was becoming the man my wife had been waiting for since she first met me.

Then, like a psychological house of cards, it all came crashing down. Because I *had* pulled my foot off the gas, my work ethic was called into question by some of my superiors. Their words were absolutely toxic to me. To imply to a recovering successoholic, who needs achievement and the approval of others to define and validate him, that he isn't working hard enough is like pouring Jim Beam into a shot glass and wafting it under the nose of an alcoholic whose favorite drink happens to be whiskey. The grounds for this accusation were that I wasn't coming into the lab to work on weekends and wasn't making it to research meetings during the week (because I had clinical procedures lined up on that day). Despite being a prolific publisher (the best in my group) and often worked well into the middle of the night, my hours had gotten to healthier levels. This meant that, rather than my assignments being completed overnight, as before, it took me a *few* nights to get things done. This was due to having twin toddlers, of course, but the field was not going to care, I was warned. Time away from family is the price to be paid to be a successful clinician-scientist, and if I was not physically present at all times, making discoveries through osmosis and saturation would never happen. This was the message I heard. This is how a recovering success addict hears things.

In actuality, I was just being warned about what it was going to take to be a heavy hitter in both the clinical and laboratory realms. It was going to take time. Lots of it. I was choosing to have two jobs, and if that was the case, I needed to double my hours. There is no such thing as a 50:50 person, the term used to describe a physician scientist who spends 50 percent of his time in the clinic and 50 percent of the time in the lab. The clinic demands—which include the uncertainty of patient issues and drop-ins and their care taking precedence over all other things—makes the designation of 100:75 or 100:100 far more accurate.

My ego would hear none of that. This was a direct challenge to my worth, sense of meaning, work ethic, and purpose. At which point OSU entered. Just as this new professional crisis was brewing, OSU started recruiting me to lead its pediatric radiation oncology program, run the adult brain tumor service, run my own laboratory as I saw fit with complete academic freedom, become the residency program director (which at the time needed a drastic overhaul and faced potential probation), help guide the search for suitable proton therapy, etc. The list of new responsibilities rattled on. I was told that I would be a leader of this new vibrant and growing department, and I would have control over how it was to grow.

This was like telling a recovering alcoholic that, up in Ohio, there was a whiskey distillery—which he could be in charge of—with a warehouse full of barrels that he had access to 24/7. Even with tangible evidence that I did not need to be "the man" to be happy right before my eyes for the first time, the addiction of work and success came roaring back with a vengeance and turned me into a drooling, career-crazed zombie again. And there would be no stopping me this time.

Susan pleaded for us to not go. We had built a home and support network during our eight years in Houston. She was a Texas-licensed medical malpractice defense attorney, and had worked and supported me during my residency at MD Anderson. I was finally on faculty at the top cancer center in the country. We were a happy young family. Going to Ohio would force her to start from scratch, both personally and professionally. But her words fell on ears deafened by my own career lust; I needed to prove to everyone who doubted me that I was the real deal.

There are no rehab centers for successoholics. In fact, you get centers *named after you* if you are an exceptional successoholic. This is a form of substance abuse that the whole society not only enables but also celebrates. And, as long as it lasts, it can conceal a myriad of other problems. On some level, we all know that a 120-hour workweek is not healthy, especially for a family, but it's still rewarded and even revered in our culture. Just when being successful had stopped feeling good to me, other people kept telling me how good it was *for* me, and fed into my pathologic need for praise. Again, that's like telling a recovering alcoholic to quit being a pussy and drink up.

I took OSU by storm. Everything I touched or got involved with turned to gold. The residency program was not only saved from probation by me, as director, but I was growing it into a training powerhouse. By 2013, we were competing for the top talent pool of medical students from across the country. My residents' performance on the in-service exam began to average above the 90th percentile via the core curriculum that I designed. My publication output was ramping up, returning to pre-success-recovery levels. I also received several grants for my research.

After just a few years of my lab being up and running, we were building a preclinical radiation testing program for childhood cancer and had applied for a patent. Every year, I was sought out by medical and undergraduate students who wanted to work in my lab. I revamped our radiosurgical program, another aspect of the department that was abysmal before my involvement. My clinical load was immense as well. In three and a half years on faculty at MD Anderson, I'd treated about 250 adult patients with primary brain tumors and metastases. In that same time span at OSU, I treated around one *thousand* patients, about two hundred of them children with cancer, the rest adults with brain and spine metastases, primary central nervous system tumors, lympho-mas, melanomas, sarcomas.

I was finally getting to do the things that I'd previously only dreamed would be possible after putting in ten to fifteen years. OSU gave me the career opportunity of a lifetime. I was assuming new leadership roles left and right and fixing anything that was broken. I was very proud of what I'd been able to achieve.

One highlight was a very stimulating phone conversation with a recruiter who was looking for a new chairman to lead a smaller academic program. Word had spread about the amazing job I was doing. I wasn't even thirty-eight years old yet, and was getting chairman offers. One of the leaders of our field described my performance as "Pelloski on steroids." This was probably not far off the mark. I had enough stress hormones and adrenaline coursing through my blood to kill a normal person.

Unfortunately, I also returned to shooting up in the bathroom with my laptop, checking email, running analyses, signing off on clinic notes—ignoring my family. Once I returned home from work, I would keep looking at the clock, just waiting to get back to work for the evening.

It was a pretty impressive run. Had I remained on that treadmill, I could have easily overdosed on success. Either I would have had a grabber right in my office or just died quietly, slumped over my keyboard, like one of those Japanese businessmen who succumb to Karoshi.

As my workload exponentially increased—and with it, treating and seeing patients die in far greater numbers than I had before—the need for immediate relief increased as well. I needed to get out from under the inhumanly high standards that I placed upon myself and lived and breathed by. So, as I always did in the past, I reached for beer. Sometimes it was the only way I could fall asleep. After a while, I shopped for beer by alcohol content rather than brand or flavor. The problem is that chronic alcohol exposure tends to lower mood. It is a very effective depressant, especially considering its area-under-the-curve effects, not just the peak level when one is actively intoxicated.

Thus the positive energy I'd gained after my children were born, which kept my horrific memories at arm's length, was completely gone. New flashbacks started to emerge. There *was* more, as I had feared. It *did* happen more than once with The Pool Man. There was another time, when I was *really* little. And there was another time, with a woman—who was a relative, too. An aunt? Jesus.

Of course, when I felt bad, I added more work to my plate (further isolating myself from friends and family) to increase the praise and feeling of achievement, while I washed things down with more alcohol when I had the chance to. But while this formula had always seemed to do the job for me in the past, I'd maxed out my limited coping mechanisms. So I returned to viewing children being sexually abused, to see how bad it really was—to remember and counter these flashbacks.

In October of 2012, law enforcement saw me do this on a peer-to-peer network and started watching me. They would continue to do so over the next nine months.

Next to pulling a trigger, I believe accessing media depicting children being sexually abused is about the quickest and easiest way to commit a felony. When I built up the "courage" to see these horrific things and was mentally prepared for the physiologic and psychological state that enabled me to recall, validate, further explore, or piece together new fragments of my own childhood sexual abuse, I crossed that legal threshold. It induced a sense of fear and despair, a flood of nausea, palpitations and chest pain, and a headache from neurotransmitter overload. It was as if my present-age spirit left my body, which became a scared kid again, within a bubble floating in the midnight darkness with only the computer monitor casting an eerie light.

It was too simple: Go to a free software download site. Get a peer-to-peer file-sharing program. Download and run it. Type in the right search terms, and hundreds, if not thousands, of files would fill up the queue, many owned by the hundreds of other users online at that moment. The whole process took about five minutes. I would click on various files, not knowing what would actually download at the moment. These networks were meant to be running nonstop, with bits being downloaded here and there over days. Sometimes I never got that far. I would chicken out at the free download site and run away.

I would never leave my computer unattended. So if I was going to see anything, it was going to be then and there. I didn't leave out the fishing net to see what I caught hours or days later. There would always be a few files that downloaded quickly within a sitting. That would be what I viewed. The forensic findings on my computer had pages of links showing 0 percent complete, meaning they were in the queue but I had shut things down before they could be imported.

The more disturbing the depictions, the greater the effect they had on me. The ones where children were in obvious pain, crying, scared, or bound were the most harrowing. But those would bring the clearest memories into my mind, as well. There could be no questioning of their validity.

Sometimes I would search for certain files that had resonated with me in previous "sessions." If I was remembering my aunt, I would look for female abusers in the media. These were rare. The sickness did not permeate the world of women as much—but those who crossed that line were just as vicious as the men.

If it was memories of The Pool Man that were haunting me, then it was oral sex or sodomy. Sometimes boys would be abused, but it was overwhelmingly girls being abused by men. The younger the victims were, the more my hands would tremble on the keyboard and the further back I could remember into my childhood. It was as if one part of me was forcing the other to watch, as some form of sadistic punishment.

The files came from everywhere: Russia, Chile, the UK, Thailand, Ukraine, Mexico, Romania, and plenty from the United States. A global problem. In many of the media, there is obvious poverty and desolation in the background, which only adds to the sadness and cruelty of this world.

When I had seen enough and could no longer tolerate the induced state, I shut everything down. I deleted everything and anything that came across my computer. I deleted titles out of the recent files folders. Then I would uninstall the peer-to-peer file-sharing program. I wanted nothing there to remind me. As if trying to clear my mind, I wished it all away. But the mind is like a computer's hard drive: you can never really erase those images. Whether an *in silico* hard drive or the *in vivo* mind, the only way to truly delete this filth is to smash it to bits.

After I shut everything down and deleted the record of what I'd done, a maelstrom of disgust, guilt, anger, and fear would swirl in my mind as I lay in bed, isolated from my family and everyone else, trying to sleep. Thanks to the beer, I'd gained weight, and overweight, I snored. I always had to wake up before anyone else in my family did anyway, so gradually I began to sleep at the opposite side of the house. When I returned home late from work on consecutive days, after my kids went to sleep, my wife would tell them I was on a business trip, even though I was only three miles away, working in my office on grants or covering the late hours of the clinic. I came and went without seeing them, as if I weren't really there at all.

I didn't know where to direct the horrible feelings I had. Was it toward my memories, realizing that very terrible things had been done to me? Was it toward the images I had just seen? Or was it toward my own deep-seated feelings of worthlessness and disappointment? What made me stoop so low as to enter that dark world? I always told myself I would never do it again. That was the only way I could ever fall asleep on those nights. But I knew I would come back.

Over the next few days, I would ruminate on what I remembered and what I'd seen. Lots of alcohol and anger would "assist" in the processing. My temper was on a hair trigger. I grew so unpredictably combustible that my wife and children became uncertain how to approach me. I especially needed alcohol for anesthesia and sleep afterwards, or else I would sweat through my pillow with my eyes wide open in the darkness. Eventually, I would start to believe that my memories weren't true, that I was just projecting what I saw onto myself, to be able to see myself as a victim. But when life and work replaced sleep and rest, more flashbacks (new, old, and from the media I'd viewed previously) would surface more often. I would make myself crazy with this cycle, and eventually feel like I *had* to look again, to verify that I wasn't losing my mind.

Through these horrific sessions I developed a very clear picture of what all happened to me. My first suspected incident of sexual abuse happened when I was around three years old. I cannot recall who the adult was. It was a stranger, though. It may have been a babysitter. It also may have been an innocuous diaper/underwear change that somehow stood out as different and spooked me. Or it could have been something more sinister. I just knew that it was not quite right or normal for me.

I remember laying flat on my back. Someone was doing something to my lower body, and I remember a strange sensation in my pelvic region and pit of my stomach. My head was turned to the side, I believe to avoid looking at the stranger, or maybe my head was turned that way for me, by the force of a big hand on my head. I stared at an orange-painted wall and could hear voices or some kind of commotion outside the room I was in.

My parents were college students at Michigan Tech at the time, and had many parties at their married housing apartment. Whenever I hear music from The Doobie Brothers, I think of those parties. They were always a fun and exciting time. I got to stay up late and I would be doted upon. I have fond memories of those times, except for this memory, which I believed might have happened at one of these gatherings.

Whatever this action was, I believe it started an amplification of my anxious and active behavior. It carried into the darkest time of my childhood. My parents left college and lived in a flat above my father's parents. Their financial woes grew, and my mother worked long nursing shifts, while my dad had multiple jobs and came home late exhausted. Arguments were frequent. Whether they were between my parents or my father and his parents, it was a near-weekly phenomenon. Home was a pressure cooker. At one point, my mother filed for divorce and was going to fly to California to be with her sister. At the airport to see her off, I darted across the boarding area, into the line by the gate, and jumped into her arms, sobbing and pleading with her to not go. The three of us cried together, and so did a few others in line. As with other intensely unpleasant episodes in my life, I did not remember doing this. I remembered being at the airport, but I probably began to shut down as it became clear my mom was saying goodbye to us, and bolted to her by instinct. My father told me this story when I was much older. He said a Hollywood scriptwriter could not have topped what I said when I was that terrified and heartbroken little boy.

It was while that was going on in my home that I had the misfortune of running into The Pool Man. He was an older man in the neighborhood who invited kids over to his pool in the summers. Of course, I was all about getting into that pool. Five-year-olds are funny like that. My grandmother, who would watch me most of the days my mother worked, brought me over there one day, after I saw a bunch of the neighborhood children playing in the pool. As I was changing into a bathing suit, in the bathroom of his home, I noticed the door was cracked open and someone was looking at me. It was The Pool Man. I'm not sure why I didn't just show up already in my own swim trunks, or if they were provided for me by the host.

There were the sounds of people laughing and splashing in the pool. The window must have been open. He stepped into the room, wearing only a robe. I had seen an adult penis before; I saw my dad naked many times. This one was different. It stood out away from the body, poking through the robe. It was fully erect, not something I'd seen before. As it drew closer to my face, the robe opened a bit to show some gray pubic hairs. This was also different to what I had seen before. I was told to open my mouth, and so it began. A big hand was placed on my shoulder and moved my small frame as needed.

At some point, I think someone called for the man, and he yelled back, "In a minute!" but kept me in his grip and had my full mouth silenced. Shortly after, my mind went blank. I do not know how long it lasted, or if or where he ejaculated, but eventually I found myself swimming in the pool, with the other kids. I remember feeling a bit detached and wondering if they all had to do the same thing to swim there.

One of the lowest feelings I had, as I started to remember more of what happened to me, was after I realized that I went to that pool more than once, and was abused by The Pool Man more than once, as well. In at least one of the other encounters, he added digital-anal penetration to the list of activities. I was so disgusted with myself that I would ever agree to return to that pool, or even want to go back. I told myself that on some level I'd gotten what I deserved for being so careless. Blaming yourself for your own abuse is common in adult survivors of childhood sexual abuse. It's also a very difficult feeling to shake. Even if your adult self rationally knows that it wasn't your fault, being stuck in the child's mentality that comes with the memory can be confusing as hell.

For the next few years, my disruptive behavior in school worsened and the disciplining intensified. And, as if I needed more problems, I had yet another encounter with a disturbed adult. It was a woman with blonde hair, about my parents' age, who was probably a distant relative on my father's side of the family. In my mind, her name started with a *D*, and I have mentally called her Auntie D ever since I first remembered what she did to me.

My grandparents took me to some type of family gathering or cookout when I was about seven years old. I found myself sitting on a green wool couch, in a densely carpeted living room with the shades pulled, only slivers of bright daylight peeking around the edges. I could hear people talking and laughing, either in a different room or outside. I remember her pressing herself against me and asking me if I would kiss her.

To a seven-year-old, a kiss means a peck. So I was surprised when her mouth met mine. It was open, and her tongue tried to pry its way past my pursed lips and into my mouth. Then she said some words I will never again forget: "I just love the way a grown man kisses me." Along with some other moaning and breathy sounds, she kept saying this, as I was sexualized. At some point, she fondled my prepubescent penis between her skinny fingers and shiny fingernails, while keeping her mouth on my confused face. I went blank then. I have no idea how or when things ended. I do know that I got a seven-year-old's version of an erection, and that part felt kind of good. Of course, this was another source of intense feelings of shame and guilt for me, once I fully remembered what happened. I felt so disgusted that my body betrayed me and responded to the skillful hands of a monster. A woman no less, whose instincts are supposed to be to protect children at all costs, not defile them.

Another common theme to my abuse episodes was that they occurred when a lot of other people were around. I could always hear some kind of commotion on the other side of a wall or window. The ones I most clearly remember happened in broad daylight. This was a realization that brought one of the biggest waves of tears. Help was always just around the corner when I was being molested, but I never got it. No one ever walked in. It also meant that I never yelled for help either. Was I too scared to make a noise? Was I paralyzed with fear? Did

I just assume that others knew what was going on and this was just how the world worked? It made my heart sink, to think that these were things I'd had to consider, so young.

Chapter Six

THE FIRST FEW DAYS after my charge went public on July 24 were difficult. The liberties the TV news media took with their coverage of my charge and affidavit created a near panic. It was hysteria. The headline "Pediatric Cancer Doctor Charged with Child Pornography" wrote itself. The insinuations that my own children were involved, as well as other children known to me, were especially troubling for my immediate neighbors, who had young children my kids played with. There were also enough breadcrumbs released in the news to make readers and viewers incorrectly deduce that my pediatric cancer patients were somehow involved.

The blogs and comments sections accused me of being a child molester who preyed upon the most vulnerable of children, those with cancer. The very first line I read in one blog was "Great. Another child molester. And he is a doctor who works with children. Is it safe anywhere?" There were several who characterized all pediatricians as pedophiles. Parents of my patients were interviewed on the TV news. Most of them at least said I was a good doctor who took good care of their kids and that they'd never noticed anything strange about me. The most vociferous, though, who wrote what was essentially a "Hang Dr. Pelloski" post on his Facebook page, was a father who (interestingly) was so noncompliant and seldom present for his son's cancer treatment that the children's hospital was considering a guardianship intervention by Child Services.

A friend of mine would later tell me that "WTF?" was strewn throughout the posts about me in Facebook. Some stuck up for me and said there had to be more to the story. Others quickly condemned me and said there was no hope for this monster. To be honest, I would have written the same thing about me, if I'd only read or watched what was said about me. I would have wanted me killed, too, if I were hurting my own children or child cancer patients.

I was now officially on house arrest and under federal supervision. I met with my pretrial services officer, Hank, on the morning following my court appearance. He would supervise me. Hank was another tall guy with big shoulders and short dark hair, but again very kind and professional. He had a female college student or intern working with him, to observe our conversation, as he laid down the ground rules.

It was more humiliation when he reminded me that "you are to have no sex toys, vibrators, dildos—nothing sex-related in the home. No adult videos, nothing of that nature." The student blushed; I could see she felt very awkward. "You are, from our perspective, in jail, but you have the privilege of being home for it."

In addition to requiring Susan's supervision in the presence of my own children, I had to stay within five feet of the back door, and I could only step out the front door to leave for preauthorized medical, legal, spiritual, or employment purposes, which had to be scheduled every Monday. Our meeting culminated with the house arrest monitoring tether being affixed to my left ankle. I would eventually develop a kind of Stockholm syndrome attachment to it, and desperately defended it against any accident or damage when wrestling with my kids. I went into a mild panic whenever it was taken off to change the battery. Throughout my house arrest I had terrifying dreams in which I would be out at social gatherings or doing mundane things like grocery shopping and suddenly realize that I hadn't scheduled it with Hank. I would awake in a full-blown panic.

Later that night, my wife returned to Columbus. She'd been on the road for the last two full days. My house felt like just a collection of floors, walls, and roof after being surrounded and violated by news crews the night before. But once she stepped into it, it felt like a home again. Our children were staying with their grandparents up in Michigan. She found me somewhat shell-shocked and already about ten pounds lighter than when she'd seen me four days before in Colorado. She looked at me with a sympathetic smile when I pulled my pant leg up to show my new tether and gave me a hug.

We had a meeting with my attorneys that week, on Friday. The size of my legal team had increased to three. There was Newton, who had gotten me through the day I was charged; Dickins, whom my psychiatrist had insisted upon; and his partner, Charles Wadsworth, who would also be working on the case. A few people I knew wondered why I decided to have three attorneys and not just one for my criminal case. Some feared it gave the impression that I had a lot to hide and needed a big team to minimize the damage. Susan, from her lawyer perspective, endorsed the decision to have a team: "Sweetie, this is your life. You have one shot to get this right. And with lawyers, you get what you pay for." It was a comment well-received by my new team. Even though it was going to undoubtedly raise the cost of legal fees into the $75,000 to $100,000 range, I reluctantly agreed.

From what I knew about Presidents Washington and Lincoln, and from my professional experiences with multidisciplinary tumor boards (a meeting where new cancer patients are discussed by a roomful of different cancer specialists), it is far better to have several opinions contributing when trying to arrive at the best solution to a problem. I knew there would be thousands of decisions to be made throughout my case, and burdening one person with all of them would be tough— no matter how adept that person was. Washington would listen to his generals argue out their differing battle strategies. Lincoln surrounded himself with contrarians. And in my experience, sometimes the person in the meeting room you'd least expected would come up with the best treatment approaches.

These three lawyers brought some very different perspectives and experiences to the table. The one who was to be my lead attorney, Dickins, was a veteran, well-respected and well-known. His new partner, Wadsworth, was my age, a young up-and-comer in his field as I had been in my own. He had an appreciation for all the computer and technology elements to my case. The third attorney, Newton, was the one I'd contacted initially, who had guided me through the day of my charge. He had an almost academic interest in criminal psychology and was fascinated by the psychology that underpinned my offense. He told me that in social and professional settings no case in recent memory had drawn as much interest and conversation as mine had, and said that many, surprisingly, felt terrible for me.

I appreciated that they all had offices in the same building and had worked cases together before. They were great guys—true professionals who assured us they would do everything they could for the best outcome. They also explained that the case would take six months to a year to unfold and would be punctuated by three major events, with lots of legal work in between. The first event was the charge, which had already happened on Wednesday. They were already starting to work toward a plea bargain, which would lead into the second milestone of the case, my plea hearing, where I would, they assumed at that point in time, plead guilty. After this, the mitigation would start. In this phase all the factors around my offense would be considered in preparation for the final key event: my sentencing hearing, where a federal judge would hand down the punishment.

I was learning so much about a whole new field.

At this meeting, I also discovered that OSU had launched an internal investigation to make sure I had not inappropriately touched any of my pediatric patients. I cannot begin to imagine what that process was like—how devastating to everyone involved. This was exactly what my wife and I did not want to happen. Not only did parents have to suffer with their children's cancer treatment, followed by, for many, their children's death, but now they were confronted with news that one of their treating doctors may have been a pedophile. It was just one more thing for them to agonize over.

My patient satisfaction results had never dipped below 92 percent, which is remarkable, given that the majority of my patients had the worst cancer prognoses and would be dead within a year. It was even more noteworthy in light of the fact that my time was frequently diverted by my myriad other responsibilities. Still, my attorneys feared that someone might seize the opportunity, claiming that I had done something bad in order to collect damages from the institutions that allowed a piece-of-shit doctor to practice medicine there. More to worry about.

I received a few pieces of hate mail over the next few days. A few stood out. One was from an old girlfriend who basically called me a monster, said she was praying for my children, and offered to take them away from me for their safety. Another was an anonymous letter with the passages from the newspaper about my children's alleged victimization highlighted and annotated with a few handwritten scripture quotes; the writer said that my wife and I were demons for abusing our own children and that God would ensure we'd burn in hell for all eternity. I received a letter from the Ohio State Medical Board asking that I permanently surrender my medical license—meaning they never wanted me to practice in Ohio again. Fortunately, my medical board attorney (the fourth attorney I would retain) interceded, and the board allowed me to voluntarily suspend my license until the criminal case was over. Still, I was told not to get my hopes up about ever practicing again in Ohio. I also received a late letter from the children's hospital stating that I was named in a child pornography investigation and it was strongly suggested that I resign (I already had, of course). To this day, I still flinch at a fresh pile of mail, like a combat solider who jumps at the pop of firecrackers.

A few of the neighbors who had small children themselves told my wife they preferred to not associate with us anymore. They cited the local TV station news reports that said I admitted to involving children I knew. That was it. Sadly, one of those homes was where my daughter went to play almost every day. She was not allowed to go there anymore.

I was told OSU and Nationwide Children's Hospital forbade my former colleagues from talking to me. I felt like a hot potato that everyone wanted to drop. Within the next day or two, the facts of the case were somewhat clarified—that there was no suspicion of improper direct contact or molestation—but by then no one was paying any attention.

We had our children stay with our parents for about a week so that we could see how it was going be on the home front. Once we were confident no bricks would be thrown through our windows, no images of me hanging, burning in effigy from a tree, no protesters camped on our front lawn, we felt safe enough to allow them to return to us. We dreaded having to tell them that they couldn't see their nearby friends any longer, right when they would probably need them the most.

My parents drove them down to Columbus, and when they arrived we kept things as normal as possible in the children's presence. Once they went to sleep, a very long, uncomfortable discussion with my parents ensued, full of anger, sadness, disappointment, and horror. They had to absorb everything at once. Not only did their son (who was until very recently a source of pride) just have his life publicly destroyed (and their own reputations too, by association and surname), but they learned for the first time that their little boy had been sexually abused multiple times at multiple hands. It was draining.

Nonetheless, before they left that weekend they had begun to process what had happened and why I was the way I was. A lot of mysteries about me were starting to make sense finally. I had a particularly long talk with my father before he left, after he'd been able to ruminate on the topic for a couple of nights. The news hit him the hardest, initially. It was extremely important to me to have his support, and I finally did.

Once my parents were gone, we needed to discuss the new rules and conditions of my house arrest with the children. It was a conversation I had been dreading, but it had to happen. Both children sat with Susan on the basement couch, with me opposite them on the shorter arm of the L-shape sectional. She started, "OK, we need to talk about some new rules. Daddy made a mistake and did something bad that made people mad at him. He is not a doctor anymore. He might be later, but not now. He is going to stay home now." My daughter's face flushed when she heard about me not being a doctor. She loved the fact that I helped sick people, especially sick kids. She had toy stethoscopes and thermometers and always took care of her "sick" stuffed animals, asking me for an occasional consult.

"So, Daddy is in trouble because he did something bad?" My daughter asked.

"Yes. He is in grown-up 'time-out,' and he has consequences."

"What are 'consequences'?"

"They are new rules of a punishment. Daddy cannot go out to places with us, or play outside. We cannot have your friends come over and visit us. Also, some of the people who are mad at Daddy don't want any of us to go over to their houses, including the moms and dads of your friends. It is not your fault. You did nothing wrong. Sometimes when grown-ups don't get along, it makes new rules for kids, too. It is not fair to you guys, I know, but that is how it is."

"So, Daddy does not have a job anymore?" she continued her questioning. At this moment, my son slowly walked over to me, climbed into my lap, hugged me, kissed my cheek, and kept his arm around me, not saying a word. He just held on to me and looked at the floor of our basement. I hid my tears from him.

"No, but Daddy will work again when his consequences are done," my wife continued.

"How long will the consequences last?"

"We don't know. Grown-up time-out takes a very long time." My daughter looked at me with disappointment. Sensing this, Susan added, "Daddy is still your daddy. He loves you and we love him. He did something bad, it was a mistake, but he is not bad. Daddy is not a bad person. Also, Daddy cannot be alone with you. Mommy needs to be there, too."

"If Daddy is good, why do *you* need to be there, too?" My daughter never misses a beat.

"It is just the rules for now."

I finally added to the conversation, "Daddy will be home a lot now. I will be able to draw, read, and build Legos now. I am so sorry that I made a mistake."

"Why did you do a bad thing?"

"You guys remember how I was 'Yelly Daddy'?"

"Yes."

"Well, I was that way because I was not feeling very good. So I was mean to you guys and did the bad thing. But I will get better and not yell so much. We will have fun with me being home. I promise." My son hugged me again, but my daughter remained skeptical. I had been Yelly Daddy for quite some time. So not only had I been mean and grumpy, but now I'd done something so bad that even grown-ups were mad at me. Further, because of me, she was losing friends that were part of her everyday life. I was definitely not on her list of favorite people at that moment.

Her personality significantly changed over the next two weeks. She sensed the tension between her mother and me, and there were all of the abrupt changes in plans and rules. Just as I did when my parents argued, she always tried to insert herself in any of our conversations to deflect our attention—often when we were discussing pressing matters. She became much more clingy, irritable, afraid to sleep by herself, emotionally labile, hypervigilant, and sensitive to any criticism or discipline. It added enormous stress to an already fraught situation.

However, I would always remember that on the day we told my daughter of my consequences, after my wife reminded her a little later not to step foot into the adjacent yard, she came up to me and said, "Daddy, I love you, but I am very mad at you that you were bad and have consequences. But I still love you," and then stomped off. Most adults cannot articulate their emotions so clearly. I was so proud of her, and I felt like an incredible loser for not being as forthright with my emotions in the past as she was, and for bringing this mess into her life.

Chapter Seven

L OVE SAVED MY LIFE. It was receiving the unconditional love and support from my wife and father-in-law that saved me that first night I was alone in a dorm room in the middle of Colorado. With each passing day, I was gifted with more of the same. Being reintroduced to my children over those five days in Colorado helped me endure the day my story broke and the night my home was surrounded. I had been an absent and angry father to them for a while, but they still loved me, and my relationship with them began healing before everything truly started.

This was critical. I was about to lose everything I'd let define me and my worth, yet people still supported and loved me, for me. When my story broke and the local TV news and Internet media portrayed me as a monster, a few days after the shock wore off, the support only increased. Neighbors and people who really knew me, whom I had feared would want me hanging from a tree, started calling me to make sure I was OK and still alive.

And Susan sent out this incredible e-mail to all the women of the neighborhood, shortly after the media explosion:

> Ladies,
> I know some of you have asked that I not contact you, but I wanted to share some information that I thought you might want or like to have. I won't contact you again unless it's absolutely necessary.
> The reason I am writing is to put your mind at ease that you will not be involved in this process. We were assured of this in the beginning, that there was no evidence or information needed from any of you; it's not that kind of case. I have asked again for confirmation from the prosecutor, but thus far I have been assured that there is no

reason for any of you to be interviewed or otherwise attached to this case other than the stigma of living by and socializing with us. And for that I am so very sorry. I know how important social perception is in this town, though I have no doubt you ladies have already done your damage control there; you're too awesome to be dinged by us.

I am so sorry for the fear and confusion that has entered your lives and what you've had to endure thus far. I am slowly coming in and out of various stages of shock and fear myself. I knew some of Chris's childhood abuse, but I had no idea what was happening until my house got raided as I was starting the bedtime process with the kids. And I am sorry I was not allowed to say anything at the time other than there was no danger to any of you (which is also why Chris was allowed some vacation, and is currently at home, and not in jail without bail). I believe him when he says it's like an Auschwitz victim looking at Holocaust photos, but I have several more years knowing him. And no, it doesn't make it less disturbing, just that I understand what he means and that PTSD manifests itself in some horrible ways sometimes. I grew up with someone in a constant fight-or-flight survival mode, so nothing ever seemed abnormal to me. And I know what I would probably think if I wasn't involved and didn't know Chris as well as I do. I still feel like I'm having an out-of-body experience.

My other reason for writing is to again plead for your help in protecting my kids. They are too young to have much information about the reality of the situation. There is enough opportunity for trauma here, and I need to minimize it as much as possible for their sake. I don't want my kind, happy, confident, outgoing kids to become withdrawn and angry. Chris did what he did, and he has to pay the consequences, whatever they may be, but my children should not have to suffer any needless or careless strain and distress. So, please, I ask that adults and kids not ask them questions (they don't know anything) or make hurtful comments, and if you see gawkers hanging out or driving by one too many times, please say something, or let me know so I can say something. Hopefully that novelty will soon pass.

In the same vein, for the sake of getting my family through this, I have chosen not to read or watch the news, and I do not want to know the gory details of what my husband was viewing. If you have investigated this, please keep it amongst yourselves. I cannot absorb that, and take care of my kids and myself. My imagination is bad enough and I don't want to actually know. What happens between the two of us will be decided in time. I have been with him for 20 years, and right now he needs my help, and I have very young children I need to guide through this mess as cleanly as possible.

For those of you that have asked my children to also stay away, I plan to tell them simply that the adults have had a disagreement that will take some time to sort out, and unfortunately sometimes in these situations the kids get caught up in it as well. So, if you get approached (my guess is by my too-crafty-for-her-own-good daughter), that's what I'm going to say.

For those still in support, I cannot ever thank you enough. It gives me extra bursts of strength when I think I have none left.

Once we have a better grasp on what will occur the next few months and what will be Chris's restrictions, we will be selling the house. Once Chris is sentenced (6-9 months from now), who knows what will happen. I will cross that bridge when I come to it. For now, I am pretty sure I will be pulling the kids from school, and that's about as far as I've gotten. They will be home this weekend, and may go to my parents as various things come up. I'm hoping to keep everything as normal as possible for their sake.

Thank you for your time, and again I'm so very sorry, and so is Chris. He cannot express how truly sorry he is that his release from this mental torment has negatively affected all of you, and mostly his own family.

I read this email with the same admiration I have when I watch a momma bear defend her den and cubs on a National Geographic documentary. The support we received only grew after it was sent out. Our neighbors rallied. And, yes, in July, when mental health professionals and attorneys were trying to package my neuroses with the more traditional labels of depression, alcoholism, and/or sex/porn addiction that the courts would understand, along with my long-standing "established" history of ADD and generalized anxiety disorder, my wife made the diagnosis of post-traumatic stress disorder. I was a bit skeptical about this. PTSD? No. That was what soldiers got from combat. I never did any combat.

Outsiders' perception of our Upper Arlington neighborhood is that it is a bit haughty and blue-blooded. Since Susan and I both come from working-class families, in which our parents were the first generation to go to college, we did feel out of place when we first stumbled onto the neighborhood. We thought the old homes looked cool and liked how the neighborhood was full of old trees and winding roads. We had no idea of the deep regional traditions and class antagonism that came with the address.

As in Shaker Heights or the Main Line, families in Upper Arlington have lived there for many generations. It was odd to be asked which UA elementary school I attended growing up. My first inclination was to say I'd gone to the Feinberg School of Medicine at Northwestern University, which would presumably have rendered moot the question of from which institution I'd matriculated primary school. Instead, I would politely say that I did not grow up in Upper Arlington. So you can imagine how terrified we were of how we would be perceived by the neighbors when my story broke—following a theatrical police raid and TV news media encampment on our front lawn. Not only were we outsiders to UA, but our presence and my offense imparted a glaring blemish to its pristine linens. Even the dignified homes and ancient trees seemed to collectively shake their heads in disgust at us. At me.

But we saw none of that. How the media and hateful bloggers treated us was *not* a harbinger of things to come. Out of all the neighbors in our immediate vicinity, all but two households were in our corner. The support from our UA neighbors was unprecedented and overwhelming. Even people we barely knew or rarely saw, or who were from more remote parts of the neighborhood, showed us unwavering support. If my wife was outside or out on the sidewalk, people driving by would stop their cars, get out and tearfully hug her, and offer anything to help her. Families brought us dinners, visited and talked with us, offered to watch our children for a while so Susan could get away for a bit. On one day in October, fifteen households in our neighborhood sponsored a luncheon as a show of support and care for my wife. There was a huge food spread and they gave her a gift card to a local fitness center that offered child-sitting services.

I heard stories of neighbors yelling at the reporters, calling them "low-life vultures" and complaining to the police about them. Children from the neighborhood who knew me were telling their parents that Dr. Pelloski is a good guy, and they don't know what they are talking about. I don't believe he would ever hurt any kids. The very next day after the media swarm at my home, a neighbor, the mother of two girls called me, and gave me her usual cheerful greeting—"Heeeeey! What's goin' on?"—to tell me that nothing had changed.

The elementary school where my children started kindergarten was incredible as well. The teachers and principal, and the parents of my children's classmates, were understanding and supportive, and made every effort to absorb any of the stressors my case could have created for my children. Susan met with the staff to see if the kids were even going to be allowed into the school. She was met with open arms and a pledge to preserve my children's well-being. So we enrolled them in kindergarten after all.

Later in the year, when they turned six, we threw them a birthday party. Twenty-nine children, mostly from kindergarten and a few from their old preschool, showed up, and they all had a blast. No one declined the invitation, cancelled, or tendered a relatives-suddenly-showed-up-in-town-sorry-we-can't-make-it excuse. The whole community rallied around my children to make sure their kindergarten experience was normal and healthy. I couldn't ask for anything more. I just hoped they would be treated well. And they were.

Even the neighbors who initially pulled away from us softened their stances over time and allowed my children to play with theirs again. One of our initial detractors made sure our sidewalk was plowed and clear for us in the winter, and reestablished contact with me and encouraged me during therapy. When my family's lives could have taken another scarring turn, compounding the trauma that my case generated, the community of Upper Arlington, Ohio, stepped up and helped my wife and children. It could have been easy for others to turn their backs on them and assume they were already damaged goods. But they did not. For that, I will be eternally grateful.

It would be dishonest to say I was never outraged over how everything played out in the media and the response it generated. On the other hand, I understand how the game is played and that many people's intentions were good. The wave of fear generated by the local news should have been of no surprise to me. It was business, not personal. Local news has to compete with twenty-four-hour news channels and Internet news outlets. When they have a juicy story, they need to milk it for all it's worth. That is what brings in the clicks and viewers, and generates revenue, which puts food on the table. And, in fact, many people don't want real news. Real news is boring. The only time C-SPAN ever grabbed a decent Nielsen share was when Clarence Thomas and Anita Hill were talking about pubic hairs on Coke cans and Long Dong Silver.

The next wave of support came from my laboratory group and residents. In their eyes I was still their principal investigator and program director, respectively. The day after my charge went public, when I was avoiding windows and doors, hiding from news crews, my chief resident's father left a bag of Subway sandwiches hanging from my side door. Since I didn't recognize him, I assumed they were poisoned and promptly threw them away when he drove off.

Eventually my coworkers and residents all ignored the unofficial and "plausibly deniable" OSU gag order and started contacting me and coming over to visit while I remained on house arrest. Over time, I was even able to do some troubleshooting on the research projects I had initiated, do a little data analysis, and give career guidance via texts and house visits. All off the record, of course.

Once they felt safe enough to reach out to me, they all did. They came in droves, and we shared texts and phone calls, potluck dinners and visits at lunchtime, TV football and beer (at least until I was forbidden to have any alcohol as a condition of my bond). They all came to see me to make sure I was OK. Many were stunned to see how much younger I looked and how much weight I'd lost. It is amazing what stress does to a body. My blood pressure, when measured during my alcohol abuse evaluation in early August (at the height of the media circus, no less), was 118/70! It hadn't been that low since high school.

I'd hovered around 145/85 for the two years before my arrest. I'd also instantly dropped twenty pounds, without changing what I ate and with no exercise during those first few months on bond.

There were also other reasons besides friendship and moral support that people reached out to me. A disturbing and tragically common theme was their own childhood sexual abuse. I was amazed by how many people confided in me that they, too, had been sexually abused as children. Many were women, but there were several men, as well. For some, I was the first or second person they ever told. Some were people I had known my whole life; others I had only met recently. They all knew that something happened to me as a child the moment they heard about me in the news. Some envied the relief I'd gained by being forced to talk about it. Yet they found solace in talking with me about what happened to them. It was as if we were members of our own secret society and had finally discovered our mutual hidden allegiance. I was able to convince a few to start counseling. For others, who did not have the time or the funds to get counseling, I encouraged them to at least tell the people close to them. Nothing beats just getting it all out. Even if the life around the sufferer is crumbling, getting it out is liberating.

Though there were quite a few tears in these meetings, there were also laughs. One of the nurses I used to work with, who'd come to visit us, noticed people driving slowly by the house and gawking after our address was pasted all over the news and Internet. So, as she drove off after her visit, she made sure we saw her pass our house going three miles an hour staring blankly out her open window—followed by a goodbye wave and her huge, infectious belly laugh that we could hear across the yard and street. Moments like that kept things light for us. These moments were all additional layers of support that proved I had many people and things to live for.

One glaring gap in my support network was the academic faculty physicians who were my primary colleagues. They didn't return my texts and refused to write a character reference or to testify on my behalf at my sentencing. Neighbors, friends, family members, students, residents, nurses, physicians in private/community practice, and basic science researchers all leapt at the chance to support me. Some were people whom I did not know well personally, and yet they still wrote letters on my behalf to my judge. Some wrote without even being asked. Many owned private companies or had law firms that were their own businesses, and thus had much more to lose by sticking out their necks for me. But no support came from medical doctors who were on faculty at the university hospitals where I'd worked. None from the people beside whom I'd fought in the trenches on almost a daily basis, for years.

Even the few academic physicians who were initially supportive fell silent as time went on. Some told me they could not talk to me or support me because of the mandate given by their legal departments (which is technically illegal, since that would be interfering with their freedom of speech outside the workplace). When I asked if they could write a letter of support on my behalf, the near-unanimous response was *Let me talk to Legal first.*

No one else, in any other line of work, including other *physicians* in the private sector, ever said anything even remotely similar to this in their responses to me. There was no need for *anyone* to check with a third party first, except the academicians. It was especially difficult to hear that many supported me or understood, but could not get involved out of fear of some hypothetical risk to their careers. One physician from the West Coast basically told me that her academic position was her entire life and identity and, while she was sympathetic to my predicament, she could never do anything to jeopardize it—whether the danger was real or imagined. This was a person I'd spent many hours with in the past, talking her down from the ledge during her first few years of grueling post–med school training. However, I would get no help from her when it was my turn to desperately need it.

It would have been one thing for them to tell me to go to hell, if they felt that my offense was unforgivable. But it was disturbing to hear that physicians—some of whom had psychology or neuroscience in their backgrounds, and were thus far better able to appreciate the long-term effects of childhood trauma than the average layperson—did in fact support me in spirit and in theory, but were being successfully bullied into involuntary silence. After all that hardcore studying, long hours in the lab courses, their twenties spent tirelessly working round the clock in hospitals and shouldering a massive accumulation of educational debt—they lacked the courage to follow their own conscience? At what point did we physicians, especially those in academia, collectively and figuratively lose our balls?

While we all know universities are notoriously competitive and are never beyond reproach, on a personal level many individual physicians and scientists within those institutions still believe in a higher cause. From the day we step into medical school to the day we leave academia, it is pounded into us that academics are supposed to be above politics and the prejudices of laypeople. For thirteen years, academia told me that private practice physicians are self-centered, unprincipled, and concerned only with money. A steadfast belief endures in many corners of academic medicine that a physician who leaves for private practice has betrayed that higher calling and joined what many in academia call the "dark side." Academia, at least for many within it, has successfully sold itself as a bastion of science and altruism, a beacon of enlightenment, an arena immune to fear and ignorance.

When it came time to support me, however, academics were dissuaded from doing so by self-centered entities concerned only with money. The irony is that, in sticking to their principles, the private practice guys were selfless in their actions despite the financial risk of attaching their names to mine. Thus, academia showed itself to be hypocritical through and through and without conviction in the principles it is supposed to represent. Further, even though academics deceive themselves that it is "not about the money," by letting others handle it, they are just as beholden to the corporate/business side of medicine as private practice physicians.

At first I felt quite betrayed by my colleagues. They'd turned their backs on me when their endorsement could have provided so much help for my family and me. This was the community in which I'd been working myself to death, shaving years (if not decades) off my life while isolating myself from those who actually loved and cared for me? This was how much I mattered to the field, which demanded that I dedicate myself to a point where all I would have to show for it would be my son coldly and distantly reciting my CV as my only eulogy while a gold medal is laid upon my corpse? It was an incredible eye-opener for me.

But a double-dose of reality crept in during my healing process. The first was that I was lucky that *anyone* would support me at all, given my charge and the public perception. The second was realizing that I could not blame those who would not publicly support me. I used to be one of them, self-absorbed and ball-less. Would I have stuck my neck out for someone in my same situation had my career continued unscathed? Probably not.

I, too, would have rationalized why I could not get involved. A physician who treats children and is the director of Pediatric Radiation Oncology cannot be associated with someone who was caught with child pornography—even though I would *certainly* have understood how someone could arrive at that activity, given my own personal history. I would have had a career to worry about. I would have had places to go and positions and titles to acquire. I could not have that blemish on my record. *No way. Sorry, man. You are on your own with this,* would have been my response, too. I would have abandoned my colleague in need and bowed to the PR interests of university administrators and legal officers, even though they did not understand the mental health aspects as I did.

So I counted my blessings for the support I *did* receive, and let it go.

Chapter Eight

A S MY LEGAL CASE EVOLVED, the decision for me to plead guilty was confirmed. There really was nothing to contest. I'd confessed, and there was ample computer forensic evidence that I had viewed child pornography. The hope was that because of this plea agreement and my cooperation, the prosecution would not ratchet up the technicalities. As another part of this deal, I was to undergo an interrogation with lie detection. The prosecution wanted to verify that I was not a physical threat to children and had no sexual attraction toward children.

Agreeing to be questioned in this fashion is seen as a good sign in and of itself. Many assume that those with child pornography charges have a lot to hide and will avoid this type of interrogation and analysis at all costs. I, however, was chomping at the bit for it. It was the first time I would get to officially talk about my case to anyone from the other side since my conversation with the detective during my home raid.

The method of testing was called CVSA, for Computer Voice Stress Analyzer. I will always remember those letters because they were pasted on the computer that sat before me on the detective's desk. The microphone clipped to my shirt collar was plugged into its USB port. CVSA is a screening tool for the more well-known and more expensive polygraph ("lie detector") test. The science behind CVSA is very interesting. When a person speaks there is a low-frequency vibration of the vocal cords that reflects the level of stress placed upon them. This frequency is not audible in the normal human range of hearing. It is in the infrasound range of eight to fourteen hertz, the same frequency range that African elephants use for communication at long distances (up to six miles) to coordinate the movement of herds and locate mates.

The stress on the vocal cords is an indirect measurement of the nerve impulses that arrive from the brain to make the cords produce sound. When you tell the truth or say something direct or sincere, the speech and motor portions of the brain coordinate and send signals down to the vocal cords. Lying requires a bit more work by the brain. A third part of the forebrain has to run some interference when what you're saying is the opposite of what you know. This extra work is transmitted via extra signaling, and this extra input causes microtremors in the cords, which are detected by the CVSA software. Thus the test is used more to verify truth telling than to detect lies.

If I failed the CVSA or the results were inconclusive, then I would move onto the full polygraph assessment. This would mean a lot more time and money spent on all sides, so the hope was that the CVSA would conclude this part of the investigation. Both sides were fairly certain I was "safe," but they needed some form of scientific documentation to support it.

Before beginning the assessment, I met with the prosecutor, Newton, and the detective who would conduct the questioning to go over the ground rules. It was September 25th, at this point, seventy-one days since the raid on my home. The interview (or interrogation, depending on whose point of view you took), was to last an hour and would consist of an open "conversation" (to verify overall truthfulness) and then a set of three agreed-upon questions run through the CVSA toward the end of the hour. No lawyers were to be present, just the detective and me. I was told if the questioning wandered off track or if I felt I was getting backed into a corner, I would have "kill-switch" capability and could stop the meeting and demand that my attorney intervene. I told them this was not going to happen with me; we could talk about anything (though of course my attorney got a little squirmy with that statement).

The three agreed-upon questions by my attorneys and the prosecutor were:

1. Have you ever masturbated to images of [your own children] in various states of undress?

Since we had pictures of them naked after baths and because of my charge, this question had to be asked. It was so difficult hearing and seeing their names in this context.

2. Have you ever derived any sexual gratification from your pediatric patients?
3. Have you ever derived any sexual gratification from [your own children]?

Again, it was agonizing to see their names.

An additional eight sample and control questions would also be analyzed to establish baselines. I signed some papers, and off I went with the detective down a corridor to the interrogation room. It was ten by ten feet, a cube of a room in the belly of the Sheriff's Department, and had the same suffocating qualities as my holding cell: no windows, all drywall and white-painted cinderblock. The microphone was clipped to my collar close to my throat. I sat across from the detective's desk with the CVSA laptop between us.

"Now, before we start, we need to be clear on some things," he stated. He was a big guy with serious eyes and a military-style haircut. Not tall, but big—his hands were weathered and massive and looked like they could easily crush a clutch of walnuts. On our way in, he'd told me a little of his time in the Marines and that he had been on the police force for almost thirty years. If he was trying to scare the shit out of me, it worked.

"We need to be clear on what sexual gratification is, because it can mean different things for different people. As far as I am concerned it is *anything* sexual. It goes beyond rape or physical violation. It is more than what we think of as molestation. It can be extra touching, like when giving children baths or, in your line of work, if you spend more time than you need to do a physical exam. Or, you can have children touch you in a sexual manner. Or it can be indirect. Photographing or filming children for your sexual arousal. Masturbating to pictures or movies of children, pornographic or even nonsexual media. Or observing children when they are not even aware of it while you are getting some sort of sexual pleasure: masturbation or lustful thoughts. Another example is showing children pornography or other inappropriate media. Basically, anything where you gain sexual arousal at the expense of children."

"I am perfectly clear on your definition and I agree with it, too." I said, assertively. "There is one thing I want to clarify, though."

"What is that?"

"Question number two: Did I ever derive sexual gratification from my pediatric patients? I want that expanded to any and all children I have ever seen: Did I ever derive sexual gratification from any child? That is what I want asked and answered."

"Are you sure? Do you want to run that by the attorneys?"

"No. In addition to the parents of my patients, I have neighbors who think I was checking out their kids. I want this addressed. My wife wants this verified!" Just about everyone I talked with about my viewing—friends, neighbors, mental health professionals—all assumed that I got off on child pornography. They couldn't understand that I was torturing myself with it and making myself remember what happened to me. Expanding the scope of the question would include *all* children. Even those in the illicit media that I viewed. I needed this clarified.

"Really?"

"Yes, there was a lot of untrue stuff about me in the media, too. I want to make things clear."

"OK. We are clear this includes *any* children in *any* media you have *ever* viewed?" he seemed like he thought what I was offering was too good to be true, from an investigator's perspective.

"Yes."

"You know, most people who are in the trouble you're in don't even want to sit down and talk, much less *expand* the scope of the questions." He looked at me for a while, expecting me to renege. I didn't flinch. He shrugged his shoulders and then took pen to paper to make changes. "OK … I will modify question two." I had just swung the door wide open. He seemed pleased that I wanted this asked. Given his line of work, he definitely wanted to ask this question. It was the question everyone wanted answered.

I gave him the thumbnail sketch of my career. He told me how much experience he had with CVSA, and then the investigative questioning began—not the analysis questions, but the credibility questions.

"OK, we are going to get to it now. Aside from the agreed-upon questions, I am going to ask you other questions to make sure you are open and honest about things regarding your case in general. The first question I have is why? Why were you drawn to child pornography?"

"The first time I had ever saw it, I was expecting 'normal,' legal porn to show up, but instead, it was something else. I got sick: headache, nausea. I could feel my heart beating, my chest hurt. Then I realized that I was made to do what I was viewing when I was the same age as the girl in the video clip."

"You were abused?"

"Yes. It was a man who had a pool and invited kids over all the time. That was the first one I remembered."

"There was more?"

"I was abused by at least three different adults from the ages of three to eight or so." I could see genuine sadness in his eyes. "I can't remember exactly what happened when I was three. The pool guy happened around five or six years old, and a distant family relative, a woman, was the third, when I was about seven or eight.

"I know I haven't remembered everything." At this point, the detective became somewhat choked up and quietly, solemnly told me that someone close to him has been abused. "Aw man, I am so sorry," I said.

"Yeah, that is why I decided to work for this task force. To protect children. To speak for those who cannot speak for themselves." I could see the warmth, pride, and concern in his eyes, behind his formidable stare. He quickly snapped back to the task at hand, however.

"Did you ever tell anyone or try to press charges?"

"I am sure the guy with the pool is dead. I am not sure who exactly the woman is or what happened the very first time. I told my grandparents about the woman, but I was told to be quiet and not be 'dirty.'"

"I know you have helped a lot of kids with your work. And so I know you understand why we are having this conversation here today."

"Yes. You guys want to ensure the safety of children. I get it. And I *do* want kids to be safe, too." We had an understanding. Sure, I knew he needed to gain my confidence and trust to make me relax—and maybe accidentally divulge some extra information he could investigate. It was all part of standard interrogation practices. But I also felt that he believed, on some level, that my concern for children was genuine, despite my offense and its appearances to the contrary.

"Getting back to the offense. How would you do it?"

"I would download a peer-to-peer file sharing program. Type in search terms. View whatever came up. And when I could not look anymore, I would delete all the files and uninstall the program."

"That is how you always did it?"

"Yes."

"You do realize that when we analyze the computers, we can check time-stamps, times of possession, and keystrokes." I knew they already had all the answers; he was testing me.

"Yes. You guys got everything. Every computer we ever owned, you have. We never threw them out because they had bank and credit card account information. We didn't want identity theft to occur."

"I can understand that. Computers are scary that way."

"Yes. Apparently they store *everything*." I was pushing my luck, trying out my gallows humor, but he just nodded to confirm my observation.

"So why your work laptop?"

"After we moved to Columbus, we never used our old desktop again. There was no convenient place to set it up. That was why it was in a heap when you guys found it during the raid. I was glued to my laptop at all times. So that was what I used. I never used any OSU servers or systems. Only my home Internet line."

"So, before your activity in Columbus, 2012, when was the last time you looked at child pornography, on that or any other computer?"

"It was in '06 or '07. I stopped once my kids were born. I thought I was over it and didn't want to pick at that scab like that again."

"So, the time-stamp on these deleted files should be '06 to '07?"

"Yes."

I believe he got what he wanted, because our attention then switched to the three questions to be analyzed. The concept of CVSA and the science behind the questions that would be asked were explained. My anxiety returned after the break that our initial discussion had provided. There were going to be six positive control questions with yes or no answers that were correct—things like *Your name is Christopher Pelloski?* (yes), or *Your shirt is blue?* (no; it was green). Then there were to be two negative control questions with known untruthful responses: *Is the wall black?* (yes), and *Have you ever exceeded the posted speed limit?* (no).

The scientist in me appreciated this approach. Several variables were controlled for here. Truthfulness, of course, but even the difference between honest and false phonations of the words *yes* and *no* were taken into account. However, the emotional human side in me became acutely self-aware. I was sitting in a cement box with an ex-Marine whose job was to tear those who harm children a new one, and who on some level suspected that I deliberately and physically harmed children. The media, bloggers and their readers, and even some from my hometown—all assumed I was a monster. All of this loomed in my mind, and the content of the questions wasn't even in the same ballpark in terms of relevance and intensity. A question about wall color compared to whether I molested my own children was like comparing a pinprick to a shotgun blast. These questions were going to be the deciding factors in all of this?

Would my own nerves betray me? Every time my children's names were mentioned, I got hot-cold flashes thinking about harm being done to them and how old I was when things happened to me. Would a rush of blood from my intensifying heart rate cause a quaver in my voice because I was responding to hearing my children's names or foreseeing new allegations against me (which were the point of the questions)—a quaver that would be interpreted as confirmation that I was indeed a monster. Sweat poured down my back as we proceeded with the questions. After each question was asked, I was supposed to pause a bit before my voice was recorded.

"Have you ever derived any sexual gratification from any child?"

"No," quickly.

"That did not register, I am going to have to ask that again." Fuck! I was getting rattled. How was I going to explain this to my wife? She would leave me, take the kids, and I would never see them again. The prosecutor's worst concerns would be confirmed, and she would come at me with a vengeance. And rightly so, based on the data from this exam—I completely forgot that a polygraph would be the backup if these results of this exam were suspicious.

"I know you want to get ahead of all of this. If you are telling the truth, it will show up. Just wait one second and then answer the questions." I took a deep breath and we proceeded. We hit all of the questions: wall colors, speed limits, and whether or not I was a dangerous sexual deviant. You know, light stuff. He showed me the voice wave patterns afterwards. There were a few lines that looked a little more jagged than the others. The wavelengths on those were a little shorter as well. But overall there was no dominant wave pattern I could see.

"We are going to throw this one out."

"Really?"

"Yes. The second time around clarifies the picture. The first time you are nervous and not sure what to expect, and that can alter the patterns a bit. You are nervous, I take it."

"Uh, yeah. Very."

"Well, if you are telling the truth, you now know how the questioning will run and what it feels like. You are more relaxed, and your voice patterns are more consistent on the second time around. If you are lying, you are now freaking out that you have to lie to the detective one more time. And so that pattern becomes more apparent."

The second time around, there were no hiccups. The big three questions were asked again and I responded at the correct time:

1. Have you ever masturbated to images of [your own children] in various states of undress? *No.*

2. Have you ever derived any sexual gratification from any child? *No.*

3. Have you ever derived any sexual gratification from [your own children]? *No.*

At the conclusion of this second run-through of the questions, he showed me the voice wave patterns again. They were strikingly clearer. Nine patterns were smooth, with equal wavelengths and amplitudes. They were nearly identical, except for the overall length of the recordings, which may have correlated with the differences in how I say *yes* versus *no.* However, two wave patterns were jagged and had varying, but overall shorter wavelengths. Were these the two negative controls? Were those the two lies I was told to make: the wall is black and I never exceeded the speed limit while driving my car. I tried to think which questions these oddball curves corresponded to and replayed the question order in my head. Was number nine the one about my address, or was that the one about whether or not I jack off to my kids? I was scrambling to remember.

Even in this setting, I could not help but analyze data like the inveterate scientist that I am. I would probably calculate the acceleration and force of the guillotine blade as it fell toward my neck, if I ever found myself in that situation—using the last moments of my life to appreciate Newtonian physics.

The detective abruptly pulled away the data and said that we were finished.

"Did I pass?"

"We will look over the results and check on your responses and let your attorney know. Maybe tomorrow we'll know the results?"

I walked out of the department with my attorney, and when we were out on the street, he asked me how it went.

"I was just asked if I beat off to kids or molested my own children. Do you have any idea how fucked up that is?" I was exasperated and exhausted.

"I know, man. I am sorry. But it is done. Hopefully we can move on from here."

It took me about twenty-five minutes to get back to my house. Later that night, my attorney called and informed me, "You've passed." Those two jagged curves *were* the control lies. I would later learn that the microtremors are strictly a function of the brain knowing it is lying and have nothing to do with the stress responses in heart and circulation. Thus questions of wall color and whether or not you have committed a heinous crime can be asked back to back and be given the same scientific consideration.

Both the official and unofficial questions had checked out on the forensic computer evaluation. This meant that both sides knew, with much more confidence, that I was not a danger. In his report, the detective said that, based on his twenty-plus years of experience with CVSA, from the answers I gave he concluded that I was honest and truthful and the voice stress analysis yielded a clear interpretation. His report read:

> Conclusion: Based upon my training and experience, it is my opinion that the subject did respond truthfully to the relevant questions. Due to the gravity of the charges, a second opinion was requested from Det. Sgt. Gregory Danielson, Franklin County Sheriff's Office. The evaluation of the charts was done "in the Blind". The conclusion drawn by Det. Sgt. Danielson were the same as the examiner, that the subject did respond truthfully to the relevant questions.
>
> Briant Watts, Franklin County Sheriff's Office.

The results of this interview and the detective's report were a turning point. This was made clear to me on Halloween night, when a local news channel was running a special on the results of the Internet task force operation. Forty arrests had been made, including mine. A lot of dangerous people had been nabbed—people whose involvement with child pornography was just the tip of their sordid iceberg. These individuals had also committed enticement, rape, and other heinous contact offenses. Horrible. My name was left out of the TV segment and the corresponding printed piece the next day, despite the tempting high-profile aspects of my case. This meant they knew I was not a danger.

It made a huge difference for my wife and children, not having their trick-or-treat experience shadowed by another public dark cloud. My wife saw no drop in turnout as she sat out on the sidewalk handing out candy, and our children happily went around the neighborhood with their grandparents. It was a welcome fresh breath of normalcy, though naturally I remained out of sight in our basement.

Chapter Nine

SEPTEMBER 25, 2013, was a pivotal day. Not only was my CVSA interrogation that day, but it was when I first met my abuse counselor, Rachel. My pretrial services officer, Hank, was getting annoyed that months had passed since I'd been declared an alcoholic, but I was receiving no counseling whatsoever. I was going to AA meetings, but that was not the same as one-on-one therapy. My psychiatrist was still pushing the alcohol angle and bandying about depression and bipolar diagnoses, for legal purposes, of course. I, too, was getting annoyed that I hadn't started therapy. People involved with my case wanted me to talk about drinking, but I wanted to talk about the people who put their tongues, penises, and fingers into me when I was a kid.

Throughout my entire house arrest, Hank was top notch—a true professional, and someone who really cared and wanted me to get better. A pretrial services officer is in the awkward position of enforcing the rules governing a defendant's bond release. These rules are especially complicated in Adam Walsh Act offenses, in which access to the Internet and unsupervised proximity to minors is prohibited. It is the kind of job that could easily cause someone to slip into the role of a harsh taskmaster dealing with a manipulative criminal. While he certainly laid down the law, he was also part psychologist, counselor, and confidant. He could laugh and acknowledge when things *were* awkward— which included his having to verify that the urine streams that would comprise my drug screenings did in fact originate from my penis, via a grocery-store-style convex mirror above a toilet. He would diffuse the tension with a comment like "Well, here is where the friendship ends," followed by chuckles.

Hank provided a human face to the federal machine that had taken over my life. He was also very sensitive to my children's psyches. He would time most of his unannounced house visits for when my children were at school. It was also his call to allow kids to trick-or-treat at our house, provided I stayed out of sight in my basement. I appreciated that gesture and his trust.

Because of a catch-22 created by the twenty-eight-day inpatient treatment requirement for "impaired" physicians and the need for twenty-four-hour monitoring by the court, I hung in alcohol treatment limbo from July until late September. Finally, Hank felt we'd waited long enough and I needed to start some kind of substance abuse counseling—not just going to AA. That was when my abuse therapist, Rachel, entered my life.

When I called her, I got her voicemail. So I left a message telling her if she needed any background information on me to just look up my name on Google. When she called back, I could hear the discomfort in her voice, "Ah … Hello, uh, Chris, er, uh, Dr. Pelloski."

"You must have looked me up, eh?"

Nervous laugh. "Yes, I did."

"It is not what it sounds like. There is much more to the story. I promise I am safe, otherwise, I would not be at home right now." Nervous laugh back.

"I would assume so." She seemed more relaxed. "I know there are many sides to the same story, and I will definitely hear yours. Let's set up an appointment."

From then on, the deep healing began. I told her my story, The Pool Man, Auntie D, my suspected assault as a toddler, the difficulties my parents had when I was very young, ADD, GAD, drinking, school, career, home raid, and my felony charge—all of it. She went through her notepad at a frantic pace, flipping pages, adding in note sheets and Post-its. At some point, she stopped me and asked if I could create a timeline for her and bring it to our next appointment, so she could fully digest my life.

Despite crying and almost throwing up a few times, I was able to recite the facts of my life. Even she looked a bit tired afterwards. "Let me see you twice a week for the beginning, so I can make sure I get everything straight before we start working.

"There is a lot of stuff here. I am so sorry you have had to go through all of this. You have lived a couple of lives, here," she said while trying to organize her papers, not looking at me. Then she paused and looked up, "When just one is hard enough."

During our first meeting, she said my story screamed of PTSD. After hearing me describe what it felt like when I viewed child pornography—that it was what put me in a state of mind to remember—she said it was obvious I had experienced dissociative amnesia when I was molested. Dissociative amnesia is a protective mechanism the mind uses to block out overwhelming stresses or trauma. By witnessing similar trauma I could dissociate enough to remember what happened to me. When I told her that watching children being sexually abused took my mind to where it went when I was abused, she said it was a classic dissociation trigger. That is why my memories remained repressed until the first time I stumbled across child pornography and saw something very similar to what had happened to me.

One of my friends who reached out to me when this began, who was abused herself, said she completely understood. She had gone throughout her adult life not realizing she had been abused, until decades later she saw the relative who had done it for the first time since it happened. Then she could remember everything.

There is a definite link between dissociative disorders and PTSD. This is because their causes and symptoms overlap somewhat. Painful, traumatic events can cause tremendous emotional and mental disruption in a person's life. So, along with developing post-traumatic stress disorder or other psychiatric disorders, a person may develop something called a dissociative disorder as a way of coping with the trauma. The process of dissociation may be protective. However, in the long term it can wreak havoc on a person's life.

Dissociation. I finally had a name for something I always did when things became horrible or unbearable for me. My world would tear away from the brain and body that housed it, whenever either one became too overwhelmed or acutely injured to retain it. I did this the moment a pile of adolescent fury fell on my knee and cracked it open sideways on the 23 yard line. I did this when I was surrounded by the news crews that created a perimeter around my home, hovered over it in their flying machines, and slithered inside via their televised defilement of my character. I did this when other predators defiled my prepubescent body and innocence. I am quite certain it was those earliest events that taught my mind how to escape to safety—a method that would be repeated and reinforced over the course of my life.

I got real good at it. I was the funniest and had my sharpest wit, giving the appearance of happiness, while emotionally rotting on the inside. So my colleagues and co-workers had been thinking all this time, during my downward spiral, that I was a real hoot, while my family bore the brunt of my anger and anxiety. That is dissociation, too.

Rachel had me take a PTSD screening test, and I scored off the charts for "PTSD with dissociative features" on October 30th. I finally had an accurate Axis I diagnosis—not attention deficit disorder, not generalized anxiety disorder, not depression. And, within five minutes of her hearing about my relationship with alcohol and the ease of my abstinence after my confession, she also ruled out alcoholism.

It took me a long time to wrap my head around having PTSD. When my wife had suggested it in July, I didn't think that was the case. I thought she was being a little dramatic. But damn, Susan had been right again. I hadn't thought of the dissociative amnesia phenomenon since medical school, either. These were psychology and psychiatric terms—and ADD and GAD were the only ones that had ever been applied to me, and I had pills for them. Radiation oncology is about electromagnetic radiation, electron volts, molecular biology, DNA damage, cancer cell kill, tumor kinetics, and clinical cancer staging—not emotions and mental health. It is hard science: physics, chemistry, and biology. I was going to need to dust off some of my books from medical school and start researching whole new sets of scientific journals.

My plea hearing was scheduled for November 15. My attorneys feared that after entering a plea of guilty I might get hauled off to a county jail to remain there during the mitigation process. Because of this concern

I had my forensic neuropsychological evaluation performed the day before I would appear in court. It was a good thing for me; otherwise I would have turned the wood floors of my home into sawdust by pacing back and forth while trying to keep bile from shooting through my nostrils. I had learned to control my anxiety and stress, but I still had reactions within the normal range of emotions. The examination would keep my mind busy. Being carted off to jail just a week or two after I was finally given a correct diagnosis and had reached a good foundation of healing with my family would have been devastating at that juncture. I was worried sick for my children at this vulnerable point.

Although the neuropsychiatric evaluation was for the purpose of establishing the underlying psychopathology for my offense, I wanted it to become an integral part of my therapy, too. It was going to be a daunting task. I knew the media distorted things to make me look like a child molester and get everyone scared, but the analysis that would emerge from this examination was going to be based upon *my* responses and my word only. I was going to be completely open and honest. Nonetheless, I felt some apprehension about truly learning what kind of human being I was.

The evaluation was exhausting: interviews and tests from 9 a.m. until after 2. Fortunately, the forensic psychologist made the day go very well. He was a slightly bowed man whom age had shrunk a few inches; his was the hunch of a learned man who read a lot to make his living. His hair was gray, long, and somewhat wild, not unlike Einstein's famous photo. And like the great scientist's, his eyes were young and lively, and a grin was never far behind as he spoke eloquently and efficiently. While he had the appearance of a quintessential academician of all things psychological (sans only the elbow patches), he sported glasses with bright neon-green frames, wore very shiny patent leather shoes, and had a stack of Post-it notes with FREUDIAN SLIPS printed on one side. This told me that he was the kind of guy who knew his stuff but didn't take himself too seriously. I felt I was going to like him.

"Do you want some coffee? I am going to work with you for a long time today, and I do not want to declare you insane because you got tired on me." Yes, I was going to like him.

"Sure, I can always use a hit of caffeine."

"Let's not jump right into substance abuse just yet." Another grin.

When the coffee arrived, his dark sense of humor came with it. "Looks like you were just stupid enough to get caught. They really didn't find a lot of stuff. Not the amount I am used to seeing. And you deleted everything?'

"Yes."

He sifted through my packet. "I appreciate the timelines your abuse counselor had you make. She is excellent. Her reports are excellent." And so it began. Once again, I was telling my life story and all of its painful details to someone I had just met, who was writing everything down and would soon give what he wrote to others to read.

This was the most comprehensive interview I've ever had. Childhood, work, feelings—we covered everything, from me getting kicked out of preschools to building cancer research programs. We even discussed my preference for classic porn from the 1970s and early '80s. It was extremely awkward to provide the details of what I saw as the "virtues" of that era versus what is produced these days. However, given what was attached to my name, it was probably a good idea to let *everyone* know that I preferred a vulva with hair on it as opposed to a bare one.

I liked the older era better because the arousal was more cerebral (not mechanical and robotic), it was shot on actual 35 mm film like a real movie (not direct to video), the performers looked like real people from the real world, and there seemed to be at least some enjoyment by the performers. In that era, they were trailblazers and so a bit rebellious in their own right. I'd always been fascinated by the history of adult cinema and found the personal histories of these pioneer performers compelling.

Lastly, they had hair on their bodies. I just did not understand the fascination with depilated genitals that has seemed to grip our society since the early 2000s. Why? That is not what adults look like. This was the kind of debate I would have with my friends at 2 a.m. in a greasy spoon somewhere after a night of drinking in college, when they made fun of me for liking the old stuff—not in a setting that would generate a report a federal judge would later read. Still, it was somewhat ironic that I stumbled across child pornography while looking for performers who actually appeared to have attained Tanner stage V.

Describing the instances of abuse was especially difficult. It was so degrading to describe what happened to me, again and again. I did not have any tears left that day, so I appeared stoic and numb, I later learned. I was tapped out. At an appointment with Rachel the day before I'd spent all my tears crying at the thought of being taken to jail.

The clarification questions were especially prodding and painful. "So this was done to you by the man who owns the pool, and yet you still went back to swim again? You didn't think there was something wrong with that, or tell anyone?" This was especially shameful for me. How could I have let my desire to swim in a pool supersede my own safety? I'd struggled with this question during my downward spiral once I realized that The Pool Man had happened more than once. I couldn't answer why. I still can't. To this day, I am not sure what was going through my mind. I was five years old, though. Did I think it wouldn't happen again, or did I rationalize it as what you need to do before you get to swim? Swimming in a big in-ground pool was fun when you were a poor kid. Having to admit that it felt good when my aunt stroked my child penis was humiliating as well. Though, in that case, I did tell my grandparents about it (and even said it was fun), for which I was deemed both dirty and untruthful, despite my insistence.

About my use of peer-to-peer networks, he asked, "What were you looking for? Girls, boys, men, women?"

"I would punch in fairly generic terms and watch whatever came up. You could never tell what was going to show up in that short period of time. When I came back to view again, sometimes I tried to finish watching something that resonated with me before and I would search for that particular thing. But you never knew what would appear from the queue. When memories of what happened with Auntie D haunted me, I actively searched for women participating in the media, several times. These files were rare, but were very jarring to me. It violated nature. Men are pigs, I get that. But mothers are supposed to lift the SUV off of their trapped toddlers or throw their bodies on them to get between them and a deranged gunman—not mouth their genitals."

He absorbed everything I said. Then asked, "Did you masturbate to this?" Again, this question. It was always there.

"No!" I made no effort to hide my annoyance. "This was asked and answered in my interrogation—with lie detection … No."

Again, the expected response followed.

"But you *did* masturbate to normal, legal porn?"

"Yes. When I was horny and wanted sex but couldn't. That's how I took care of things—just like every other guy I have ever known within ten years of my age who wants sex but can't have it at the moment. It is an outlet." This question was really starting to bother me quite a bit. I'd had to masturbate to porn in cold, sterile fertility clinics when my wife and I were having trouble conceiving, and no one had an issue with that. I couldn't just walk into an exam room, drop trou' and deliver my fluid in a cup on command. Like every other grown man who has ever produced a clinical semen sample by himself, I needed (heaven forbid) the natural visual cue of pornography to get things going. Thousands of people owe their existence to, and had their sanctity of life begat by, the miraculous modern procedures performed within maternofetal medicine clinics throughout this great country. And pornography certainly had both a figurative and literal hand in it, too.

"How often?"

"I don't know. Once or twice a week sometimes during the large spans of time that my wife and I were not intimate? Pretty much the frequency with which I wanted to have sex but couldn't."

"Why weren't you?"

"Well, I was rarely home, and when I was I was either yelling at everyone and making my kids cry or working or drinking. Not the most romantic formula for regular lovemaking."

"So, you viewed regular porn frequently. How often was the child pornography?"

"When I was actively viewing, it would be around once every two months. Whatever the affidavit says." My tone started showing my exasperation. "I didn't schedule it on my calendar, and the police were watching me the whole time. They could answer that more accurately than me. That was pretty much my pattern, even before they started watching me. I would view, hoping it would be the last time, and then months, sometimes years, would pass in between the times I viewed. There was a long period of many years in between the two periods of active viewing."

"So you really only viewed during those times you were connected to the peer-to-peer program. Not in between."

"That's right. So I viewed five times while the police watched me for over nine months. I probably have viewed ten to fifteen times over an eight-year period, with a four- to five-year break right in the middle. So much for a fetish, huh?"

"Fetish? Why do you say that?"

"Some cop in the news said it was disturbing that someone like me had this *fetish*."

"Well, was it a fetish for you?" He probed at every opening in the conversation.

"I would think a fetish is something you would like doing more often. And it's not like I kept doing it more and more frequently. I wasn't ramping up my activity. I even took a long hiatus." I needed a comparison. "Come to think of it, my real *fetish* is baseball."

"Baseball?"

"Yeah, during those eight years, I probably did a baseball-related activity—I am counting practices, games, bullpens, workouts, and just watching games on TV—probably, what? … Let me think." I started doing the math in my head. Once a week is about fifty times a year. Twice a week over a year is about a hundred times. "Yeah, twice a week for eight years is about eight hundred times. I certainly liked baseball. I did baseball eight hundred times, even with how busy I was as a doc. Does ten to fifteen times compared to eight hundred times over an eight-year period sound like I enjoyed it to you?"

"Good point." I think he conceded to contain my then-mounting anger and frustration. Without skipping a beat, he moved on. "Did you ever drink and view child pornography?"

"No. I wanted to be stone cold sober when I viewed."

"You mean, you did not drink to get drunk and give yourself

permission to do something illegal?"

"No, this was one of the few times I did not want to be numb. I wanted to remember. Once I built up the courage to look, I did."

"So this was not an enjoyable experience for you?" he still hammered away at this point.

"No! If it was, I probably would have had a few beers while doing it." He could tell I'd had my fill of this line of questioning and tried a different tack.

"There are many reasons why people view child pornography. For a decent-sized proportion of the offenders, it is nonsexual. Or, well, for nonpleasurable sexual reasons: boredom, the sense of belonging to something, the thrill of doing something illegal, curiosity, sexual fantasy, sex addiction, porn addiction—and your reason." He said as he pointed to me, "You are not the first person to tell me it helped you remember your abuse. Your sporadic and infrequent use certainly supports that."

I felt a sense of relief knowing I wasn't the only one who'd lost his mind the way I had.

But then his tone changed from empathy to frustration. "The bottom line, however, is that it doesn't matter what the reason for NP/NCs is, for viewing…"

"'NP/NC'?" I asked, interrupting his train of thought.

"Nonproduction/noncontact—meaning you did not produce child pornography, nor are you a hands-on, contact child molester. And most of your Internet offenders are just that." He paused a bit and then recovered his train of thought. "Yes. It doesn't matter what the NP/NC offender's reason is for being there. The bottom line is, whether it is for sexual or nonsexual reasons, you are never going to do that again."

He sat back in his chair and smiled a bit, "As a matter of fact, I would bet had the police came to your door and said, 'We are watching you,' you never would have done it again."

"Yeah," I said, dejected that this wasn't how it happened.

"'Yeah' is right. That is the case for just about all of you NP/NCs. We in the 'business' call it Door Knob therapy."

"'Door Knob'…"

He cut off my question. "It's when the police turn the door knob of your house before they raid it. It is highly effective, and probably accounts for the bulk of the near 100 percent success rate." He said this with a smile that quickly evaporated before he delivered his next line. "But this is something people don't want to hear. They make these incorrect assumptions. So we have the public floggings that you had to go through." Then his tone became more positive. "Ironically, the viewing of child pornography is the least of the NP/NC's problems. Although society screams about it, you guys have other more serious issues going on, which eventually get addressed, and that also contributes to the low repeat offense rates."

He continued, "People find it difficult to believe that offenders might view child pornography for nonsexual purposes. There is clearly data to suggest that this is true, but it is never the person the detectives and prosecutors are going after. The defendant who is currently in question will always be viewed as actively being in the progression from just viewing child pornography to committing hands-on offenses—even though there is no data to support that assumption either. Actually, whether someone does or does not masturbate to it has no bearing on them becoming contact offenders either."

"Well, to me, people seem preoccupied with the masturbation question because the terminology is misleading."

"What do you mean?

"It is not porn. Porn is something you giggle about and get horny to. The other stuff is childhood sexual abuse and rape. 'Porn' implies fun for all. Child porn is not fun. But, I guess if you called pictures of Auschwitz or Dachau porn, people would wonder if you masturbated to it when you viewed it, too."

I could see in his eyes that he agreed with me and knew that I had been thinking about my offense for a long time. "We could discuss that topic all day, if time permitted. But there are those who feel there is a slippery slope between legal and illegal porn. How are you any different in this argument?"

"There is a vast difference between fully sexually developed participants, with bush, and prepubescent children. And there is a vast difference to why I looked at both."

"Wow. So you engaged in this highly illegal activity, that is very easy to detect online, that cost you your career and reputation—and you didn't even enjoy it? That is pretty masochistic." He started forming his image of how my mind works. He continued, almost perplexed. "And you had this horrible childhood, and then you take care of young people who have cancer and will die soon, and heaped this overwhelming career on top of it. That is pretty masochistic, too." There was a very long pause. "Did you want to get caught?"

"I don't know. And you are not the first person to ask me that."

We both took a moment to digest this very loaded question. Of course there were days I was furious about what happened to me as a child and the way everything all panned out. But, there were other days I was relieved that this happened, that I was no longer struggling to keep my head above water and gasping for air in the world I'd created for myself. At the moment he learned of my charge, a close colleague who'd always worried about my mental health and the amount of effort I expended on my career wondered if my offense and getting caught was my escape.

The closest thing I can compare my viewing to is the well-studied self-harm, or "cutting," phenomenon. The classic example is exhibited in about 70 percent of people with borderline personality disorder. They cut their skin, typically on the forearms. There are a few theories about why these patients do this. One is that those who feel completely dissociated need proof that they are alive. The pain and tangible damage inflicted on their skin provides this proof. Another posits that some individuals may transfer their pain, anger, or powerlessness onto their skin to gain some semblance of control over at least one type of pain that plagues them. Yet another theory postulates that this practice preoccupies the person with a new pain, allowing them to avoid dealing with a different, more chronic psychological pain. Some have concluded that the true purpose of self-harm is as an indirect method of drawing attention to their pain and "asking" for much-needed help. It is probably a combination of a variety of motives and triggers.

I can certainly see the parallels in my viewing, though. I had no control over the suffering I saw in my patients while at work. I had little control over when they died. I had no control over the intrusive thoughts and memories of my abuse that were surfacing during this horrible stretch of my life. I had no control over the sexual abuse that was dealt to me, or how others interpreted my behavior as a young child. When I exposed myself to the trauma of seeing children being sexually abused, at least I got to decide when I did or did not see it, and determined for how long it would last. I had the power to shut it off and make it stop. If I doubted that my memories were real, viewing children being abused would serve as some kind of verification that I was not imagining it, that it did happen to me—that there were adults out there who did this to kids, and this was the proof. If I was numb, depressed, or dissociated from the dull pain of my real life, the surge of adrenaline and other stress hormones into my bloodstream while viewing—the physiologic terror/stress response—certainly convinced me I was still alive.

There is a huge difference, though, in these two methods of self-harm. One requires a knife or razor; the other requires the exploitation of children's suffering, children who have already suffered enough. The similarity of these coping mechanisms ends at the personal cause and effect. The two are wholly and drastically different from a moral, ethical, and therefore legal perspective, and the latter only furthers the pain of all involved.

To this day, I do not know if I broke the law on purpose, subconsciously wanting to get caught. My instinct for self-preservation says no, but the relief I felt when everything came out makes me say yes. I needed something drastic to stop me from hurting myself, to give myself permission to stop and have others force me to stop—not just viewing, but all of the anguish I heaped upon myself. I needed my life as I knew it to stop. I needed a grown-up time-out.

The interview continued, delving to great depths into all the topics of my life. Then came the personality tests: the Minnesota Multiphasic Personality Inventory—2 (MMPI2), and the Millon Clinical Multiaxial Inventory—III (MCMIIII), which collectively consisted of over seven hundred random, and at times bizarre, true-or-false phrases, like:

I have diarrhea once a month or more.

I like mechanics magazines.

Once in a while I think of things too bad to talk about.

My hands and feet are usually warm enough.

Evil spirits possess me at times.

During one period, when I was a youngster, I engaged in petty thievery.

It was endless.

Given the day, the questions, the thoughts of pleading guilty to a felony and going to jail on the following day, I was completely exhausted. I just wanted to crawl into a hole and disappear. When the psychologist returned with the test results, he had a grim look on his face. "Wow, you are fucking bat-shit crazy." Then a smile broke and he continued, "Nah. Just kidding. You are not crazy. Or sociopathic. Or violent." He became a bit more serious again. "But, you are very troubled. Do you see this graph? This is a profile of someone with deep-seated emotional scars which have their origins in early childhood." He showed me the saw-toothed graphs of the MMPI-2. "A 'normal person' [said with air quotes, to soften the blow to my soon-to-be revealed massive ego] would have a nice smooth line that runs in the middle. Yours is very jagged, with significant peaks and valleys, my friend. This is the profile of someone who has been thoroughly traumatized."

He showed me the other graph, from the MCMI-III. "In the personality disorder spectrums, you scored high on the narcissistic and masochistic areas. You were moderate in anxiety and depression. I know you don't have these personality disorders; otherwise you would have no friends and not be as nearly successful as you have been." True personality disorders were always explained to us in medical school with the following scenario: if you had a room of twenty people and one of them had a personality disorder, everyone in the room would have a problem with that one person, except the person with the disorder.

"But there are some traits there," he continued. "It probably was what you developed as a way of surviving the traumas. And, as far as I am concerned, probably every physician, politician, or other type A person would have this kind of profile, especially the narcissistic part." He showed me another graph. "You also scored highly on the Axis I disorders for PTSD, anxiety, and only moderately for alcohol dependence." PTSD again. My wife, my therapist Rachel, and now the personality tests.

The composite summary further characterized me as an emotionally immature and self-indulgent adult with a profile reflecting unresolved and deeply ingrained disturbances. An adult who at one point was rebellious against authority and became estranged and alienated. Who would react compulsively without considering ramifications. There was a pattern of disillusionment and resentment, fearfulness and frustration. This manifested in a strongly contradictory but ever-present preoccupation with success and demonstration of self-worth, while simultaneously possessing an underlying fear of humiliation with anxiety surfacing and depressive thoughts recurring. All of this culminated in a negative perception of a world that I could not comprehend, along with a self-critical stance that prevented me from enjoying meaningful relationships and a manipulative interpersonal style. The data suggested that I was at my core an often sullen and resentful man who likely became angry, if not rageful, when frustrated.

This was a massive punch to the gut. I had heard similar judgments about me before, presented as complaints at different junctures in my life and in different scenarios. But never delivered impartially like this. It was an informative moment. I had always suspected some of this, but now I had words and data to confirm it.

I'd also noticed many of these traits within the academic medical field in general. The career path I had chosen in my life resonated with my pathology. Narcissism and masochism are the engines of academic medicine. You need to both promote yourself and sacrifice an enormous amount of yourself at the same time to make it in the field. Although "making it" is a metric that remains ambiguous to all, and is most likely an ever-receding target, especially when it seems almost within reach. Academia itself is a perpetual existential crisis, in practical terms (*Will my research get funding?*) to a more fundamental ones (*Will my research ever matter in the grand scheme of things?*).

To avoid becoming a serf in the feudal system of academia one must be prepared to enter a war of attrition—to see who can sacrifice the most of their personal life—and I was clearly shooting for the aristocracy. This was always painfully evident when I ran into people I'd trained with who went into private practice. They seemed to have shed the masochistic element and saw academic medicine as just a continuation of training, with a chairman replacing the residency program director. Those in private practice tended to smile more and talk about places they'd recently vacationed, or what their children were doing in school and their kids' extracurricular activities. I could never really contribute to these discussions; I could only talk about my work and give a vague update about my kids: APGAR scores, current age, approximate height and weight and overall health, to the best of my knowledge.

There are many apparently well-adjusted individuals in the field who seem impervious to this status quo, can check their pride at the door, and are content with being serfs—but clearly I was not one of them. The way this resonated with me, however, was more like aeroelastic flutter—always pushing the amplitudes of the peaks and troughs higher and lower, until my mind ripped apart like the Tacoma Narrows Bridge in 1940. Not even my beautiful family, our healthy and happy children, a meteoric career trajectory, and financial security (finally) could dampen these effects. I could never accomplish enough.

"This is good news for you, actually. Well, legally at least." The psychologist snapped me out of my moment of revelation and back to the test results.

"How so?"

"Well, if you were 'normal' [air quotes again] the judge would say, Get the hell out of my courtroom you fucking pervert, why were you looking at child porn? And then throw you in prison for a long time to think about it. If you were crazy or dangerous, you would get locked up for a long time for the sake of public safety. But it is clear—and I know you were answering honestly; there are a lot of cross-checking algorithms to rule out false or misleading answers to sway the results one way or the other, and you were honest—it is clear you had a rough time growing up."

"Jesus. OK, so you ruled me out for being crazy or a deviant pedophile. But it looks like you ruled me *in* for being an asshole. Is there any hope for me in the future? Can I get better?"

My admission and genuine concern was met with an understanding, reassuring laugh. "That is entirely up to you. You are really going to have to take a long, hard look at yourself. And you need to work through your trauma with that excellent counselor you have. Don't just talk about your legal case with her. The case will come and go, but you really need to focus on fixing yourself if you want to really do it."

On my way out of the office, he assured me that I would not be carted off to jail the next day. He said I would have in the past, but for nonviolent offenders like me, "they are realizing that it is best to keep the current therapy going, before prison time. It is easier on everyone that way. People get fixed faster and more efficiently." Had it not been for this last bit of knowledge, I would never have slept that night.

My attorneys, however, remained very concerned by the judge assigned to my case.

Regardless of my career choices and legal trouble, I realized I had bigger personal problems to deal with. The most severe of my traumas came between the ages of three and seven. I was sexually abused several times. My young parents teetered on the edge of divorce, frequently arguing and fighting, while my other main caregiver, my grandmother, lived at the frenetic pace of what I was starting to realize was probably also full-blown and untreated PTSD. I got myself kicked out of two preschools during this time, because I was acting out. I was reeling from all the shit that was done to me and happening in my life. This cycle of acting out and being reprimanded continued for years after, like ripples in water. This in turn reinforced the self-concept that I *was* bad and worthless.

So my emotional development had basically arrested in this setting, where the world truly *was* unstable and unsafe from my point of view. A wounded five-year-old had been running the show ever since. This child became very angry toward and distrusting of authority. Well, hell, of course he did. There were a lot of adults letting him down during this time: physically harming him, saying he was bad, ignoring boundaries, and ignoring him when he was trying to tell them something vital. Eventually, this child had a major score to settle and a cinder block–size chip on his shoulder.

In hindsight, I believe I developed some sort of attachment disorder from about the age of four to eleven. I displayed nearly half of the identified features: delays in school-based learning (I really couldn't read very well until the end of second grade; I only learned things I was interested in, like the names of the bones in the body and the structure of atoms), poor relationships with peers, preoccupation with fire (I couldn't stay away from lit candles or our fireplace), hyperactivity (the suspected ADD) and very little impulse control, inappropriately demanding and clingy behavior. I drove my family and teachers crazy.

I recalled how, as a young adult home from college, I once watched home movies that my mom had made of my brothers and me when we were little. As an adult, I found myself getting annoyed by my child self on the movie screen. I could not hold still. I was an attention-seeking ham. I kept jumping around and mugging for the camera, sticking my face in the lens. I could see my mom's hand frequently trying to move me away so that she could film one of my little brothers crawling for the first time or taking their first few steps. I felt compelled to yell at my child self, *Calm the hell down, you spaz!* I can only how imagine how difficult it was for my folks to deal with me. After just sixty seconds of home movies I'd had enough of myself being so incredibly annoying. It is amazing my young and struggling parents did not beat the crap out of me on a daily basis—and that they actually had two more children after me.

Many trauma and abuse researchers believe that emotional development is somewhat arrested at the time of the inciting action—or at least the achievement of milestones subsequent to the insult is severely jeopardized. When I reexamined Erickson's psychosocial stages, I saw that I had taken on a variety of unfavorable crisis resolutions: suspicion, fear of future events, feelings of shame and self-doubt, confusion over who and what I really was, and the inability to form affectionate relationships. Normally, the stages flow smoothly and sequentially from one to another, but instead, mine were strewn about and severely damaged, a multicar highway pileup caused by a thick fog.

Unfortunately, that child became more empowered and assumed a larger role in governing me when he started to do well and succeed by all measures of authority and society. I starting showing people that I meant something. I could prove them wrong, even if I didn't believe it myself: *You see that, you bastards? How you like them apples?* the wounded child would say every time he accomplished a new achievement despite the sea of doubters and naysayers. He became drunk on success.

I became a cancer doctor to ease people's suffering. My medical school classmates nicknamed me "The Cancer Man," not just because I was obsessed with all things cancer and founded a medical student interest group for cancer, but because I had made cancer my sworn personal enemy. It had killed my mother-in-law a month before my wedding and my maternal grandmother a month later. These were two people who'd had a profound stabilizing effect on me at critical phases of my life, and I was pissed that both were gone. My classmates knew all this, because when I imbibed at cathartic post-test parties, my contempt for cancer would emerge, and in my booze-enhanced Midwestern drawl I would essentially challenge the disease to meet me in the parking lot after work so I could kick its ass in front of a cheering crowd. It was a display of passion and dedication that provoked both amusement and awe among my fellow students.

But, on house arrest, thinking over my life, I started to doubt my true motivations in becoming a top-flight academic physician-scientist. This was particularly disturbing for me. Of course I wanted to help people, ease suffering, and make a difference. That is what a doctor does. That was why I chose that career. But the manner in which I made the decision to be more than "just another doctor" may not have been entirely altruistic, and it was definitely driven, in part, by a needy inner child. At some point along the way, the line between helping others and working toward my own glorification became blurred, and eventually I crossed over it in an attempt to satisfy some pathological need for a sense of worth.

All of this could be described as trying to fill a bottomless hole inside of me, constantly attempting to placate this inner five-year-old child so that he felt significant and loved. I could have cured cancer, won the Nobel Prize, and been the first human to communicate with intelligent life from other planets, and it would never have been enough. It would never have come close to the high I got from that eighth-grade algebra quiz. This is what abuse and trauma during childhood can do to someone (in addition to setting them up for a variety of medical and psychiatric disorders).

It was a revelation. I realized the very success of my therapy depended on nurturing this wounded child, thanking him for getting us so far on his own, and then taking over the reins from him. This is what the personality tests and the forensic psychologist were trying to tell me. Understanding this was critical to healing from my traumas and becoming a better person. I could no longer afford to be defensive about who or what I was while pointing to my success as justification for the unhealthy parts of my psyche. It was almost as if I needed my external validation to be razed to the ground so that the wounded child could no longer be enabled by the accomplishments achieved on his watch.

Chapter Ten

AS I RESEARCHED PTSD and dissociative amnesia, it was like discovering the Rosetta Stone of my life. Since I was barred from the Internet, my former residents and lab workers printed out scientific journal articles from PubMed and dropped them off at my house. I would read them on my elliptical machine, as I'd finally started exercising again. My PTSD symptoms rattled off the checklist right out of the DSM-5 (the American Psychiatric Association's *Diagnostic and Statistical Manual of Mental Disorders,* Fifth Edition, is the most widely accepted resource used by physicians and researchers for the classification of psychiatric illnesses):

> Recurrent, involuntary, and intrusive memories ...
> Dissociative reactions (e.g., flashbacks) ...
> Persistent effortful avoidance of ... [t]rauma-related thoughts or
>   feelings ... Inability to recall key features of the traumatic
>   event (usually dissociative amnesia) ...
> Persistent (and often distorted) negative beliefs and expectations
>   about oneself or the world (e.g., "I am bad," "The world is
>   completely dangerous") ...
> Persistent negative trauma-related emotions (e.g., fear, horror,
>   anger, guilt, or shame) ...
> Irritable or aggressive behavior ...
> Self-destructive or reckless behavior ...
> Hypervigilance ...
> Problems in concentration.

However, it turned out that the best summarization of PTSD had been prepared for me about a year before my official diagnosis. My children started calling me "Yelly Daddy" because of my ever shortening temper and the increasing boom to my voice. My observant daughter drew a fairly accurate picture of me in the midst of a PTSD crisis.

"Yelly Daddy"—My daughter drew this picture of me when she was four years old. It captures the essence of someone in full-blown PTSD crisis.

It also appeared that I had the Selective Type of dissociative amnesia, as described by the DSM5:

Here, the individual is not able to recall all that happened in an event, just a select few tidbits. For instance, a rape victim might be able to recall just parts of the event of rape and not the full event in its entirety ... Individuals suffering from dissociative amnesia also tend to report symptoms of depression, anxiety, depersonalization, trance states, analgesia, and spontaneous age regression. The disorder usually also co-occurs with sexual dysfunction, impairment in relationships, self-harm and suicidal impulse, as also aggressive impulse.

I read the FDA's Advisory on PTSD, provided by the Sidran Institute (see the Addenda section at the back of the book for the full statement), and large sections of it seemed as if they were written with me in mind.

> [C]hildhood sexual abuse was a very strong predictor of the life-time likelihood of PTSD. The trauma most likely to produce PTSD was found to be rape, with 65% of men ... who had been raped developing PTSD ... Epidemiologic studies demonstrate that PTSD is a chronic problem for many people ... Child sexual and physical abuse may not only produce PTSD in some, but may increase PTSD susceptibility in response to later, adult stressors ... Many people with PTSD turn to alcohol or drugs in an attempt to escape their symptoms. Clients who are dually diagnosed with substance abuse and PTSD may benefit from trauma treatment instead of ... traditional model substance abuse programs ... Schools increasingly report disciplinary problems with no understanding that some children may be suffering from violence-related trauma disorders rather than ADHD or ADD. Consequently, they are improperly treated with Ritalin, while their real problems remain unaddressed.

I wondered how many kids get hit with ADD or depression misdiagnoses, are improperly medicated, and live in frustration as I had.

I also came across a phenomenon PTSD researchers call generational reverberation. PTSD sufferers can pass on a genetic trait that makes them susceptible to PTSD to their offspring. And since the parent has undiagnosed/unmanaged PTSD, and therefore poor control of their emotions and responses to stressors, they induce active PTSD in their offspring. Seeing parents flipping out, losing their temper, or yelling is always somewhat traumatic for a child as it is. But for those with the PTSD susceptibility trait, it is as if the parent is yelling into an amplifier with the volume set to 11. Another article gave a specific example, discussing the high transmission rate of PTSD to the offspring of Holocaust survivors and subsequent generations. It widened the scope of my introspection. Looking beyond myself—a mystery that seemed to be unraveling right before my eyes—to the experiences of my entire family.

After reading this article my thoughts immediately went to my grandmother and what had happened to her. I started putting pieces of her story together: bits from my grandmother directly and from my grandfather, father, and things my brothers had said she told them. I began to form a harrowing picture as I finally allowed myself to think and feel for her. She'd survived captivity in Nazi prison camps and God knows where else, from the age of ten to fifteen or sixteen. She was abducted by the SS from her hometown of Klagenfurt, Austria, and thrown onto a train— not for being Jewish but for the purposes of political intimidation.

She died in 2006, and I never heard the details from her. I don't know if she could have told the full story; she rarely talked about it. She bore a scar on her inner arm where there had been a prisoner ID—tattooed or branded, and at some point crudely removed, leaving a fleshy, disorganized bed of keratin. It was as if both her mind and body had tried to erase the experience. The few times she tried to talk about it, my parents told me it was with clenched vocal cords, followed by

My beautiful grandmother at ages 16 and 21. As with me, the emotional scars remained deceivingly well hidden.

silence and her abrupt departure from the room. Keeping it in was a physical demand for her.

She was taken walking home from school. When she disappeared, the town officials, Nazi puppets, publicly declared a child killer that plagued the area's woods had abducted her. However, just before her abduction, her father had forbidden his children to join Hitler Youth and the other Nazi programs that came to Austrian cities and villages after Anschluss, in the spring of 1938. I believe her father was told what really happened, because after my grandmother was abducted, he acquiesced and let his remaining children join the programs. My grandmother was most likely used to set an example for those who would not comply. I am sure he passed the information along to other dissenting households, because there were no further abductions of children from the village by the "child killer," and the participation rate in mandated Nazi programs was nearly 100 percent. My great-grandfather abandoned his moral stance in the interest of his children's lives, though the forced conscription of his three sons by the Third Reich later meant he was unable to protect them in the long run.

Children typically had no use in the Nazis' labor and concentration camps. When they got off the train, they were lumped in with the elderly and those incapable of manual labor, and were gassed and incinerated right away. But there was something about my ten-year-old grandmother that spared her this instant fate. I believe I now fully understand why. I know what adults are capable of doing to children. This evil was augmented by a situation in which civilization, supervision, and accountability no longer existed.

My grandmother was lovely her entire life, even up to her death. In her final repose, her still face was beautiful. She looked like a movie star when she was young—perfectly symmetrical facial structure, piercing, clear dark brown eyes, and teeth a cosmetic dentist could only aspire to create.

It was not until I let my mind fully go and began to think of my grandmother as an incredible survivor that I came to some very disturbing realizations. I am quite certain she caught the eye of a guard or officer and, with the right nod or hand signal, was relegated to a role that is reprehensible, unspeakable, and horrific. I cannot imagine what was done to her, how often, or by how many. From the ages of ten to fifteen, she survived these atrocities, and endured. What terrors and pains did she experience? What other atrocities did she bear witness to?

How does one so young possess the survival skills to make it through, after being stolen away from her mother and father, to transition from child to adolescent while being repeatedly assaulted by wicked and evil demons? Even after she was liberated from the camp, or perhaps escaped from her captors (she never clarified), she had to wander a war-torn countryside to get back home to Austria. Again, her survival skills were tested. At some point she was caught stealing a loaf of bread and had to serve time in a makeshift post-war jail. Later, this "criminal act" nearly cost her the ability to emigrate to the United States, though by then she was married to an American, my grandfather, who'd met her while serving in the U.S. occupation force, and they had a child (my father). My grandfather had to write to one of Michigan's U.S. senators and threaten to renounce his citizenship if his family was denied entry into the States.

When my grandmother returned to her family's pig farm after the end of the war, only her mother recognized her. Her brothers had been all killed in the war, so her sister was her only surviving sibling. My father spent his early childhood in Klagenfurt, and he told me that the atmosphere around the dinner table was so tense even he could perceive it, despite being so young. It makes sense. The person who'd married my grandmother and was sitting across from her family members had been on the side of the war that had slaughtered her brothers and now occupied her country.

How could the adaptations to handle all of these traumas *not* alter someone? Not just the behavior they exhibit for the rest of their lives—as I saw in my grandmother, and now fully understood—but biologically.

In fact, it has been shown that trauma does cause *biologic* alterations—all the way down to the molecular level. As I researched PTSD further, I learned that traumatic episodes and prolonged exposure to a threatening environment can directly alter someone's DNA, specifically the genes that regulate neurotransmitters, stress response hormones, and neuron metabolism. These are all components of the normal fear response, the building blocks of the fight-or-flight sympathetic nervous system. If you have any doubt about whether slight modifications in brain chemistry can affect behavior or emotions, go to a local emergency room and observe people who have taken PCP, cocaine, LSD, ecstasy, etc.

Similarly, with trauma, especially repeated or ongoing trauma, modifications can occur that alter the concentrations of key neurotransmitters and hormones. These alterations can keep the sympathetic nervous system of some people in a perpetual high-alert state and prime them for developing PTSD later in life. These modifications are epigenetic, meaning that the actual DNA *code* is not changed, but the *structure* of the DNA is chemically modified and therefore read differently by the genetic machinery. One such epigenetic process is called DNA methylation, in which the methyl group (CH_3) is bound directly to a cytosine (the C in the T-C-G-A four-base DNA code). Having this extra chemical attachment changes how the genetic instructions are read from DNA. (See DNA Methylation Mechanisms in Trauma and PTSD in the Addendum section at the end of this book.)

I'd researched the role of methylation in the formation of brain tumors toward the end of my residency and beginning of my assistant professorship. Never could I have predicted then that I would be thinking of methylation in the context of the emotional well-being and the behaviors of my family and myself, years later.

DNA methylation can cause a quick environmental adaptation within a generation or two. This is different from genetic mutation, which relies on the DNA sequence itself to change and thus (if it's successful in terms of survival or reproduction) requires many generations before the advantage is realized by the species. Methylation can not only induce changes in the appearance or behavior of a living thing within the subject's lifetime, but it has been shown that the subject can pass this change on to its offspring. So it is almost like an expedited evolution in some way.

One fascinating experiment demonstrating this mechanism involves taking mice embryos from a litter that are genetically identical (same DNA sequence, like identical twins) and implanting them into genetically different females, which carry the embryos to term. One set of the females is given a normal diet, and the other nearly starved.

When the pups are born, the starved ones are smaller, as you'd expect, but later in life, these mice become obese compared to their normal counterparts, who remain within normal weight limits—even when both sets of growing mice are given the same amount of food. When the DNA sequences of the mice are compared, they remain identical. But when the methylation patterns throughout their DNA are compared, the differences are striking, especially on the genes governing metabolism and so, ultimately, body weight. The code-within-the-code is entirely different, and it yields a very different phenotype.

So what does all this mean? Methylation can prepare the next generation to be ready for something—some kind of stress. During gestation, the lack of food leads to changes in DNA methylation that tell the starving mouse embryo, *Hey, you better absorb and retain as much energy and nutrients as you can (by storing it as fat and becoming obese), because food is going to be pretty scarce.*

What messages were encoded in the methylation changes my grandmother underwent: *The world is a shithole that is no place for a child or any human to live?* or *You better have your head on a swivel at all times, because something horrible is going to be around every corner?* She had numerous miscarriages before having my father. My mom had always assumed they were a result of anatomical injuries my grandmother had endured. But I wonder now if her suffering was so severe and profound that her body, completely distrusting the world, simply refused to bring another life into it. The most basic threshold of her faith in humanity had to return before there was enough to carry my father to term. I am quite certain that DNA methylation played a role in this.

So, broadly, PTSD susceptibility trait can be imprinted onto a trauma victim's DNA through methylation, and this alteration can be passed down to future generations so that the constantly-on and exaggerated fear response is activated. A step further in this elucidation observed by other researchers is that different types of abuse, at different intensities, can leave a unique methylation signature on the DNA contained in the cells of different parts of the brain and sympathetic nervous system. This means there can be a molecular "scar" left within the developing nervous system's DNA that is specific to whether the person was raped, beaten, emotionally abused, or neglected in a chronic versus single-event exposure. This certainly describes a plausible molecular mechanism behind the intergenerational transmission of PTSD in Holocaust survivors.

The silver lining to these discoveries is that it suggests there may also be a molecular/epigenetic basis for therapy and recovery, such that it can reverse the pathology. I certainly seemed to experience that during my therapy. My therapist and I often joked that I just needed to re-methylate—only in the right way this time. Our levity about my therapy was not that far from reality. The technical term is *epigenetic reprogramming*. There are studies showing that with psychotherapy alone ("merely" talk therapy, no medications), the methylation status of key neurotransmitters can be altered, with a resultant positive change in symptoms. Similarly, chronic exposure to alcohol can alter the DNA methylation patterns of stress hormones and key mediators of the immune, limbic, and sympathetic systems in an unhealthy way. Detoxification and treatment can reverse these aberrant epigenetic changes as well, and improve cognition, stress response, and emotional functioning. These are examples of mental illness phenomena and traditional forms of successful "low-tech" therapy that are finally gaining a cutting-edge, hard-science explanation: physics, chemistry, and biology. There is a massive paradigm shift on the horizon of psychiatry and all other branches of mental healthcare. The molecular revolution is coming, if it has not arrived already.

Of course, I latched on to these molecular discoveries. That is what I do. This is the language I understand. It served as an intellectual bridge between my hard-science world and the world of mental health. But I went further and began to examine the emotional havoc that PTSD has wreaked upon my family for generations. The long-term impact of my grandmother's childhood experiences governed her behavior and personality for her entire adult life. I rarely saw her sitting calmly; she led her life at a constant frenetic pace. She would clean her entire kitchen, including mopping the floor, at 2 a.m. Then she would wake up at 5 or 6 a.m. and start another day of nonstop action. She collected the mail and walked the dogs of people throughout Ferndale and Royal Oak who were on vacation. In the summer, she mowed lawns; in the winter, she shoveled snow. (I got so much crap from my friends and friends' parents who claimed that I "made" my grandmother shovel the snow from our driveway. She did it before I even knew we had an accumulation.) She was also our taxi service for school—there was always a ride in the morning if we chose that mode of transportation.

Her main love, though, was being a cafeteria worker at my elementary school—a lunch lady. She was there for over twenty years. She started when I was in fifth grade, and I became "The Don" of big chocolate chip cookies for all my friends. She was my supplier. She "retired" three different times over those twenty years, but the kids kept pulling her back. She was always worried about them not thriving in her absence. I estimate the school district lost thousands of dollars in free cookies, milk, and extra hot lunches that she gave to children at Roosevelt Elementary School. She could not stand to see anyone not eating, and would have followed the kids around on the playground with a food cart if she could have. They all called her Grandma, for her huge heart and equally huge smile. I missed every one of her retirement parties; I was too busy with medical school and residency to bother. I was given grief for even considering leaving my ivory tower medical training to see my grandparents on their deathbeds, and I had to fight tooth and nail to go to their funerals. So there was no way in hell I would have been granted leave to see my grandmother retire from being the lunch lady of all lunch ladies.

Her mind was a steel trap, too. She remembered everything. Every detail of every person's life was permanently recorded and readily available for retrieval and sharing. It would frustrate her when you couldn't keep up. "You know the one … the one." The one woman she met in line one day at the grocery store whose son was going to Wayne State Law School, who needed her dogs walked every Thursday night because she played bridge with her sisters in Port Huron. The one neighbor who'd just had a below-the-knee amputation due to diabetes-related gangrene and now needed his lawn mowed. The one. She remembered everything about everyone. Silence and uncertainty were her enemies.

I understand now. Any break in her kinetic energy would have allowed her mind to slow down and, potentially, remember what she went through when she was just a girl. Those thoughts and terrors had to be beaten back with nonstop activity and conversations. These memories could not seep into her consciousness; that door had to be bolted, boarded up, and nailed shut against the evil that tirelessly hammered on the other side trying to get in. I recall how fidgety and uncomfortable she once became as she stood by me during the afterglow of our high school's production of *The Sound of Music*. I played Rolf, costumed in a Brownshirt uniform, complete with the red armband and its black swastika embroidered inside a white circle. My grandmother hugged me reluctantly and then immediately looked away. Not until decades later did I fully understand.

I also remember, when I was much younger, that whenever I spent the night at my grandparents' home, she would come in, thinking I was asleep, sit down beside me, and run her hands through my hair, looking down at me. I could feel her thinking. I sensed she was relieved to see me warm and safe, but I could tell that her mind was elsewhere. Was she remembering? Was the presence of innocence her visual security that the evil done to her was gone, and the sleeping child in front of her the proof that she needed to know the world might finally be safe? These moments were the only ones when I saw my grandmother slow down.

Though my father would be the first one to deny it, I strongly believe he carries the PTSD susceptibility trait as well, inherited from my grandmother. My grandmother directed a lot of her pain and anger toward my father. Her fear, anxiety, and near-manic approach to life made his childhood beyond difficult. She was a harsh disciplinarian. It was very difficult for her to show affection toward him; she seemed to reserve her kindness for others outside of the family. There was no therapy back then. People did the best they could, without any help. My father most likely was born with the PTSD-susceptibility trait, inherited from her. The sensitivity, high energy, and neediness of children with this trait, coupled with my devastated grandmother's parenting style, must have made for a constant cycle of punishment. He carried the experience into adulthood. Early in my childhood, the frequent arguments my parents had were explosive. They were very young and poor and doing the best they could with a little kid to worry about, too. My father worked multiple jobs to keep food on the table and brought his anxiety and exhaustion home. Combined with my hyperactive and needy nature, it was another generational bad mix.

Like my grandmother, my father is a natural genius. He joined a fledgling paint application company and assumed the directorship of Research and Development when the owner caught wind of all the science courses he took in college. My dad was driving the forklift at the time, and trying to wrap up his college degree. Over the next few decades, his innovations and numerous patents would go on to help this company grow from its humble origins into a massive, worldwide power in industrial anticorrosion coatings. Under the hood of most automobiles, the gray metal tubing and fasteners are coated with a paint he invented. Brakes, rims, and gas tanks that avoid the oxidization created by the addition of ethanol to gasoline are just a few of the other applications for coatings developed under his watch.

During this time, my father's existential stress and anxiety went from figuring out how to survive and keep a roof over his family's head to worrying about multimillion dollar contracts failing because the customer's machine settings were incorrect or something in the quality assurance testing was amiss during the development of a new coating. In his mind, a financial disaster loomed around every corner. He took any product failures personally. Further, he felt responsible to all who worked under him, as if they were part of an extended family. Failed products and busted contracts meant layoffs and job losses, and it was his burden to bear. Many times, my father would help out people who worked in his lab if they were having a financial or family crisis. In the same way my grandmother worried about the kids at my elementary school, my father worried about the people at his work.

The frustration, anger, and anxiety followed him home. The family prepared for his return from work the way a small town in a movie Western reacts when the bad guys roll into town for the big shootout with Johnny Law—women, children, and shopkeepers scrambling to get off the street and behind closed doors. The arguing between my father and me became especially heated when I was in college, when I was becoming emotionally and intellectually independent while still being financially dependent upon him. The clashes of a stressed-out father and son are never pleasant, and we had many such clashes. Classic PTSD reverberation.

So the starting material for my mind was constructed by two generations in which the susceptibility and sensitivity to trauma were created, passed on, and reinforced. I desperately needed an emotionally warm and secure childhood environment to ward off those molecular demons, but I experienced just the opposite. While what I had to endure was peanuts compared to what my grandmother and father endured, I was programmed to react strongly to even the slightest of traumas.

Perhaps the greatest outcome of my case and therapy is that this familial trait was identified. The reverberation will stop with the next generation, and they will enjoy a much better emotional life than my forebears and I have.

Chapter Eleven

I WAS AMAZED TO LEARN that PTSD can be a lifelong condition (if never treated properly) and that childhood trauma, sexual abuse in particular, primes the mind to develop symptoms later in life, when confronted with adult stressors. I was able to pinpoint several periods of my life where I was presented with an existential crisis in the form of financial, career, life, and relationship uncertainties. The greater the number of these uncertainties, the more severe my symptoms were during those periods. When I mentally reviewed the years preceding my arrest, when I was at my absolute worst and in a personal free fall, I came to realize just how great an effect treating children with cancer had had upon me.

Despite the TV news media's persistent portrayal of me as a pediatrician, I am not. I am a radiation oncologist. I happened to treat children, and had the title of Director of Pediatric Radiation Oncology at OSU and Nationwide Children's Hospital. But of the over two thousand patients I have treated in my career, probably less than two hundred of them were children.

The residency training for radiation oncology is four years long and commences after a general internship year, which is the first year of training after medical school. During the four years of radiation oncology training, residents are expected to participate in and/or perform between 450 and 750 treatment cases. Of these, only 12 need to be pediatric cases. There is no formalized or required fellowship in *pediatric* radiation oncology. Pediatric cases account for less than 1 percent of all radiation treatment deliveries in the United States, so this is a very rare subspecialty. Because of the low numbers of cases, economics dictate that children are usually treated at the same centers as adults.

A typical radiation treatment machine costs around $3 million, plus another $500,000 in annual operating costs. For a machine to be financially viable, it needs to treat about twenty-five patients per day, but even a metropolitan area will have only a handful of children on any given day who require radiotherapy.

The preparation and training of pediatric oncologists ("chemotherapy docs") is very different than that of pediatric radiation oncologists. After a three- to four-year general pediatrics residency, where every patient is a child, the oncology fellowship begins, and it lasts for three years. Thus, for five to seven years, these trainees are trained and surrounded by experienced physicians and support staff who care for children and only children. Coping with the suffering and death of children is part of their ongoing curriculum. Conversely, in most radiation oncology departments, there is only one radiation oncologist who treats children. This work is done in relative psychological isolation from the rest of the department, as most people prefer to avoid children with cancer.

When I would interview faculty candidates for radiation oncology positions and ask what area of subspecialty they preferred (breast cancer, GI cancer, etc.) a very common answer was that they absolutely did not want to work in the pediatric sector. It is too depressing. Initially, I, too, avoided treating children. From 2006 to 2009, I treated only one or two pediatric patients per year as a licensed radiation oncologist at MD Anderson. Given my difficult childhood, I felt I couldn't relate to children. And since I wasn't yet a parent, I had no clue about kids. I also felt I couldn't relate to parents.

But then, in 2010, the job in Columbus was offered to me. When I was considering the position, my wife, several friends, and even several colleagues at MD Anderson, openly expressed their concerns and questioned if I could handle treating children. I had been so opposed to treating children during my time at MD Anderson that this move was confusing to them. But, I told them (and myself) that having my own children and seeing them thrive enabled me to "get it." I understood all things "kids" and could now relate to parents. Plus, it was my nature to take on the toughest jobs around and attack them head on.

Going after the brain tumor, glioblastoma, arguably the worst and most incurable adult cancer there is, was an example of this mentality. Taking care of children with cancer was an even scarier and more demanding subsection of radiation oncology, intellectually and emotionally. But I was finally up to the task, and I *had* to do it, to show how tough I was. Plus, the pediatric directorship was a *title*—my first leadership title, ever. On top of that, being "Director of Pediatric Radiation Oncology" gave me a 40 percent pay raise. The OSU offer was a once-in-a-lifetime opportunity, and taking care of pediatric patients was part of the deal. With this self-deception and rationalization, I accepted the position.

My lack of training, especially in coping with the suffering and death of children, the isolation within my department (I was the only radiation oncologist treating these patients, and I was rarely physically at the children's hospital with the other pediatric specialists I coordinated with in patient care), and my own history of abuse and undiagnosed PTSD meant that I was not emotionally prepared for this part of the job. Further compounding the difficulty was that, typically, if children required radiation as part of their anticancer therapy, it was a bad sign, medically. I did not see the more common and favorable acute lymphocytic leukemias, which have an 80 to 90 percent cure rate using only chemotherapy (which doesn't cause the brain damage, growth abnormalities, and secondary cancers that radiotherapy does). I saw mostly the kids with brain tumors, bone tumors, and soft-tissue sarcomas—the ones who were in the most dire shape. Thus, I saw the worst cases of the most difficult cancer patient demographic there is—children—with very little preparation.

This was an entirely new storm system entering my mind's already complex climate. I had never dealt with this kind of weather before. The technical aspects of delivering radiotherapy to children came easily to me. I quickly became proficient at it, and understood the concepts well enough to effectively teach it to my trainees and students. But the emotional component never caught up with my newfound expertise. In fact, as time went on, it lagged further and further behind. Obviously hundreds, if not thousands, of radiation oncologists have treated children over the last hundred years across the world. Did any of them implode and commit a despicable affront to common decency the way I did because of this same lack of training and preparation? Probably not. However, it certainly played a role in my ungluing. Because, for me, dealing with this part of the job was nothing short of a psychological kick in the teeth.

There is a bit of gallows humor that provides an explanation for why the pediatric oncology fellowship lasts three years. During the first year, the trainees meet and treat their patients. In the second year, the patients recover from their treatment and are in remission. During the third year, their cancers come back, and many die. Thus the entire unfortunate life cycle of children with very dire prognoses is encapsulated within the setting of a three-year training period. The fourteen pediatric cases I'd "logged-in" over eight-plus years in Houston as a trainee and faculty physician were no match for the carnage I was about to see.

I had twenty pediatric radiation oncology consultations in the month of December 2011 alone. As I entered my third year in the position, the number of deaths, cancer relapses, and children being rushed over on life support for emergent treatment began to pile up and wear away at the peace of mind I thought I'd developed when my own children arrived. I took each treatment failure and death personally, and would perseverate on my treatment plans in these cases, looking for evidence that I was indeed to blame. My rational mind would conclude that nothing else could have been done, but the other parts refused this explanation.

Cancer is a well-documented childhood trauma itself, and the children being robbed of a normal childhood resonated with my own lack of a normal childhood as I spiraled into a PTSD crisis. It was getting more and more difficult for me to consciously think about what I was saying during consultations. I would stand before crying parents and an adorable, sick child who would either succumb to his or her disease within about a year or be maimed for life by the radiation I was about to deliver. In a few instances I could feel myself dissociating— stepping out of my body—as if to let my physical shell handle the difficult task of interacting with the families. This separation was especially strong if the children looked, acted, or said things that reminded me of my own kids.

There was one little girl with a medulloblastoma who could have easily been my daughter. She was the same age and had the same sense of humor, extremely bright and beautiful. Over the course of her treatment, I watched all of her hair fall out from the whole-brain radiation and concurrently administered cocktail of chemotherapy. The addition of chemotherapy made the probability of her hair growing back (or at least looking like it used to) very unlikely. The dose of radiation to her spine, administered in the hope of sterilizing her spinal column of any tumor cells that might have seeded it, would most likely permanently lock in the five-year-old size and bone composition of her vertebrae, making her trunk disproportionately shorter than her limbs and shortening her final adult height. The most horrific side effect would be that this bright little girl, with her great wit and comic delivery, would become dull over time. She would not maintain her expected trajectory of intellectual and cognitive development due to the radiation dose I was delivering to her entire brain. At that dose, along with the chemotherapy and her age, she would probably have a final IQ in the upper 80s—assuming the tumor did not recur, fatally, and there was about a 40 percent chance of that happening.

At about the same time, I was treating a woman in her thirties who had had precisely the same kind of tumor and treatment when she was the exact same age as the little girl. The impression that radiotherapy left upon the woman was striking. She was in a wheelchair, her hair was thin, her spine and skull malformed, and she had a very flat affect. Her medical chart was composed of four sections, each about eight inches thick. Pounds of paper chronicled the life of a childhood cancer survivor: endless hormone replacement monitoring, neurocognitive test results that plateaued over time. What was not documented in those charts was the hollow, withered, emotionally exhausted countenance of her devoted mother, who over the last twenty-five years had lost a career, a husband, and countless friends while caring for her daughter's special needs. Needs made acutely special by the large doses of electromagnetic radiation that had been shot through her child's vulnerable and then developing central nervous system when she was just five years old. This was the very same treatment that I was forced to give to the little girl in the next room, to prevent the same tumor from killing her. The grown woman's latest ailment was the development of a glioblastoma, a brain tumor that gave her about a fourteen-month life expectancy. It was most likely induced by the radiation exposure used to treat her childhood cancer.

I felt nauseated when I watched the little girl with her family and our staff members, the way she would make them laugh while she endured her treatment with fearless innocence. I would look at this beautiful angel and see only the blank stare that would greet me in the next room, knowing that—in the best of scenarios—that would be her fate, too. I had to keep myself dissociated; otherwise, if I allowed myself to clearly process the human drama playing out in front of me in real time, I would have lost all professional composure and sobbed uncontrollably, frightening the little girl and her family.

Having these cases juxtaposed in my clinic was maddening. It was the cancer treatment "before and after" right before my eyes, without the respite of the intervening decades. It was an exquisitely cruel trick played on me by the Cancer Gods. They knew, full well, the state I was in—and how poorly I would respond to their morbid and perverse foolery.

Oftentimes, I would quickly leave the clinic to gather myself in the hallway, or I'd close the door and cry in my office. While avoidance is a common behavior of PTSD sufferers (for example, a near-drowning victim avoiding water), I could not avoid children suffering. It was very difficult for me to hear children crying in my department. I think sound is especially difficult for me, because out of all the senses that compose my fragmented memories of my abuse episodes, it was the sounds of people and normal activities on the other side of wall that remain the clearest in my mind. The sounds of children suffering were there every day, and I could not talk about it. I was isolated within my department, and I certainly couldn't talk about it when I left work. It turned people into wrecks when they heard about my cases. My wife would cry, and people at social events would quickly change the subject if I even hinted at what I'd dealt with over the previous week. Many nights I would come home to a dark and quiet home, my family already asleep. So often it was just me and my sixer of the strong double-IPA cough syrup that allowed me to, for a brief hour or two of intoxication, break the surface for some air. My brain's elaborate mechanisms for self-preservation were breaking down.

I probably will never be allowed to treat children again, because of the nature of my offense. However, without question, those three and a half years of doing so were the most rewarding work I ever did, despite the toll it took on me. Words cannot describe the honor it was to have been part of their path. I had no idea how spiritually and physically resilient children could be. I once treated a four-year-old and a forty-year-old with the same tumor and treatment regimen at the same time. The four-year-old was running up and down the hallway, fighting with his brothers for a hat or toy. The forty-year-old was curled up in the fetal position in a dark room, averse to loud noises and bright lights.

Of course, children heal and bounce back faster; that is their physiology. But there is something beyond that. Children are tough. Of course they are scared, but they are open and honest about it, and their fears can be addressed. With adults, getting to the root of the problem and figuring out the true cause of fear or uncertainty can be exhausting. Children are straightforward. They haven't had time to develop the complicated walls that adults have to conceal their emotions. Their innocence, grace, and dignity under what can be horrific conditions are truly inspiring.

I was not the only one who saw this in my clinic. There was a huge difference in the attitudes of my adult patients, depending on what time of the day they were treated. The morning patients rarely had many complaints during their weekly on-treatment visits with me. I would ask if there were any issues or problems, and in the morning the typical response was "Nope. Doing just fine. See you next week." Whereas in the afternoon, encounters tended to run a little longer, and mundane complaints like "My skin is itchy" or "Sometimes I get a headache that goes away with Tylenol" seemed to take up an inordinate amount of the appointment.

It wasn't clear to me what caused the difference until one day a morning patient of mine, who was in his seventies and getting palliative radiation for a bone metastasis from prostate cancer, clued me in. After I good-naturedly kept badgering him about not having any problems that I could fix, he looked me square in the eyes and said, "Doc, I see those little kids you treat every morning. Whatever problem I've got is nothing compared to what they have. I can manage."

My adult patients who received their treatments in the morning saw the majority of my pediatric patients. The very young ones who required anesthesia for treatment deliveries were among the first treated in the day, since that was when the anesthesia teams were available, before they went on with the rest of their day in the adult hospital. Seeing those children gave the adult patients perspective, and they bucked up out of respect for what the kids were going through.

Many of the adult patients grew attached to the little ones. They would bring them toys and treats and make them laugh. The children got doted on, and they loved it. It was a nice reprieve for the family as well. Being the only pediatric patients in the entire medical center, each attained a sort of celebrity status in the eyes of many there. While the children would cry in the beginning of their treatments because the machines were big and scary and what was about to happen was unknown, they would also very frequently cry at their last treatment because they were going to miss seeing all the friends they had made while visiting our department. It was precious. They were so precious. I will truly miss them, and taking care of them.

Chapter Twelve

NO SOONER THAN I had those important breakthroughs of personal introspection and early healing but I was reminded of the massive blast-crater of a legal case my actions had created. Susan and I spent the first few weeks of November getting our wills and power of attorney documents in order. I made a notebook listing where to find all the bills that needed to be paid and how to draw out more money from our retirement accounts. It was a great distraction from the fact that I would soon surrender my right to vote and admit that I did a horrible thing to the nation. We were draining our life savings to maintain stability for our children as long as we could, to enable me to repair the relationship with my family without any additional stressors. It was a painful financial decision, but worth far more to our children's emotional futures. I was making great strides in fixing my relationships with my children. The grim prospect of being carted off to jail after entering the guilty plea, however, created a visceral panic. I needed more time.

In the roughly four months between the police raid and the day I pled guilty, my attorneys worked with the detectives and prosecutors on my plea deal. Because of the way the statutes are written and the technology I'd used to view, I could easily have been eviscerated by the technicalities if a purely black-and-white interpretation of the law was applied. Peer-to-peer networks, by definition, are distribution-and-receiving networks in and of themselves, but from the way I used the technology, my honesty and openness in describing how I used it, the voice stress analysis interview, and the forensic evaluation, it was clear that my intent was only to view, to access. I did not leave the system running all day and night, contribute to the distribution machine, or amass a huge collection. I only viewed whatever came up during those ten to fifteen times over eight years that I visited that world. Thus the files that came into the queue during those ten- to forty-five-minute "sessions" that I didn't download were not counted against me. Technically, this constituted an *attempt* to access, but given the randomness of my searches and what I viewed within that narrow time window, it was clear I was not attempting to acquire those files specifically. I also deleted every file after viewing, meaning I did not have a stash that I could go back to or potentially distribute in the future. So I believe that what I pled guilty to appropriately reflected my infringement upon society's mores and was not maximized by jargon or technicalities, at least from a score-keeping perspective.

Still, child pornography offenses are steeply penalized and scaled by levels according to the Federal Sentencing Guidelines. A level 18 is the baseline offense for accessing/possession. Then enhancements are added to the baseline in an attempt to reflect the full culpability of an offender. I was given a +2 for using a computer, a +2 for the presence of prepubescent victims, a +2 for having 59 confirmed deleted files (the range for this enhancement is 10 to 149 files), and a +4 for the presence of sadism/masochism/violence (I'd viewed some horrific stuff). Two points were deducted because I accepted responsibility for my crime, and one more point for notifying my intent to plead guilty in a timely manner.

After the plea deal my offense score (which took in all the factors of my offense) was 25. According to the guideline recommendations, my punishment was to be fifty-seven to seventy-one months' imprisonment, five years to life on probation, and a fine of $10,000 to $100,000. This information literally made me vomit up a stomach full of coffee and bile when I read the first draft of my plea agreement one cold November morning leading up to my hearing. I asked my attorneys if there was any way I could be either a physician for a seriously underserved area (inner city, rural area, American Indian reservation, etc.) or do cancer research at the NIH—for free, no salary—as my sentence instead, so that the federal government and society could get something useful from my punishment. But my attorneys informed me that service could not replace prison. It is preferable that my extremely rare skill set be wrapped up in an orange jumpsuit and rendered idle to the tune of more than $3,000 per month of taxpayers' money than to have me address areas of critical healthcare need within our country at no cost.

The sentencing recommendation was why my attorneys advised me to prepare to be hauled off to county jail. A lot of times, judges who know a person is going to spend time in prison will get the clock started and have them start serving their term before the final sentence is handed down. This practice came about at a time when most defendants in child pornography cases were assumed to also be child molesters. I was sure that someone would want to take a swing at the pervert doctor who was on TV when I was in the county jail. I would be a great prize for someone who didn't have much more to lose. I hadn't been in a fight since seventh grade. How in the hell was I going to defend myself?

My plea hearing was on November 15, 122 days since the raid on my home. I woke up early so that I could shave, shower, and put on my suit. Everything I did that morning, I did with the thought that it would be for the last time ever—simple things like brushing my teeth or taking a shower. My jail time would dovetail with my prison time, and the house would be long since sold by the time I was released. Most of my worry, though, was for my family. Was there going to be another media circus at our home, like when I was charged in July? Would the roof rattle again, in the helicopters' downdraft?

My children had grown accustomed to my disheveled hair, stubble, and whatever clothes I'd slept in the night before as I made them breakfast and packed their lunches on early school mornings, so they were surprised to see me in a suit. I made sure their lunches were to their liking and threw in a few extra snacks. I turned up the thermostat so they could be treated to a nice hot air blast from the heat registers as they got dressed for school. As I helped my wife get them into their car seats, I gave silly answers to their questions before the real answers, just to hear them laugh.

"So Daddy, why are you all dressed up?" my daughter asked.

"Because I need to go swimming after you go." I said straight-faced, and then waited.

"What!?" she said, smiling.

"It's way too cold, dude!" my son added. *Dude* was his new word, picked up from the big kids at school.

"Oh, yeah. Maybe I should just get into some shorts and flip-flops, then?"

"Oh, Dad! It's too cold for that, too!" my daughter pointed out, laughing.

"OK, OK … Daddy just has a meeting this morning." I always told them I was going to a meeting whenever I had a scheduled appointment for lawyers or therapy. "Daddy just wants to look extra good for this one."

"Oh. OK," my agreeable son said, satisfied with my answer, as the seatbelt buckling continued.

I hugged them both for so long, fighting back any tears, that my daughter finally said, "OK, Daddy, we need to get to school on time!"

I laughed through my burning throat for them. Keeping things normal otherwise. As they drove off, I asked myself if there had been enough time for us to heal, and was worried sick there wasn't. I could see their little heads bobbing in their car seats as they looked around, oblivious, assuming it was just another day. I had stopped being Yelly Daddy. They noted that. I could draw cool sharks and explained science to them using the chemistry and paleontology sets my wife bought for us to work on. I could make them laugh. They knew I was trying to get better, and would call me out if I was getting too huffy or impatient. My son told me during one of our play sessions, "Dad, you are cool now. I like you." My daughter was far subtler in declaring our relationship improved. Despite Christmas being several months away, I managed to crack her exclusive wish-list, which consisted of three items:

1. A puppy (or pupp*ies* would be OK too).
2. Magic powder that confers the ability of flight (of course).
3. For Daddy's consequences to be over.

I was ready to accept prison in the spring, but I needed more time to be with them. My work wasn't done yet.

We did not tell our children that I might be going to jail that day. They never would have gone to school—well, not quietly at least.

They would have been terrified and angry, especially my daughter. My in-laws had originally planned to come down to see the kids' first Irish dance recital, but now they were coming to provide moral support during my hearing, and potentially to soften the blow of my unexpected departure for my distraught family. They were also on standby while en route from Michigan, in case my wife and children had to leave Columbus to avoid another siege of our home. The contingency plan was that they would turn around and prepare for my family's arrival if the situation warranted. One of the kids' teachers, who was also the mother of one of their friends, volunteered to take them to her home to wait out the aftermath of the hearing. It was another incredible example of the love and support our neighborhood and school district gave us.

After my family left for school, I had one last moment to sit on my porch. I was starting to sweat through my clothes. I had not worn a shirt and tie in over four months, and my body was not used to having so much of its heat trapped. I had a cup of coffee, looking at the fuzzy frost on the blades of grass in my yard for maybe the last time and wishing I really was going swimming somewhere warm. I had sat there to read, write, smoke Marlboro Lights, and reflect. I'd spent four months watching summer give way to fall and winter starting to announce its arrival. This was where I had mostly talked with my visitors and well-wishers from OSU, to avoid the kids' overhearing details about the case and to give my wife some distance from the place that, in her view, eventually broke her husband. We dubbed it The Therapy Porch. I needed my time there more than ever to collect my thoughts and cool off.

When Susan returned from dropping the children off, she came to the back door and looked out at me though the window, motionless, her face wearing a kind of terrified calm. She didn't object to the lit cigarette in my hand as she normally would have. Today was different—a cigarette or a brick of Valium would be entirely permissible. Then she nodded imperceptibly and disappeared to get ready.

Of course, it took her all of fifteen minutes to go from just-woke-up to stunning. She wanted to look professional, but not like an attorney. She wanted to look like a family member, but not too casual. And she got it just right. She and I had discussed how much she wanted to be present. She would not walk with me into or out of the federal building. Doing so would open up the possibility of her being photographed with me, which would forever bind her to me in visual media. It would jeopardize her future job prospects and our children's future. So we would stay separate.

She also did not want to hear the gory details of what I'd viewed, nor about all the rights of citizenship that I would be losing. She wanted to wait in the hallway outside the courtroom, and come in only if needed—to rescue me if it looked like I was going to be sent to jail. She would attest, on the witness stand, that I was not a monster and that she was perfectly comfortable with me being around her children.

This well-laid plan was crushed within the first five minutes of our arrival at my attorney's office.

"Oh. No. You *will* be there," Charles said, politely but assertively wagging his finger toward my wife with an earnest smile. "This *will* turn into a bond hearing. You need to be there. The judge needs to see that you are there, and how you react during the entire proceedings."

Susan had been keeping it together for the whole drive to the office, but she broke down at this news. But here is where the young attorney exhibited his great ability to manage people. "You are going to do great," he said. "Do you know why?"

"Why?" between sobs.

"Because you have to," he said with a big smile. My wife started to laugh and immediately pulled out of her dive. She was ready.

My attorneys had my wife sit in a very conspicuous area in the gallery: front row, stage right, next to one of their associates. This was to let the judge know who she was without tipping off the reporters. Susan later told me that during the hearing the judge did indeed look over at her, and did so for a particularly long time when deciding if I was to remain on house arrest or go to county jail. Every time he looked over at her, she said she felt as if the column of air above her suddenly became a hundred times denser, and she could feel it pressing down on her shoulders and coating her lungs.

The courtroom had a cathedral-like feel to it. It was immaculate. The ceilings were high, and the bench was a massive mountain of varnished hardwood. I expected these structures to dwarf the judge, but they actually made him look bigger. He was kind, extremely informative, and deliberate with me. I almost took pride in being allowed to speak to him. He had that air. I wanted to be as polite and forthright as possible, and atone for my sins.

When he asked about my highest education level and what institution I'd graduated from, I cringed when I told him, "Medical Doctorate, from Northwestern University Medical School." He did a double take; he'd earned his JD from Northwestern University School of Law. The two schools are right next door to each other in downtown Chicago, in the shadow of the John Hancock Building. Oftentimes, the medical and law students shared conference rooms and auditoriums. All the early morning lectures during my first year of medical school were held in Lincoln Hall, a striking facet of the law school's historic Levy Mayer Hall. Lincoln was a beautiful, scaled-down version of the British House of Commons, complete with stained glass windows that caught the morning sun off of Lake Michigan and massive dark wood benches that each student could convert into their own mini-office. I am sure he and I had sat in the same rooms as we learned our respective crafts. I felt so ashamed to share this common history with my judge but to be standing in his presence as a criminal.

Standing before the court is about as humbling experience as anyone can endure. My hands felt as if they'd been dipped in an aquarium of cold and slimy water. I stood at attention, my knees locked, and never shifted my weight for the fifty minutes or so that the hearing lasted. Both of my arthritic knees felt completely ossified, my legs painfully fused into a single rigid bone by the time it was over. Bending them to walk again was excruciating, as if I had to break them first.

The rights that I would surrender as a felon were listed aloud: no voting, no military service, no firearms, no elected public office.

To verify I was mentally capable of making the decision to plead guilty, I had to say I had a history of ADD and generalized anxiety disorder and that I was currently taking Zoloft. The PTSD diagnosis and the determination that the other disorders were misdiagnoses were still too new to be included in my mental health history, but during this hearing the truth started to come out. As the statement of facts was read, the true nature of what I'd done came to light: first the fifty-nine files, all of which had been deleted, not actively collected. But then the gruesome details of what I saw were read as well. I cringed, knowing my wife was right behind me, hearing it all. Bondage, penile penetration of children as young as five or six years old by grown men, forced oral sex.

To the statement of facts, I said, "Your Honor, I plead guilty."

My voice sounded calm, but the air I used to say those words felt like superheated gas from a blast furnace that charred my throat, nose, and mouth on its way out.

Then came the bond hearing, as promised. A sidebar was called and elevator music played so that what was being discussed could not be heard in the gallery. I was close enough to make out some of the discussion. I tried to stare at the federal seal that hung in front of me, but I occasionally stole a glance at the group. I heard all the attorneys, including the prosecutor, argue for me to remain on house arrest. I could see the judge nodding and heard the words "voice stress analysis," "ongoing therapy," "family counseling," and "No, no, your honor, not a threat." At one point some of them glanced over, past me, at my wife. They must have been confirming who she was to the judge, although I am sure he knew from the start. When they finished, the judge returned to his bench and began to recap my behavior up to that point.

"Dr. Pelloski has been cooperative from the beginning. He returned from Colorado of his own accord to surrender himself." He asked my pretrial services officer if I had been in compliance with the conditions of my house arrest.

Hank, always professional, stood tall and reported, "Your honor, to my knowledge, the defendant has been in full compliance with the terms of his bond. I have no concerns or indications to the contrary, either, sir."

The judge then took a long look at my wife and continued thinking out loud. "Doctor Pelloski has never posed a threat to the children of the community." He repeated this statement several times, but saying it as if tacitly asking my wife, *Is this guy really OK?* She later said she was too numb from the weight of his gaze to recollect what she did when he made this statement. She couldn't remember if she nodded or just looked terrified, but apparently he got his answer from whatever she did.

He continued, "Dr. Pelloski is currently undergoing active therapy with several health professionals. It is the court's wish that this continue." There was another long pause. "I will continue Dr. Pelloski's home monitoring for the remainder of the duration of this case, provided he remains in compliance with the terms of his bond."

I was so relieved I couldn't remember what was said after that. Regardless of what my final sentence would be, this was an incredible personal victory. There was still time for me to heal with my family and explore and treat my very new and finally correct diagnosis of PTSD. My children's emotional futures may very well have been spared that day. For this reason, I will always be grateful to the prosecutor, magistrate judge, and district judge for allowing me to remain on house arrest. They trusted me, when I'd given them little reason to do so. They did not have to, but they did.

The media tone changed slightly after the hearing. Write-ups described me as polite even when declining to talk to reporters. Most of the sinister insinuations were omitted this time around. They did continue to say that files had been found on my computer, giving the impression that I had stockpiled the stuff rather than deleting it—but it was a far cry from what was said about me in July. I was thankful for that. One of the newspaper reporters even had a tone of sadness when she wrote, "Today a meteoric career in oncology came crashing down."

The only visual media used was a video shot of me leaving the federal building carrying my ankle monitor case and then entering a car. We'd made arrangements with the TV news crews in the hope that if they got the shot they wanted—the "perp walk"—they would not set up shop at my home. They honored our implicit request. Not a single soul came to our house.

To bolster my spirits of after pleading guilty to a dark felony, a few of my friends texted me over the weekend to tell me that their grand-mother/sister/cousin had said they thought I was good-looking. So at least my attempts at grooming and hygiene didn't go unnoticed. I had been exercising. I kept off the twenty pounds that I'd immediately lost after the burden of holding in my abuse secrets was relieved. I'd even had to get my suit retailored so that it fit me properly and I didn't look like some kid borrowing his father's for the prom. I also made sure to get some direct sunlight as often as I could during my house arrest, to avoid the pale, sickly appearance of a predatory Nosferatu.

I didn't tell my friends I didn't need cheering up. I was still going to be around for my family for a while. I was still going to heal with them and get myself better. That was all I cared about on that day. I slept in until 2 p.m. the next.

Chapter Thirteen

OVER TIME, people from my more distant past began to reach out to me during my house arrest. When I talked with several people I'd grown up with from elementary school through high school, and even some college friends, I was amazed by how many had made observations about me that were similar to each other. This was especially true of the girls I'd dated or those who had an interest in me but never connected with me—the ones who "got away." Many were not surprised that I had been abused once they found out. They told me that in one way or another they always knew that something was wrong with me but could never articulate what it was until everything came out.

One phone conversation was especially poignant. It was with someone who was always very close to me but never officially more than a good friend. She finally had some closure about why we never became more involved. Her words cut like daggers: "There was always something about you. But I could never put my finger on it. You had an edge. You were the kid who knew everything about sex—when no one else did. People always gravitated to you when they were curious about it, and you would hold court, at lunchtime or on the playground. In grade school you already seemed to know how everything worked. In high school, you were far too confident in that area. You were way too intense. It intimidated me. It kind of scared me away from ever dating you. And I know I was not the only girl who noticed this about you."

When I got off the phone, I felt yet another pang of sadness, and a profound sense of loss overcame me. I never really went through that awkward phase of discovery with a girl, as most boys do when they are starting to learn how to "make out." I never had that sense of anticipation or fear of getting caught by parents or wondering if I was making a fool of myself while trying to be a teenage Casanova. I never felt any bashfulness or butterflies when deciding whether or not to hold a girl's hand or initiate a kiss. I was robbed of my innocence at such a young age that I never truly got to experience it. I already knew what the end game was about. I knew how the parts worked already.

While this helped me a lot in college with hookups and making a good first impression on satisfied repeat "customers," it drained the warmth and romance out of any long-term relationship I ever had. A complaint I universally received after a while in my more long-term relationships was that sex with me was too goal-oriented—more about the destination than the journey. Despite my positive attributes and technical skill as a lover, being with me became both undesirable and tiresome. I had always struggled to put sex in a healthy context. Was it that I needed to prove myself in the same arena in which I was violated and confused as a child? Was it something I needed to do to make me feel safe and wanted, yet at the same time I needed to remain emotionally distant so that I could maintain my numbness and not expose any vulnerability? By both controlling it and distancing myself from it, was I declaring victory over sex and the intimacy that is supposed to accompany it?

Through my therapy and healing, I began to realize that I often dissociated during intercourse, and this may well have been the source of my partners' eventual discontent and the lack of satisfaction I perceived. The advantages to dissociating were only fleeting, of course: I could last longer without having to resort to thinking about baseball stats—a strategy some of my friends used to ward off premature ejaculation. I had the false appearance of a confident lover who was in control. But in actuality, I was just numb. I had to force myself to think about sex so that I could finish. I'd dissociated when I was molested and could even now really only remember the beginnings of each episode. I didn't know how long things went on or what all transpired. I often felt this way about sex.

Dissociating during sex made me not fully process that a moment had been shared. No intimacy. It is like the way people who watch

TV while they eat tend to eat more and are then hungry again later because their minds did not fully process that they've already had a meal, because they were distracted by the television. Throw in the cultural pressure, stereotypes about men as sexual conquistadors, and the overall biologic drive to reproduce, and it is not surprising I have been a mess in this area my whole life.

I experienced personal highs and lows throughout my house arrest. The conversation with my friend from childhood and its revelation induced a profound low that lasted for some time. Was not *anything* spared from my abuse? Whether it was making out in junior high or being a trail-blazing leader in the oncology field, the traumas were like shrapnel that tore through my life, taking whatever chunks of me they could. The scars ran deep.

Still, though, I was healing. While each realization like this one was painful, it pushed the process along. I felt better physically and mentally when I turned forty while on house arrest for a child pornography felony than when I turned thirty and was a high-flying resident at the best cancer center in the United States. (How sad a comment was that on my life?) It's because by my birthday on December 29, I was in full swing with my therapy.

Reading Viktor Frankl's *Man's Search for Meaning* during my house arrest, I came across a quote that Frankl borrowed from Benedictus de Spinoza's work *Ethics,* which defined my recovery, acted as a guide throughout the whole process, and continues to help me to this day: "Affectus, qui passio est, desinit esse passio simulatque eius claram et distinctam formamus ideam" (in Frankl's translation: "Emotion, which is suffering, ceases to be suffering as soon as we form a clear and precise picture of it"). I was getting there.

The only way to treat PTSD (and childhood sexual abuse, for that matter) is to directly address the underlying and inciting trauma(s). This is achieved most successfully with cognitive-behavioral therapy and, to a much lesser extent, with medications (Zoloft is the only FDA-approved drug for PTSD). In cognitive-behavioral therapy, one talks through the anguish. It is painful. Talking about traumas is like draining abscesses. The cutting open and squeezing at the beginning is characterized by an excruciating pain—10 on a ten-point scale—but it's followed by a near-immediate relief, with only some subsequent soreness and drainage to endure as you get the rest of the junk out. There is data showing that people with major depression who have a history of childhood maltreatment do not have the same success with medication management alone as their counterparts who had normal childhoods. The effect of child abuse is that latent and pervasive. (It certainly limited the life span of the effectiveness of Ritalin and Effexor in treating my symptoms.) Important components to this psychotherapy are talking, writing (like, say, a book), and pursuing other forms of artistic expression with the purpose of identifying the trauma, the reason it happened (and accepting it if there is no reason), its meaning, and, lastly, organizing one's past and present emotional responses to it. That is much more difficult to do than remembering to take a pill every morning.

I cannot stress enough how life-changing this type of therapy can be, though. It is difficult, yet it is so simple. It is just talking. But it is important to be talking *to* someone. It really cannot be done alone. While having a professional counselor is ideal, just telling *someone* about one's trauma is a huge and important first step. It is a near-impossible burden to handle alone.

There are no expensive experimental drugs or technically challenging procedures required to get the ball rolling and make a massive difference in one's life. Knowing what I know now, I see how incredibly misguided and damaging it was to hold things in. There were nights during my house arrest where I would awaken, drenched in sweat, from dreams in which I was back at work, as busy as ever, and back to no one knowing about or acknowledging what was really going on within me. While the incessant paging, emails, patient problems, resident strife, and the latest crises in the lab were certainly painful to revisit, the real nightmare was that in these dreams, things had never changed for me. Then, once I would realize that I was home and in therapy, even though I'd lost my career, could not leave my house, and was facing a federal child pornography felony, I was beyond relieved that my secrets were out, and I could easily go right back to sleep.

I can't believe it took this colossal sledgehammer to make me deal with the abuse. It is such a difficult choice to make though, when one is lost in the fog of guilt and shame. If anyone were on the fence about whether to start to talking about or sharing their abuse or traumas, I would implore them to not wait any longer. The sooner one drains the abscess, the better it will be for every aspect of their overall health. If someone has a mental illness that seems refractory to the typical medications and other forms of therapy, I would strongly advise them to take a comprehensive inventory of their early-life experiences and ferret out any events that even remotely smack of abuse or trauma, subtle or horrific.

I also had to heal that wounded inner child, or else I would be destined to handle the next major calamity that life threw at me poorly. The child who ran the show needed to experience what a healthy childhood feels like, and then quickly grow up. This was the next phase of the therapy process. One of the most helpful exercises I did during my recovery was to look at that picture of myself as a little boy, around the age I was abused, and write him a letter. It was gut-wrenching, but I was so relieved after I did it. And it took another huge emotional burden off my shoulders. Healing the wounded inner five-year-old and integrating him into the rest of me was critical to my recovery. Telling him it was not his fault was simultaneously symbolic and therapeutic.

Me, at four years old, right around the time in my life when the die was cast.

The page I wrote the letter on is mottled by many briny patches of dried tears. It bears these words:

> Hey, little man. You couldn't have stopped anything. You were so small, you couldn't make the grown-ups stop. Don't think you are bad because of what happened at the pool. That man counted on kids wanting to go swimming. It is what kids like to do. I know you really wanted to go swimming. And that piece of poop knew it too. And don't get mad or feel bad that your penis got hard and felt kind of good when your Auntie D touched it. Penises are supposed to do that when they get touched. Your Auntie D knew how they work and you didn't. She really shouldn't have done that to kids. It was not fair to you. She should only do that with grown-ups who understand.
>
> I am so sorry all of this happened to you. Grown-ups are supposed to protect you and take care of you. A lot did not. They took advantage of your trust. All of this is going to make you scared and unsure of yourself for a long time, but you will get better. I promise. You will still do great things and help a lot of people, even though you will feel horrible about yourself. You will do even greater things when you feel better.
>
> Just be ready. People are not always going to like you. They will think you are really bad. But you are not. Just hang in there. People will eventually realize that you are good.

It turns out, if you need to heal an inner five-year-old child as an integral part of your therapy, then hanging out with awesome five-year-old twins is about the best medicine there is. I got to teach my kids how to read, watched them ride their bikes without training wheels for the first time, pulled out their loose teeth when they were afraid to, saw them off for their first day of kindergarten, became an expert Lego builder all over again, and taught them the life lessons and nuances of the *Star Wars* and *Lord of the Rings* series. There were many laughter-filled battles throughout the house with Nerf dart guns. Every time they returned home from school, they yelled for me, to update me on their day's adventures.

My wife did such an amazing job, shielding them from the anguish and worry about the future that my case created for her. She gained stress weight and took on the internal crisis mode that had once been mine: always on guard for the next legal uncertainty; acting as ambassador for her husband, the sex offense felon; bracing for impromptu house-arrest visits by Hank—all so that I could be with and focus on my children. At first, I thought I was teaching and helping my children and repairing my relationship with them. I thought *I* was doing the work and they were benefiting. But eventually, I realized it was *they* who were repairing me. They showed me how a normal five-year old sees the world, with love and wonderment and without prejudice. It was an incredible time with them. I do not think I could have healed without them.

My profound change was put to the test many times as I went through therapy. New memories surfaced. More details of the sexual abuse events emerged. But rather than trying to block this pain and disgust with overachievement, chasing away the stress with a few gallons of heavy beer, projecting my anger onto the people I loved, and viewing child pornography to validate these memories, I just told people about it. My therapist, my wife, friends, and family. That was it. A new set of memories would bug me for about a week and then I moved on from it. It wasn't a big production or some elaborate psychological concealment scheme. It was duly noted, mourned, and then left alone to take its place in my life's experiences. It was so liberating to do it that way, much better than trying to figure out what to do or think in isolation at 2 a.m., drenched in sweat and terrified. The memories were incorporated into a healing process this time around; I had a program.

As the fog of PTSD and pain of my own abuse began to abate during therapy, once I was able to consider my offense with a clear mind I began to feel an enormous sense of shame and remorse. While self-harm and dissociation may be psychological explanations of why I tortured myself by viewing children being sexually abused, how I feel about my offense is probably most analogous to an alcoholic drunk driver who, upon sobering up, realizes that he killed someone the night before. The driver did not intend to kill anyone. The driver, too, knew on some level that he was hurting himself by drinking and creating a danger on the road by deciding to drive, but he did so anyway. There may have been something in the driver's past or heredity that made him become an alcoholic. The driver was not himself while under the influence of alcohol. However, as a consequence of his choices and actions, a very significant harm was done. Someone was killed.

I was both horrified and angry with myself. I'd perpetuated the abuse of those children I viewed. I exploited their suffering for my own therapeutic gain. I was part of the problem of online child pornography—regardless of my reasons, I was there. I knowingly committed a felony, destroyed my career, and jeopardized my family's future, all with one horrendous activity. What a fucking disaster. How stupid, reckless, and selfish was I? I know my healing process will have to continue indefinitely on this issue, because this guilt is going to take a very long time to go away, if it ever does.

I also had the task of trying to unsee what I'd seen when I subjected myself to viewing. Seeing other children being abused created a new set of flashbacks and images that were intermixed with visions of my own sexual abuse. I had thrown a new heap of traumas onto an already-size-able pile. This realization made me miserable for quite some time.

As I continued my abuse therapy, I came to deal with my anger. I figured this would be an easy subject for me, since I was fueled by anger my whole life. I was always in touch with it. It propelled me to incredible achievements. Anger is an emotion, and it can give you energy, especially when the need is critical, like a king-sized candy bar can right before a marathon. However, like a candy bar, it was emotional junk food: high in calories, but not much nutrition to go along with it. After a while, you become malnourished if that is all you eat.

One of the anger questions raised was *Can one forgive their abusers, and is it even necessary for healing?* This was a snag I did not expect.

Of course my initial reaction was *Uh, hell no!* I had been robbed of most pleasures in my life, even the ones I worked so hard to attain. But then a moral dilemma smacked me across the face. How could I not forgive my abusers when I was simultaneously begging for others to forgive what I had done, for the harm that I'd created? I was asking not just the judge presiding over my case but *everyone*. Could *I* forgive myself for what I did? As I worked through this concept, I rationalized through the abuse that was done to me.

Maybe the very first episode truly *was* innocuous. Maybe someone was just trying to help my young mom out and was doing some sort of childcare function for me, and the high-alert status of my little brain interpreted it as something wrong or unsafe. I could let that one go, even though it really bothered me that I was so young.

I could even give The Pool Man a pass. He was a stranger and a man. Men have a lot of problems. Hell, I used child pornography as a means of remembering that I was abused. I was quite familiar with the male predilection for very bad coping mechanisms.

What I really struggled with, though, was that a female relative had molested me as well, and at a family gathering, where young children were supposed to be protected, cared for, and doted on. After the abuse from my aunt, no physical space then felt safe. It was a tearful discussion, one of the most painful with Rachel, when we covered this topic. I discussed how difficult it was for me to search and see women sexually abusing children when I was viewing online. The pain in my chest when talking to her about it was similar in intensity to what I felt when I actually saw it while online. I remembered how the women often would look into the camera when abusing their child victims, as if responding to direction or to placate some other demon who may have completely destroyed them or perhaps threatened them with violence. I remembered how each time a female perpetrator would lock eyes with the camera it tore my own eyes out of their sockets. It was actually harder for me to see women doing anything remotely inappropriate with children than some of the more disturbing things perpetrated by men. But I could never articulate that, until that session.

My aunt sexualizing me was to be the final time I was molested, but this one really sent me into a tailspin. I concluded it had happened in the summer of 1981, when I was seven. This was the summer right before my second grade year, the year in which my behavioral problems at school and at home reached their peak. That's when the notes and phone calls from the school were the most frequent. There were whole weeks during that year when I had to stay in my room (except for dinner) in an effort to improve my behavior. I may have had the strongest dissociation during the encounter with my aunt, too. I was probably really good at dissociating by then. The details of what happened with her took the longest to come back me, yet that abuse occurred when I was older, so the memories should have come sooner and been clearer.

Of course, Rachel redirected me and told me that most women are not like that. Even most men are not. She understood my reliance on humor and used it to talk me off the ledge frequently. She gave the example that lost children are told to look for a mom with children to get help. It is an instinctive and intuitive piece of advice that we all give to our children. She had me consider the women who did abuse children and how broken those souls had to be. How dissociated had they become from their own nature to do that to children.

In addition to my last abuser being a woman, there were several other aspects to this event that made it much worse for me as an adult in the process of recollecting. I got an erection during this molestation. It was not until well into my sexual abuse counseling that I learned that this is a common reaction experienced by victims of childhood sexual abuse. Adult abusers, equipped with knowledge of how the body works, use this to their advantage to exploit children. It has dually horrendous consequences for the victims in that, first, it tricks children into believing that since it feels good, it must be OK. Second, it provides a deeply rooted platform of shame that can follow and haunt them into adulthood, as the victims feel they were complicit in the activity.

I'd shared another common experience of survivors due to this encounter as well, when I tried several times to tell my grandparents about what happened. Oftentimes, unfortunately, when children do share their experiences around the time the events happen, they are ignored, the events are minimized, or they are accused of lying. My grandparents reacted the way you'd expect given their generation: I was told that I was fibbing, being dirty, and should not talk about stuff like that.

Between my normal sexual organ response and my grandparents' reaction, I endured a very common double-hit that often has deep and devastating consequences for the self-esteem and self-worth of many childhood sexual abuse survivors. Thanks to these events and messages, victims carry with them thoughts that they are inherently bad and good only for sexual purposes—a self-view that is carried well into adulthood. While my mind blocked the factual events from my memory, it did not block the emotional effect on me. My mind never knew why it always felt the way it did. It just did.

This therapy session was almost unbearable for me. It showed me there will always be surprises during therapy; there will always be a few more pockets of the abscess that need to be lanced open and drained, even months into intensive therapy. My aunt was a destroyed woman. For her to tell me that she liked how a grown man kissed her while she fondled my seven-year-old penis and attempted to French kiss me borders on demonic possession. Something horrific might have happened to her, too.

Chapter Fourteen

THE WEEK LEADING into my sentencing hearing, which was scheduled for a Friday, May 2, 2014, was the longest a week had felt to me since the time between my home raid and when I was charged. These two weeks were bookends, with 290 days in between. So much still had to be accomplished, and after months of waiting, everything had that last-minute feel to it, despite all the work that had been completed already. Witnesses needed to be lined up and prepped. I needed to work on my statement. I had multiple meetings with my attorneys that week. My wife and I, again, had to prepare for my sudden absence from the household, in case I was taken into custody immediately on the heels of my hearing.

Judge assignment to federal cases is a random event, decided by a computer. This was always unnerving to me, since the judge can have such a profound effect on the outcome of a case. How each judge plied his or her craft with different types of offenses could vary widely, but the selection of the judge, which appears to me to be the biggest factor in the outcome of any nonjury case, is ordained by a roll of the dice. I was used to the oncology field, where specialists were trained to handle specific problems. A patient wouldn't be randomly directed to a lung cancer physician if he had prostate cancer.

On top of the random selection, there was another issue with my judge. He was on the board of trustees at OSU and Nationwide Children's Hospital. I was a former employee of both institutions, and my case was high profile. The judge's connection made current employees—administrators and physicians—reluctant to publicly support me, because they knew a trustee would see any letters and testimony, even if they were sealed from the public. Administrators especially, who attain their titles by climbing a steep political mountain, would be endangering their positions. So none of the institutional brass would speak or write on my behalf, out of fear of reprisals from the board—real or imagined. The effect was so pervasive that even my treating psychiatrist was reluctant to write a letter of support on my behalf, as he did not want to cross the wishes of the board.

Many of my supporters also feared that the judge's trusteeship also gave both sides of the trial a built-in basis for appeal, regardless of his sentencing decision. His ties with OSU and the hospital could be cited as either the reason he chose to punish the hell out of me (for bringing shame to these places) or for giving me a slap on the wrist (to protect a former employee). This issue was brought to the judge's attention when he was first assigned to the case in October, but he decided to stick with my case.

Technically, judges are only required to recuse themselves if they have a direct financial conflict of interest; it cannot be due solely to an association or familiarity with someone. A lot of judges in small towns know the defendants and/or plaintiffs in municipal cases, so it would be impractical to have a wider basis for recusals. One can imagine how frequently judges might need to be imported from other jurisdictions if a reason as broad and common as often eating at a restaurant owned by one of the trial's litigants applied. It would be a mess. Also, in Columbus it is difficult to find anyone who does not have some kind of connection to OSU. So there were no legal grounds for my judge to recuse himself. He originally offered to seal the testimony, which I appreciated, though I don't think it helped.

Tempering my frustration with the judge's OSU connection was the fact that he'd allowed me to maintain my house arrest. This judge did not usually do this for defendants with my offense. Those six months he gave me were, without a doubt, what saved my life and family. I had gotten the help I needed. The therapy was intense, and I was able to devote all my energy to it. I was able to accomplish a lot of reading, writing, and reflection in the setting of my home and family—things that would not have occurred if I had to look over my shoulder every few minutes as I rotted in a county jail during mitigation.

Nonetheless, the perceived "OSU effect" on my case included the mysterious disappearance of witnesses and letters of support that I was hoping for. The desertions tended to occur after my former colleagues met with OSU's legal department. I quickly learned that *Let me talk to Legal first* meant that I would never hear from that person again—and forget about expecting a letter of support. This was the case with all the university-based hospitals. Not a single clinical faculty member or administrator from OSU wrote a letter on my behalf. My OSU support came from students, lab technicians, and trainees. The omission of character references from OSU MDs and faculty PhDs was glaring and almost comical, given that I had letters of support from physicians all over the country—some from satellite centers of superior institutions.

When I'd worked at OSU, my assistant, who'd watched me slowly implode and hide, crying, behind the closed door of my office, voiced her concerns for me more than once. But she, too, was apparently scared into silence by someone. My supporters told me that when they approached her about writing a letter on my behalf, she said she could lose her job if she got involved in any way, and she was visibly shaken by the mere mention of my name. I wonder what was said to her and who said it.

One of the more troubling incidents, though, was when a nurse backed out from testifying on the witness stand a few days before the scheduled sentencing hearing. She was my ace in the hole. She'd worked with me extensively because of my pediatric service and Gamma Knife procedures. She saw how good I was with patients and families up close and every day. However, after she finally met with the OSU legal department, late into my house arrest period, she said she could not jeopardize her position or her tuition waiver for nursing graduate school. Again, I can only wonder what was said to her.

Another discovery during sentencing week was that a research paper I had submitted for publication had finally been published—with a glaring omission from the authorship line: my name. This paper was the product of the laboratory work I had spent a year and a half working toward. My lab and I had determined that a very aggressive form of a childhood sarcoma could be sensitized to radiation by adding a new drug to the treatment regimen, thus killing the tumor cells more effectively. It was a very exciting finding for my relatively new and independent lab. We did extensive studies on patient samples and found that the molecular target of the drug (the protein FANCD2) made tumors more lethal for patients, too. It was great confirmatory and complementary data.

My lab performed the majority of the work, I wrote 90-plus percent of the paper, and had submitted it as the corresponding author three months before the raid on my home. I was in the process of finishing the revisions for resubmission when I was charged and resigned my position. All the revisions were completed under my supervision, and there was really no need to delay the publication. Many students and trainees who'd helped on the project needed a publication under their belts to help as they moved on to their next academic levels. However, my restriction of access to the Internet as a condition of my bond meant I could not complete the online resubmission process. So I'd asked that my chief collaborator take over as the corresponding author to minimize delays in publication.

Now I learned that a few of the higher-ups at OSU and Nationwide Children's Hospital had demanded that my name be removed from the paper during the resubmission process, so as not to besmirch the names of these institutions. I'd had my ideas stolen before, but I was usually given at least the common courtesy of having my name among the authors of the final published paper. I'd anticipated that I would no longer be listed in the coveted first or last authorship position for the paper, but I still expected credit for my work. Instead, I was put in the acknowledgments section—without any title or affiliation. The acknowledgments is the place in a paper where people are thanked for their help in getting the manuscript to press, but a mention there does not imply participation in the research aspect. This legal technicality really doesn't matter though, because in the spirit and practicality of academic and scientific principles and ethics, a mention in the acknowledgments of a publication doesn't allow you to cite it on your CV. And if you cannot cite your work, as far as the record is concerned, it never happened. In this way, I was struck from my own work, regardless of what contrivances had been spewed forth in defense of this action.

This amounted to forcible abortion of scientific ethics and principles for the sake of public relations. It was frightening to realize that a handful of people could pick and choose who does or does not receive credit for their scientific work, based on whether the researcher himself is in favor or out. Having the legal department scare potential supporters away was one thing; it was simply protecting the clinical "brand." But the commission of what appeared to me to be, at least morally, an example of academic fraud—this was a whole new level. It's highly unlikely that anyone outside the field of oncology would have noticed that my name was included in the list of authors. So, in effect, this action was nothing more than a ceremonial pissing on the eviscerated corpse of my career.

At first I panicked. Did this also mean that every other paper I ever published or any lecture I'd given would be redacted and purged because my name was on it? Would it stop with my publications? I'd first stumbled across and viewed child pornography when I was still a trainee—meaning that everything I'd accomplished since becoming a licensed and practicing academic radiation oncologist was done after the commission of a felony. Did that mean the thousands of years of additional life expectancy I gave to children and adult cancer patients needed to be returned as well? How would that be done? In what device (obviously one that could warp space-time) would those recovered years be stored? Are there Death Panels that go around killing those who benefited from the skills and knowledge of unsavory physicians, since the contributions of these deviants are to be struck from the record?

Shortly after the publication, I asked an intellectual property lawyer (attorney number six in this story) if he had ever seen a case of someone being erased from his own work. He took a while to answer. He first scanned the table before him, which was covered in the paper trail—notes from OSU meetings, printouts of emails between the journal editors and me when I was acting as the corresponding author, the data

I'd generated and analyzed, the revisions I'd coordinated among my group, and the original submitted manuscript where I was the senior author—as if to assure himself that he was actually seeing what was in front of him. He then quietly said, "I have never *heard* of this happening before." He sadly added, "Universities are supposed to be bastions of enlightenment, not ones which cower to an ignorant, uninformed, and outraged mob." He pointed to the strewn papers. "This plays right into and legitimizes the witch hunt they all mounted against you." He trailed off, shaking his head, "Just terrible. Damn salt in the wound. I am so sorry for you."

What we couldn't figure out, though, was why the journal had gone along with omitting me from the authorship line on an article for which I was initially the corresponding author. All organizations that produce a scientific journal or periodical have a scientific ethics policy and code to which they strictly adhere. For any change in authorship (to add, drop, or rearrange the order, for example), *all* the authors are supposed to unanimously sign off to the change on an author-change form. But I'd never received this form.

We later discovered that one of the same higher-ups at my former institution who had mandated my removal from the manuscript also happened to be the chairman of publications at the organization that published the article. So connecting the dots was not hard. What made this an especially bitter pill to swallow was that this same man had previously come to me whenever a VIP patient or prominent university official needed radiation treatment. Because I was the go-to guy.

Aside from the "alleged" interference my previous employer was running, there was a lot of unnerving talk from concerned neighbors and supporters about my judge's sentencing history as well. They told me that he tended to punish white-collar crimes much more harshly than others. "You'd have been much better off selling crack cocaine than committing your kind of crime or mortgage fraud," they would say. These offenses tended to get a blanket punishment without considering the offender—and that was the worry.

My judge was known for giving out the harsher penalties for child pornography cases in the Southern Ohio District—although this district, overall, is known for its leniency in my kind of case. The district has a formal policy disagreement with the Federal Sentencing Guidelines. And my judge still handed down sentences shorter than either the guidelines or the national average. Still, I was looking at four years—the prosecution's and probation officer's recommendation—which *was* less than the guidelines'. Four years was a long time relative to my children's lives (and to my medical career, if there was to be any hope of salvaging it).

Additionally, I was reminded that after my prison term, I would also receive a multiyear probation period as well as inclusion on the sex offender registry. *I was to register as a sex offender?* This was really confusing to me. Law enforcement had felt my behavior was safe enough that they could simply watch me for nine months. But after a thorough investigation and my lie detection test, after my computers were analyzed, after my children and my patients were investigated, and after I completed my sexual abuse counseling and cognitive behavioral therapy for PTSD, *now* was the time to blacklist me? After all the intensive vetting I underwent to show I was not a physical threat, I should have been marked *safe for the general public* even more than the public itself. One is far more likely to find a pedophile or child molester by randomly knocking on doors across the country—because they certainly won't find one in my home. That declaration comes with a mountain of data behind it.

So as the week wore on, I became far more nervous about the future of my children and just how long they would go without their father. I became fearful that factors outside of the details of my offense, mental health, and subsequent rehabilitation were going to weigh on what my sentence would be. Judges are human. They have their agendas, pet peeves, and sympathies. Seeing OSU undermining my support while the judge presiding over my case sat on its board of trustees scared the shit out of me. None of it smelled right, and I worried that I would become the sacrificial goat used to keep this college football town's innocent, wholesome sheen intact. Given that notion, coupled with the other sentencing concerns that were being bandied about by those around me, it's no wonder I didn't sleep well that week and lost another five pounds—this time from a truly unhealthy lack of appetite.

It wasn't all gloom and doom, though. I finally got to read my letters of support. The final count was forty-three. I had to meet with my medical board attorney, in case I was in custody when my suspension appeal hearing occurred and I needed to testify to the board remotely. As she showed me my file, she handed me the pile of letters. I asked for a moment to read them and she excused herself. They were beyond moving. Phrases leapt off the pages:

"The best doctor I ever worked with in twenty-five years," from a support staff member.

"Always made time for others," from one of my radiation oncology residents.

"A once-in-a-generation talent for our field," from a fellow researcher.

"He could make dying patients laugh and feel human again," from a nurse practitioner.

"A great teacher," from a student.

"Dr. Pelloski saved my career," from another resident.

"I would not be in medical school if not for Dr. Pelloski," from another student.

"This man has suffered enough. He needs to get back into the cancer field," from a neighbor.

Then came the absolute heartbreaker, written by a woman I'd gone to grade school with: "When I was a kid, my uncle molested me. This is the first time I have ever put those words into writing." It reminded me just how universal the problems I have dealt with are.

I could not stop my eyes from slowly and silently producing massive tears that dropped like fat water balloons all over the letters and my trembling hands. My throat clenched and burned, as I pored over the pages, alone in my attorney's office. I had forgotten these kinds of words about me—since most of what I'd seen in print about me in the last nine months was filled with either hate (blogs, news articles) or horrific details (affidavits and presentencing reports). My attorney joked when she returned, after I apologized for losing my composure,

"Oh stop, I always have you physicians crying in my office. That is what I am known for!" We both laughed.

"It is like I died, and this is the nice stuff people would say about me at my funeral," I said. "It is such a bizarre feeling. These letters go above and beyond the typical letter of recommendation for school or a clinical position. This is so much deeper. It is about me and my good attributes—as a human. Not a regurgitation of my CV."

"They *are* little eulogies. We tend to not hear the good stuff much that matters, when we are alive. Sounds like you were very kind to all kinds of people and helped them. Not that vision of an arrogant doctor who shits on his subordinates."

"Have you read *all* of these?"

"Yes, and after reading them, I am certain that you will be a doctor again. You need to get back out there—once this gigantic mess is done."

"These letters will help?"

"I defended a doctor where *one* letter made the difference. You have forty-three, and ten or so of them are from physicians. I cannot promise anything, but I am much more optimistic for the Ohio Medical Board giving you your license back than when we started out last summer. Other states will and should take you in a heartbeat."

The ups and downs of this trial had become rapidly cycling again. Sometimes these highs and lows were only minutes apart. Reading that I was a monster who deserved to burn for four or more years in prison juxtaposed with being called a wunderkind physician-scientist and educator whose kindness and contributions are already being missed by society was exhausting. I felt pulled in opposite directions with enough emotional force to rip me apart.

Many told me, when this all began, that I would never be a doctor again—that I should just go into sales or "something." Apparently, twenty years of elite biomedical education and experience grows on trees these days. Still, I certainly hope I can be a doctor again. At the age of forty, I estimate that I have a remaining career of twenty to thirty years. During that time, I could treat another ten to fifteen *thousand* cancer patients. I trained at one of the best places in the world. I can treat rare and common cancers, and can perform procedures that many in my field do not even attempt. All of which is significant, given that the American Cancer Society recently estimated that almost a half million cancer patients will face barriers to their care, as access to life-saving treatments and procedures will be limited primarily due to an anticipated cancer specialist shortage over the next decade. Further, specific to my specialty of radiation oncology, it is estimated that there will be only one radiation oncologist available for every ten who will be needed to meet the increased demand for cancer care in our aging baby boomer population. I estimated that during that year alone, had I not been under house arrest, I would have treated over two hundred cancer patients.

Further, our society has, in the form of tax dollars, financed my medical education and training in an amount that easily exceeds $200,000. Aside from the expectation of this debt being repaid with interest, there was an original hope that the final result of this investment would be a competent physician who could help meet the healthcare demands of this country. I know I can still honor this expectation. The list of people in this world who can do what I can do—who have my combination of training, knowledge and experience—is an extremely short one. That statement is not arrogance; it is accurate. Ironically, it is when I am finally emotionally and mentally healthy, which would make me an even better doctor than I was before, that I am confronted with the prospect of never being able to be one again.

My continued absence from the field of radiation oncology, if it is prolonged, will have a number of unintended effects. In addition to continuing to punish me after my sentence has been served, it will also penalize the society that has invested so much in me. Is it worthwhile to risk the lives I might otherwise save due to an ongoing obsession with a past act that the legal and psychiatric establishments agree is highly unlikely to recur? The fact is that, despite advances in treatment, we are far from winning the "War on Cancer." Cancer continues to kick our collective asses on a daily basis. There has only been a *five percent* decrease in mortality rates from cancer since the "War" was declared in 1971. Given that, you'd think every available able-bodied soldier would be needed for the fight—especially those who have distinguished themselves on the field of battle and are still in their prime.

Regardless of what medical boards say about me in the future, the support I received from my criminal case was unprecedented. People who commit my offense typically do not get this. Usually their wives leave them and only a handful of relatives remain in their corner. The greatest display of support, though, in relation to stature in the field and perceived risk to career, happened a few days before my hearing. Right before one of the last-minute meetings with my attorneys, the conference room door swung open, and my main research collabora-tor, Richard Herrington, who had been instrumental in getting my lab established, was standing there. I was stunned speechless, and just shook his hand like some awkward, starstruck teenager, unable to express my appreciation for what he was about to do for me. Richard, one of the most prominent scientists in all of pediatric oncology, with thirty years' experience in the field, was going to speak for me, *on the witness stand,* at a federal sentencing hearing. And he would do so despite the judge's trustee position and despite the heat he was receiving from the hospital administration. As one of my attorneys later said, "This guy has balls as big as the room."

After Richard had declared he would write a letter on my behalf and testify during my hearing, he was visited in his office several times by the hospital's top administrators. Legal department emissaries made multiple visits as well. They all begged him not to support me with the same fervor and paranoia that a superstitious medieval peasant might have displayed talking about the dark forest that surrounded his vil-lage. One of the hospital attorneys resorted to telling him that, if he supported me, the NIH would revoke his research funding. I secretly hoped, for Richard's sake, that this sage legal counsel was thorough and concluded with the proper decapitation of a live chicken, so that its still-warm blood could be poured over a bowl of fresh garlic bulbs, thus warding off any future plagues that could have ravaged his home.

Richard also had an understanding of what childhood sexual abuse can do to someone psychologically. He'd reached out to me when all of this first started. Like several others, he'd already sensed that some-thing had happened to me, as a child, before I said a word to him. He'd seen what it did to some of his family members. From the beginning, he offered to do anything to help and urged me to get better. But I never imagined him actually taking the stand for me.

He was untouchable, though, and he knew it. He *was* cancer research at Nationwide Children's Hospital. If he were asked to leave for standing by me, the grounds would have been baseless and obvious and would make the administration look like vindictive bastards. Further, his departure would render their pediatric cancer program almost academically insignificant from a national perspective. He was a true scientist and did not give two shits about politics and PR, and he wasn't intimidated by hospital lawyers the way my clinical colleagues were. The way my authorship on the paper had been handled disgusted him as well. A part of me believes he was daring them all to fuck with him for doing what he knew was the right thing.

Richard articulated his disgust to me once during a visit: "If academia was at all concerned with achieving its mission, which is the betterment of the human condition, it would fight tooth and nail to preserve its pool of talent and innovation—not entirely desert it at the slightest hint of adversity. But the field has been hijacked by self-interest and corporatization. So *you*," he said, pointing a mock-chastising finger at me, "you, my friend, are a perceived threat to the monetary bottom line of their multibillion-dollar company, unfortunately. You went from being 'all good' to 'all bad' in their eyes. So, you are left to twist in the wind—with no care whatsoever to what your absence does to the field."

He was right. I was only useful and had value within the system when I was producing. When this suddenly stopped, on July 24, 2013, I no longer mattered, and my swift dismissal was met with the same indifference that was bestowed upon those poor souls in Sinclair's *Jungle* who fell into the vats and later became portions of Durham's Pure Leaf Lard.

I also learned from Richard and another former collaborator during that week that the four projects we'd launched together had resulted in amazing data that would provide the scientific rationale for *two* future clinical trials. I got great satisfaction from knowing that my first-time independent research program and high-risk approach—something I'd developed with my team—was the right way to go. Our novel experimental system was going to move the pediatric cancer research field forward by "leaps and bounds," according to Richard, not just provide incremental data sufficient only for the self-aggrandizing accumulation of publications. He had been waiting for an experimental system that could faithfully recapitulate clinical radiation treatment for thirty years, and he was amazed that I'd delivered it to him in two. He has said of the research my lab was doing, "For the first time in the field of pediatric oncology, there is a real clinical radiobiology research going on for pediatric cancer. Each experiment itself could form the basis for a clinical trial while yielding biologic correlative samples at the same time." I was four for four in the ratio of meaningful discoveries versus total attempted projects during a brief two-year stint, on top of an additional patent born from my research. That is pretty damned good in lab-based biomedical research.

Sadly, I may never be able to continue this important work, because to most universities my PR deficits will far outweigh my value as a researcher. I was just getting warmed up; two and a half years is a blink in the span of a career. If I think how much difference I could have made—what I might have accomplished for countless pediatric patients over the next twenty to thirty years—I become excruciatingly depressed.

Nevertheless, it was comforting to hear good news from Richard during the week my legal case and life were both coming to a head. It was another reminder that I am not a horrible person. These findings were going to help children with cancer. No authorship shenanigans or abject abortions performed against science by charlatans could ever take that fact away from me.

Chapter Fifteen

FRIENDS AND FAMILY came to Columbus from all over the country. They made the pilgrimage to my home to participate in our 'Twas the Night Before Sentencing vigil. Each arrival was heralded by a longer than usual embrace, and then something inane would be said to break the tension with forced laughter. Some had not seen each other since so-and-so's wedding years before. For all practical purposes, it was a wake. The only difference being that the deceased was at the door to greet the visitors as they rolled in instead of lying in a coffin in the dining room.

My attorneys told me that not only would the judge give me a sentence measured in years but that he had never allowed a self-surrender for these types of offenses. Meaning that I would be taken right from the courthouse to a federal prisoner distribution center in Oklahoma and stay there for weeks until my "parent institution" (final prison destination) had a spot open up for me. I was told that this pre-prison detention is a miserable time. One is completely cut off from the outside world and family while waiting, sometimes mixed in with violent criminals, as the expensive suit that was worn for the sentencing hearing erodes into tatters and eventually reeks of pungent ball-sweat.

Self-surrender—which is the other option if prison time is handed down—gives the future prisoner time to prepare for the determined prison term. He continues on house arrest and can make plans and say goodbye to the family before surrendering himself to the parent institution when notified to do so. It was difficult to stay positive, but my dissociative talents (better wielded after therapy) allowed my sense of humor to keep everyone laughing, as I always could.

After the initial gathering in our living room broke up into groups of people scattered throughout the house, talking and catching up, I was alone with my parents. Ever since they arrived they'd both looked like they were watching me get run over by a truck, in slow motion. We just kind of stared and sighed, not sure what to say. The background noise of the guests became more jovial and boisterous, providing an incongruous soundtrack to the moment. Eventually, my mom asked to hold me.

She began trembling the moment her head rested on my shoulder. "I am so sorry, Chris. If I had known what happened to you, we would have gotten you help. I just didn't know. We didn't know." She sobbed, no longer needing to maintain a stoic front for others, and her heart was finally able to completely break.

"I know, Mom. I didn't say anything then, either. I don't know why I didn't. Maybe I was scared. I didn't remember myself, eventually. And I can't even remember when I stopped being able to remember it." I felt devastated for my mom. She held onto me like I was just a kid again, as if she too was trying to nurture the numb little boy that I once was. "You did all that you could, based on what you knew." I tried to reassure her. "You knew to tell grandma to not let me go to that pool again. Who knows what else you prevented from happening, and that was just on your gut feeling." I hugged her back.

"Well, maybe it was a good thing I didn't know," my dad chimed in to lighten the mood. "I would have sat in prison for most of my life after killing those people who hurt you." I smiled, and my mom laughed through her tears.

"I know, Dad. You and Mom did the best you could." I put my arm around him and the three of us stayed that way for a bit. Their pain was like a fuel-air explosion, sucking all the oxygen out of my lungs and the room, suffocating. A few of the wake attendees would step into the room, see my anguished family's huddle, and then promptly mime an apology for interrupting, turn, and leave. "I was a handful when I was little. I was a wild child. We all know that. I understand why now. It was not because I had ADD or anything else. I wasn't a bad kid after all."

"I know. We understand now, too. Everything makes so much sense. But we were so tough on you. It was not the right way to go for you. I am so sorry, honey." My crushed mom continued to sob.

"The worst time was with Dad's cousin or aunt. She really threw me for a loop. Remember how much trouble I got into in second grade? Remember all those notes home from the teacher and principal?" My mom slowly nodded. "I figured out it was because that summer before second grade, that stuff with her happened to me then."

"You were asking for help," my mom added. "We didn't hear you." She started to compose herself and talk with more clarity. "Just like I think you did what you did and got arrested—because you were asking for help. You needed help and you didn't know what to do or how to ask. You were trapped, and getting caught got you out of it. When people ask me why you did this, that is what I tell them. That is what I wrote in the letter to the judge, too."

"I know, Mom." The hugs continued for quite a bit longer.

Ever since that embrace, my parents and I have had a new understanding and a deeper love. We were able to conceptualize the "what and why" of my childhood and the relationships we had as I was growing up. We did this in a setting of honesty, love, and complete vulnerability. The moment may have lasted for only a handful of minutes, but it defined multiple lifetimes. It is the kind of closure that I am fortunate to have, made possible perhaps only by the "grown-up timeout" that was imposed upon me and the fate that awaited me the following morning. If left unresolved, it would have haunted and anguished me for the rest of my life, long after my parents had passed.

Unfortunately, many never get this chance to make amends before time and mortality make it impossible. Even right up until the eleventh hour, there was still opportunity for yet another layer of guilt and remorse to be peeled away. This should not have surprised me, though, being a cancer doctor who treated some of the worst cases. I have seen the prospect of certain death that cancer bestows on its sufferers bring families together. Families that had been fighting, hurting, or estranged would gather around the loved one who was stricken with the disease and, confronted with this bigger issue, make amends. All crises have a silver lining.

Eventually, my parents and I rejoined what had become a noisy, full-fledged party. As our tears evaporated into salt on our sleeves, we decided to enjoy the last night of my relative freedom with our friends and family, smiling.

Later that night, though, I lashed out a bit. It was inevitable, even for a *normal* person subjected to that much stress in a week—and I was a recovering PTSDer on top of it. My outburst came in response to an issue raised by one of my friends, who was very concerned about how I was perceived back in our hometown. During a lull in a group conversation, he said with a grave expression, "Your lawyers, or at least how the press handled your defense, completely backfired. You lost a lot of people's support when it was said you were impoverished. And then the abusing alcohol part—it seemed like it was just thrown in there. The whole article was like they were just throwing everything they could out there to make excuses for you and see what stuck. All of the usual defense lawyer bullshit that people are tired of hearing about." Damned alcohol issue again, I thought.

"It *did* say I was sexually abused by at least *three* adults, though, right?" I asked him, annoyed.

"Yes."

"So people just looked past the fact that I was sexually abused and focused on my parents' tax bracket—and hung me on that?"

"They just remember you from high school, when you guys had a sailboat."

"See, we *were* poor," I said with a tense jaw. "If we were rich, we would have had a fucking powerboat." Crickets. My humor did not go over well with this friend—not that I was making any effort to diffuse the tension. My case had had a deep and adverse effect on him. He openly struggled with it. Many couldn't fathom that a Ferndale favorite son had fallen so catastrophically. He was one of them. "My family *was* poor when I was very young, when all of that shit happened to me. Yes, we did well financially later in my life, but my family struggled from the time I was born until I was like eight or nine years old."

"I know that. But the people reading back home don't know that."

"Well, if they take the word of those damn reporters and don't bother contacting me or asking me directly what in the hell happened, then why should I give two shits about what they think?" The volume of my voice rose, so I tried to level it out. "Listen. I am getting sentenced tomorrow. By a federal judge. Do you think I care about that other shit right now? The other side is expecting an empty courtroom and maybe only one letter of support—from my mom. But there are going to be a lot of people in that courtroom tomorrow. They are going to be there for me, because they know who in the hell I am—because they reached out and asked me what the hell happened. So I told them. Sorry if not *everyone* is with me."

"Well, I am just saying you don't have much sympathy back home, now."

"Would it be better if I went back to carrying the flag for everybody back home? Would it be *easier* on everyone else if I went back to being the big shot doc that 'they all knew so well' [air quotes] and went to school with, even though my wife and kids hated me—even though I hated myself? Sorry to let everyone down, but I'll be damned before I ever return to that pathetic state again!" My voice quavered; I hadn't been this openly pissed off in over a year. I had learned to control my anger, but I wasn't emotionally castrated. The subject was quickly dropped, so as not to further dampen the mood of the gathering. Someone alluded to the Steve Martin movie *The Jerk,* in which Martin's rags-to-riches character claims he was born a poor black child, and the discussion morphed into a joke to smooth things over.

It stuck in my craw, though, long after the company left that night. Eventually, I became frustrated with myself for getting so worked up over the lack of love from back home. I hoped this would end up being one of the last remnants of my deep-seated narcissism and *how-dare-they?* attitude, which is apparently difficult to shake. I had to remind myself that worrying about what others thought of me, those whose opinion didn't or shouldn't matter to me in the first place, had always been part of my problem.

Then, in a moment of clarity, I finally asked myself, *When were "They" ever right about me anyway?* When I was a scared and scarred little boy, acting out, They said I was stupid and uncontrollable. When They extolled my glory later, in school and with my career achievements, I was a cauldron of self-loathing, hypervigilance, and anger. I hurt those closest to me with my outbursts and maniacal approach to everything, and They thought I was great. So why should I not be surprised that, even though I was finally comfortable in my own skin, They were now calling me horrible things, based on assumptions and misinformation? This is how it has always been for me. My outside world never seemed to match my inside world. I should be used to this by now.

The big difference this time around, however, is that I now know *exactly* who I am and how I became that person. I healed from my childhood traumas during the most stressful time of my adult life. My demons are now laid to rest, because I exorcized the shit out of them. I have an inner peace. I know my wife and children unconditionally love me. My friends and family support me. I am beyond fortunate and blessed. There are a lot of cancer patients, childhood sexual abuse survivors, and sufferers of PTSD who could use my help, knowledge, and insight. I have a lot of good left to give, if society grants me the opportunity to give it. Even better this time around, is that my drive to help others will *only* come from a place of health and happiness. It will be intrinsic and organic—not to gain some abstract form of approval that I previously pathologically sought. It will be real.

There is nothing that I need to prove to myself anymore, either. If I have anything to prove to others, it will be to show those who believed in me that they were right, not to prove doubters and detractors that they were wrong. I can no longer afford to preoccupy myself with worries of what people who do not know me say about me. If there is one thing I have learned from this whole maddening journey, it's that is it far easier to deal with people hating you than it is to deal with hating yourself.

The longest interval of sleep I had during the night before my May 2nd sentencing hearing was about five or ten minutes. Whenever I woke up, I would start reciting my sentencing statement. I was not going to read it off of a piece of paper—that is not genuine. I had a lot to say, though. I didn't want to omit anything. I kept going over what I wanted to say as I suited up in the morning. I was awake before everyone else.

The plan was for my wife and her closest friend since grade school to drop me off at my attorney's office at 9:30. I was to get a ride to the courthouse from my attorneys for my 10:30 hearing. My wife would get to the courthouse early and hang out in the cafeteria, to stay out of the media's lens. People showing up in the gallery for my support would wait in the hall adjacent to the courtroom to avoid interfering with the hearings scheduled before mine. My attorneys were still a bit skeptical when I'd given them a supporter head count of around thirty. That was way too many for a child pornography hearing. After only my wife had been present for the plea hearing, I don't think the other side was expecting much of a turnout, either.

When I walked into the waiting area in my attorney's office building, the adorable older receptionist, who had worked there for years said, "Oh, come here, Doc. Let me give you a hug. This is a big day for you." She gave me a hug and pinched my cheek, "Well, at least you will look good, no matter what happens to you today." Her smile warmed me up. "Coffee? Black, right?" I had been there enough times that just a quick nod was needed to confirm my order. She came back with a steaming cup. "Well, Doc, the boys are all down at the courthouse and will give us a call with instructions. Just have a seat. And don't pace, you will get all sweaty in that sharp suit." It was 9:45—forty-five minutes to my hearing.

I started getting texts over the next fifteen minutes. I told people to arrive at the courthouse by 10, to allow time for parking and wrong turns.

"We are on our way," from a neighbor.

"Hang in there," from an old college friend.

"Thinking of you," from a high school girlfriend.

"I am here. Where are you?" from one of my residents.

"Wow, lots of people here!!" from a past research associate.

"I just met your parents," from another resident.

At a little after 10 my wife texted me from the underbelly of the courthouse. "Ah … Are they going to come get me or what? Are you at the courthouse?"

"No. Not yet."

"WTF?"

It was getting a bit concerning. I went up to the receptionist and sheepishly asked, "Uh, are we, uh … doing this today?"

"Well, Doc, that is why they have been down at the courthouse all morning. They are talking about your case with the judge, and I was told they would either call for you to go down there or they will come back and let you know what is going on."

"Wait. So they said it may not happen today?" I asked. One of my lawyers had called me the night before to say that some issues had come up that needed ironing out in the morning but I should be ready to proceed. I didn't think it was *not* going to happen. I was told to expect a possible delay, which I assumed would be measured in units of minutes or hours.

"Well, Doc, they said it may get postponed to a different day when I last talked to them."

"When was that?"

"About ten minutes ago."

I briskly walked into the bathroom. I had to do *something*—splash water on my face or force a stream of urine, anything. I couldn't sit still anymore. I had used the bathroom in this office building before and it always had the smell of cigarette smoke. Someone there was old-school, and I wished I knew who it was. I would have hit them up for a cancer stick and gone over my printed statement with a far less shaky hand in that makeshift smoking lounge. I didn't know if I would be in federal custody or back home within the next two hours. But with the identity of the building's smoker unknown and an uncooperative bladder, I returned to my seat. Texts continued to come in from confused supporters who were wondering where my wife and I were. At least I could release some of my anxious energy with rapid thumbing.

At 10:23 the call came in, and my heart stopped so as not to distract my eardrums with the internal noise that coursing blood makes. I could only make out bits and pieces of the receptionist's conversation, but then the last part came out clearly: "OK, I will tell the doc to stay put." The tension in my shoulders gave; the door opened up. "Well, Doc, it is not happening today. But, still, let me give you another hug. This wait has got to be unbearable for you." I got another grandmotherly hug, and it had its desired calming effect. "The boys are coming back, and so is your wife, to go over what all happened this morning."

I texted all the people that I knew were there. It *was* around thirty people, as I'd predicted, so three sets of group messages went out thanking them for showing up but explaining that due to legal stuff, it had to be delayed. Nearly everyone sent back, asking me to hang in there—and to let them know the next time, and they would be there again. I texted Richard, as he was waiting for a ride, too, to take the witness stand: "I feel like the blindfold was put on, the firing squad shot blanks, then the blindfold was removed!" He quickly shot me a text which contained nearly audible chuckling and a bid to stay strong. Even up to the last moment, people were there for me.

When my wife came to the door, she had a big smile on her face. My attorneys had given her the news before me. My judge had recused himself after all. I was going to live to fight another day. I don't know if it was this turn of events that made her happy or the fact that my attorneys had told her when they met up with her in the courthouse. She'd received crucial news about my case directly from them—*before* me. It was a move that showed they trusted her. She was officially part of the Pelloski Defense Team. After seeing how she handled everything, how she stood by me, and how well our children and I did with her at the helm, she was now within their inner sanctum. It meant a lot. To both of us.

I have no idea what was said at the courthouse, in the judge's chambers, or what led to the recusal. My attorneys kept quiet out of professional courtesy, so I could only speculate. It could have been the fact that many of the fourteen letters of support selected by my attorneys and submitted as evidence under seal were written by OSU students and trainees. Or that Richard, my highly visible collaborator from Nationwide Children's Hospital, the giant in the pediatric oncology field, was going to speak on the witness stand for me. Maybe it was the combination of all these factors. Any of these issues alone would bring the institutions under more scrutiny while under the judge's watch.

The letters of support and witness roster were not submitted until the day before sentencing, for last-minute effect. With all this new information coming to light on the day before the sentencing hearing, I can only surmise that it became clear to all sides that the appearance of impropriety loomed on the horizon. The complexion of my case had become different than in October, when the judge was originally assigned and I was expected to have no support. This would make the likelihood of appeal much greater as well. Everyone hates appeals. It leaves a bad taste in the judge's mouth, as it implies the original decision should be second-guessed. It makes more work all around, and lawyers from either side have enough cases to keep them busy. Further, whichever side initiates the appeal has to deal with that annoyed judge later on in future cases. Recusal was the right thing for all.

So I was told to relax. I was not on a bus to Oklahoma—be thankful. They advised me to enjoy the group of friends and family who'd come to town to support me, have a weekend-long party, and hug my kids that night. I was reminded, several times, not to consume any alcohol, though. I was also told to not tell anyone of the recusal until it became public knowledge. We were to let the court and media handle how that information was to be shared. My defense team fell on the sword for everyone, too. The official party line was that we asked for a continuance, for more time to gather witnesses.

According to my therapist, who was in the courtroom (the rest of my supporters were herded into the hallway), a very odd hearing was put on the books. It lasted for only a few minutes. There was a lot of scurrying back and forth between attorneys, the bailiff, and the judge, and plenty of whispers. Then it started. They asked if I was present, got no as an answer, and they said start anyway. My team asked for a continuance. The prosecution had no objections. The continuance was granted. Hearing over. My therapist told me it was one of the strangest things she had ever seen.

Of course, the TV news media were oblivious to what really happened and swallowed whatever was spoon-fed to them. Or they were told by the powers-that-be to keep quiet. Quite frankly, I am not sure which reason is more frightening. At any rate, the media promptly, faithfully, and predictably disseminated the misinformation in a way that implied my team and I were stalling.

The hearing having proven disappointing, for whatever reason, one member of the media resorted to the court of public opinion. A friend related some interesting things she'd read about me online: A local reporter posted a poll on Facebook asking if my childhood abuse should be allowed as an "excuse" for my offense and its punishment. This was an odd question, from a logical standpoint, given that I'd pled guilty and taken responsibility for my actions. I didn't enter a not-guilty plea, nor did I ask that the charges be dropped. I never made any excuses. People asked me why I did it, so I told them.

If we return to the drunk driver analogy, this would be like asking if the driver's alcoholism is an excuse for his DUI or committing DUI manslaughter. Is it an excuse? No. Is it a mitigating factor? Yes. Alcoholics do, in fact, drink alcohol, which is requisite for all DUI-based infractions. Does my childhood sexual abuse excuse what I did? No. Did it contribute to my horrible decision to do what I did? Absolutely. Nothing gives me the warm and fuzzies more than minimizing someone's childhood sexual abuse to garner attention.

At least one brave soul actually stood up for me in this online meeting of the minds, though. She happened to be the mother of one of my former pediatric patients. Because of this, she was deemed biased by the e-mob. Since I'd saved her child's life, her opinion was dismissed as a vulgar display of homerism. The dissenter was therefore promptly buried in a pile of virtual vitriol. Saving people's lives, children's especially, just doesn't have the same value it used to.

Chapter Sixteen

THE RECUSAL DID, in fact, turn the sentencing gathering into a real weekend party. Of course, the beer and wine flowed. Unfortunately, I was relegated to consuming Bitburger's alcohol-free beer substitute, which was thrill-free, to say the least, but it still served as an excellent hangout prop. I had to tell my parents what actually happened. They'd canceled travel plans and taken great pains to make it to my May 2nd hearing. They were not buying the smoke screen so readily accepted by the news lackeys: that *my* side was the one that asked for a continuance. When I told them what actually happened, my father went right into full-blown Dad Mode and started looking at the dollars and cents immediately.

"What do you mean he recused himself because he had OSU ties? He wasn't aware of his fucking OSU ties when all this shit started back in the fall? This is horseshit. Now how much longer do you have to wait?"

"Another two or three months," I answered, already knowing what his response would be.

"Another two or three months?! More legal fees? More time in limbo? More time eating away at your life savings? What about all these people who traveled long distances to get here? That fucking judge should reimburse you for all the legal costs you guys have racked up over the last six months and all of the extra months that are ahead. No skin off of his back— unbelievable!"

"Dad, Dad. It's OK." I said smiling and laughing. I was amused by his anger on my behalf and appreciated it. That was his love for me. "In those six months a lot of good has happened. I spent time with the family. I got my brain fixed. It wasn't a waste of time. I could have easily sat in jail this whole time, but he let me stay home with the family." My father calmed down a bit, as my words sunk in. "Plus, they don't have to start all the way from the beginning. Just a few more months to get the new judge up to speed."

"Still, it burns me up. Damn government pushing you around like that."

"I know, but Dad, the bright side is I don't have him as a judge anymore. Maybe I get one that might be a little more understanding about what I did—at least there will be no pressure from OSU. And I'm not in a bus on the way to Oklahoma right now. We are all together this weekend. Look, everyone is smiling and having fun," I said with a long sweep of my hand toward the crowd at my house. Friends from high school and college, both sets of parents, my brother-in-law. They were all catching up and laughing.

He lightened up after that. "OK son. I just worry about all of this … Oklahoma?"

"Dad," I put my arm around him, "I think I dodged a bullet today. This is a good thing. Better than I could have possibly imagined. I would have been hauled off, right out of the courtroom today, if my hearing proceeded as planned. Right now everyone would be devastated, especially the kids, who would keep asking where I was and why people were crying or upset."

Emotions were going to run high that day. Everyone was amped up since they'd been prepared for the worst to happen—and at that point they had nowhere to direct the extra energy. They all had what amounted to a case of sentencing blue balls. With the abundant ethanol flowing to help them come down, more outbursts of frustration would follow my dad's. Running on forty-eight hours of consciousness, I was hoping to remain a numb spectator and just take things in.

At one point, I needed a break and went to sit out on the patio by myself. I wanted a moment to myself, to choke down the fake beer and feel semi-normal. Of course, I positioned the aluminum lounge so that it was within five feet of the garage door, so my ankle monitor wouldn't go off. My solitude was short lived. I would soon become the anchor of the biggest powwow of the weekend. Among the first to join me were my two closest friends from my hometown: Dave, my best man at my wedding and a friend since fifth grade, and Will, another close child-hood friend. The third was Robert, a friend I'd made during the year I took off in between undergraduate and medical school, academic year '96–'97. He was a former Marine, war veteran, and now a criminal defense lawyer. My childhood buddies were a bit numb themselves, but Robert, who knew me only as an adult, wanted to talk.

"So, Doc, what exactly did you do to get yourself in this mess?" He was always direct. Dave and I had lived with him during that year off, which ended for me with my marriage and a send-off to Chicago so Susan and I could start law and medical school (hence the nickname "Doc"). There were five of us who lived together, but three was always sufficient for a quorum, so we had quorum on my patio.

We had called ourselves the Virginia Crew, because our rental house was on Virginia Avenue in East Lansing, Michigan. We borrowed the Rolling Stones' "Sweet Virginia" as our theme song. My four house-mates were working on their degrees from Michigan State. We were an eclectic collection, with the only commonality being the roof over our heads. How we got there and where we were going next were entirely divergent. Robert, the defense-attorney-to-be, first joined the Marines and did a few tours in Iraq before earning his law degree. In addition to getting his JD, having gone through Marine basic training and serving as an officer in combat had sharpened his eloquence and intensified his passion. If I'd experienced combat as he did, I would have become an instant Section 8, just like Private Hand Job in *Full Metal Jacket*. Robert also played guitar in a band in college—a true modern-day warrior poet. The rest of the Crew was rounded out by an engineer, a teacher, and Dave, a web designer/advertiser.

I would soon realize that Robert's law degree had only sharpened his already excellent tools for debate. I could see he was getting them ready with this loaded question. When he'd first heard what happened to me, he vociferously defended me and implored the rest of the Virginia Crew to do so. When the others initially hesitated, he went ballistic, questioning their loyalty. He was an absolute pit bull on my behalf. And he did his homework on the laws and theories surrounding my case. He'd come to Columbus to support me, but he wanted to hear the full story from me, too.

If there was one thing the Crew was noted for, it was its ability to debate, and he was always in the middle of it. Many epic intellectual battles on social issues had carried over from late at night into the early morning, as empty beer cases piled up around us. The more controversial the topic, the more spirited the debate—sometimes leading to fisticuffs or the destruction of rental property. His primary advantage over all of us was that his eloquence and logic were enhanced in direct proportion to both his blood alcohol content and the passion that he carried for the counterpoint.

As I explained to him what it was that I did—what my offense was based upon—the verbal cage fighter was awakened. "So, wait a minute. You would view a few things that you would download, and delete them all afterwards, and then months or years would pass before you looked again?" he asked.

"Yes."

A few more joined the circle, my dad and brother-in-law among them. By then, there were seven or eight people sitting on chairs in a circle. Most had their heads down, silent, knowing they were in for an escalation but too situated to leave. All that was missing was a flaming log in the fire pit. Our discussion continued as more people settled in. Robert sipped from his beer bottle and the fire in his eyes was back. If not for his face, weathered from flying helicopters in combat conditions, the flecks of gray in his jet-black hair and stubble, and the crow's feet around his eyes, I would have thought it was some 2 a.m. in 1997 again and Bobby was holding court. "Fifty-nine deleted files and all of this shit happened? So you didn't even have a collection stored somewhere?"

"No. My attorneys once told me that my case was one of the least egregious child pornography cases they had ever seen in the computer era."

"Egregious? So you didn't pay for anything—you didn't have an association with anyone involved in this? You didn't do this for all of the reasons usually assumed; you just went to where you can access it within minutes and … Wait, so how long is the prosecutor asking for?"

"Four years."

"Four years? Are you fucking kidding me? There are rapists and child molesters who get less time than that. Four years?" He kept uttering this, stuck on this fact, his voice fading a bit. Then he returned. "I think your prosecutor has political aspirations."

I thought that was a stretch. "Well, I *did* break the law. And there are sentencing guidelines. This four-year recommendation was actually lower than the usual guidelines as it is. She is just doing her job, to uphold the law."

"Yeah, I get that, but prosecutors have some discretion over their cases. What a fucking waste of everyone's time this all is! I am not even sure if what you did was criminal."

"Whoa, dude, I was there! Online. I was *part* of the problem. I was another guy in that peer-to-peer queue, regardless of my reasons for being there." (So much for my plans of being a numb spectator.) "Besides, the prosecutor is a huge child advocate, and she is known for going for the bad guys' jugulars and cutting off their balls. I respect that. She let me stay on house arrest. I heard her argue *for* me to stay with my family at my plea hearing, for Christ's sake. She knew I had kids, and since she believed I was safe, she let me be with them, instead of sitting in jail. She could have had me locked up from the get-go, but didn't. That made a huge difference with how all this went down."

Robert then dove into criminal law theory. "Look, there are two components to a crime: the *actus reus,* which is the guilty act, and the *mens rea,* which is the guilty mind. So I beg to differ. Your reasons for being there—the *mens rea*—do and should factor into your culpability. You were not there to enjoy it or conspire with others to promote the abuse of children. You were not ever going to physically harm anyone." He softened his tone a bit. "OK. You can kill someone, which is the *actus reus,* and the *mens rea* determines whether or not a crime was committed and to what degree it was—if it was in fact a crime. The intent determines if the death was an unavoidable accident, manslaughter, second-degree or first-degree murder." It was comforting to see my friend holding court, as he always did. Only this time, he got to flex his new skill set. "Right now, the way the laws are written, there is no *mens rea* to stratify the culpability. It's all based solely on the *actus,* and that is bullshit. Yours is a strict liability crime—no room for mitigation and no questions asked. That is a very primitive and meathead approach to law."

"Well, I am going to get *some* time. I know that. The way the laws are on the books these days. And if I don't get any time, all I will hear is the endless shit about how I 'got over' and got to walk. It will look like I got away with something. I don't think I want that hanging over my head either," I said, resigned to my fate.

"I don't think you should do *any* time. I mean, Jesus, you have been punished enough already. You have been publicly shamed. You have derelicts who don't know what in the hell they are talking about calling you a child molester. You lost your career and are now burning through what money you ever made or saved. What in the fuck else needs to be done?" He then changed his voice to nasal, mock condescension, "Chris, have you learned your lesson? Or do you need to go to your room to think about it some more?"

His voice immediately shot back into the jagged diatribe: "How is you sitting in prison with your thumb up your ass going to help anyone? We have all—and I mean *everyone*—been punished already by you not being allowed to be a doctor and researcher during all of this time. And, to be honest, I find it a bit scary that accessing something that is free, readily available, and requires no membership or illegal association is a crime. This is tantamount to a Thoughtcrime. I can't look at something that is already there? What if it was on a billboard? If it is *that* bad, then get rid of it. Create some damn computer virus to seek and destroy any file with a known child porn hash-value and wipe that shit out. Paint over that billboard. Don't just go after the guys looking at it!"

This new line of reasoning had my friend scanning the yard, looking for the words. "And even if it is the thought crime everyone assumes, you are not guilty of it, because there was clearly no malice in your intent to view this shit. You were fucked up when you were a kid ..." He trailed off and then lowered his voice, "Oh ... uh, sorry." There was another sip of beer to refuel the dissertation. I motioned to him that it was OK about the fucked-up childhood part. It was the truth, after all.

At this point, Will, who'd flown in from Seattle, who had supported me since day one and remains the smartest person I have ever known, entered the conversation. "Well, I wouldn't say Chris is *not* guilty. He did do something wrong—and he is not blameless, either."

Will is a career physicist (PhD), with a degree in literature as well. And he is a childhood cancer survivor. He had Hodgkin's lymphoma, which relapsed. Relapsed Hodgkin's is a scary business. He'd gone through hell, twice (including radiation) in the 1980s, when the treatments were much less forgiving than they are today. His life had been tested, and he'd handled it with grace and dignity. In high school (during the second round), he was always upbeat, never openly felt sorry for himself or asking for pity, and took great pains to make sure he did not miss anything—from hanging out with the guys to completing homework assignments. After treating children with cancer, I'd come to appreciate his struggle and triumph in a far more profound manner than I had before. With his experience comes perspective very few have. So whenever he weighs in on something—*anything*—all are compelled to listen. His words bounce off many more neurons on their way to becoming sounds compared to the average speaker's.

I signaled that I was in agreement with him. I did this to show my appreciation for his support in my argument, as well as to let him know that I took no offense at his observations regarding my *actus reus*. "I agree. It doesn't matter that I did not make money off of it or put money into the system. Even if it is free and publicly available, my presence in that system created a demand. No matter how brief it may have been. No matter what my reasons were. At a minimum, it told the others already there it was OK to engage in this activity. It's not OK."

Dave remained quiet through all of this and kept his eyes fixed on the ground between his feet. He and Robert had driven to Columbus together, and I got the impression they'd already had the same conversation on the four-hour ride—and that he wanted no more of it. It was difficult for him to see me on the legal ropes as I was. Robert, on the other hand, armed with specific knowledge newly obtained directly from the defendant's mouth, still wanted to fight.

"Well, I can see *your* attorneys have trained you very well, to buy into this warped logic—which only enables and validates the bullshit system, if you ask me." He paused, recognizing his own hypocrisy and surrender to the system. "It's fine. I do the same thing with my clients, when they need to admit to the 'horrors they created' [air quotes] by having a bag of weed on them and then acquiesce to the asinine drug laws we have." The bitterness in his voice was unmistakable. These were clearly words he'd recited mentally and vocally many times. "It's no different than the God-damned Spanish Inquisition: making people confess to witchcraft right before they were gonna get burned at the stake anyway."

I felt stung by his skepticism and was about to defend my sincerity, but Will beat me to the punch. "Well …" he interjected, trying to steer things back to the issue of harm that I created, "there can be a weird personal gain, too. Like, say, some guy who has some rare file gets off knowing that it was downloaded X-many times by so many other people. It is not a monetary gain, but a gain nonetheless—at the expense of children. Chris had to have some kind of gain there, too. Otherwise, why else would he keep going back to view it? Just *being* there is the harm, albeit a theoretical one." I nodded, apologetically, but in agreement with him.

Robert pondered that point for a while and then seemingly conceded. "Fine. Harm was done. But if you need a few paragraphs and a whole lot of hand-waving to define this harm, then I strongly question the wisdom behind the laws and necessity of these prison sentences, which are measured in *years* and remove people from their families and society." I began to wonder if someone had spiked my friend's beer with equal parts rage and cynicism.

"If you maim someone, take away their life, or livelihood, or steal from them—I get that. You *should* lose your freedom, for quite a while. But what the fuck is this?" he said, pointing at me. "And I don't buy the 'continued-abuse-by-viewing' argument either. If that were the case, every time we all hooped and hollered over the aerial footage of our smart bombs blowing up a transporter full of Iraqis or destroying some enemy building, that would mean that all of those people who were killed—yes, people are actually *killed* in those sports highlight reels—that would mean all those people would keep getting rekilled, revaporized, or reblown to bits over and over, every time someone else watched that shit. I may be totally wrong here, but I don't think it is physically possible to be rekilled. And why is viewing one crime against humanity celebrated with high-fives while viewing another is criminalized?"

Dave then chimed in, "Yep, whenever terrorists release a video of some European journalist getting their dome lopped off and it gets viewed millions of times, there are these little men that reattach their heads to their necks between each viewing. It's probably those same gnomes that turn off the light when you close the refrigerator door. But, by reattaching the heads, people can be decapitated over and over. Decapitation porn certainly draws a lot of web clicks. The best thing you can do in marketing is to give a 'warning' that the content is graphic. That is a great placement for 20 percent off on running shoes or an all-inclusive vacation to Belize!" While Dave, remained quiet for most of the roundtable discussion, he could never resist a cynical pile-on, especially when it pertained to his area of expertise.

There was an uneasy pause in the conversation. A consensus seemed to have been reached that *some* kind of harm was in fact generated. But the moment of fragile accord was brief.

"The bottom line here is fear, though," Robert returned to the tirade. "Everyone is afraid of sex offenders. Ahhh!!" he said, wildly waving his hands in mock hysteria, letting his tongue flop about. Then he got serious again. "Open discussions about child pornography are not happening, because the mere mention of it has people heading for the hills. People fear it and have no understanding about it. That is why a rational discussion is not happening. That is why you are in this unnecessary situation," he said, pointing to me again. "That is why we have people spending longer times in prison for viewing this shit, compared to those guys who actually molest or rape children. And those bastards are harder to catch." This claim was a new one for me. Of course, I would have to research this later. So I filed it away.

"Still, what I did *was* a red flag, though," I prodded him some more. At this point I just wanted to see what he would say next, just like in the old days. "It was a red flag that I did what I did, given who I was and what my position was. *And* I finally got the help I have needed for so long." I was trying to promote the silver lining, as well.

"Right! It *was* a red flag. And after all of the suspicions about you being a fucking 'monster' [air quotes] were cleared up, with your lie detector crap and all of the other investigations—and you got all of the help that you needed—that should have been it. There is nothing left to address here. All of this shit should have stopped! But it didn't. What are we all doing here, now? What is the point of this case now? Why isn't there an off-ramp from this?" He waited for answers but received only silence.

He thought a bit more, and his tone became conversational. "What was the pediatric cancer you were doing research on?"

"Rhabdomyosarcoma."

"Yeah, what if my kid gets rhabdo-whatever-oma, and rather than you developing a breakthrough that could save his life, all of this bullshit is happening and continues to happen and your insights never come to fruition and so my kid dies? I would be pretty fucking pissed about that. Of course our reactionary society can't see it like that."

With that closing statement the defense rested. Whenever a veteran complains about the country he risked his life to protect, their words are always given a bit more credence and have a greater heaviness. I had the same veneration for my grandfathers, who served in World War II, whenever they spoke about the politics or social issues of our nation. Live enemy rounds and ordnance being hurled at someone puts their beliefs to the test and provides clarity.

The hearing was adjourned with one final swig from his beer bottle. I didn't have an answer to what he'd said—and since it was my fate we were talking about, I didn't particularly want to draw it out anyway. My commitment to academic discourse can only drive me for so long. He'd given me a lot more to think about, though.

I looked over at my father, and he looked back at me and nodded with tears in his eyes, his face and ears flushed, as they get when he's upset. He would later tell me that Robert had expressed exactly what he felt about *all* of this, but he could never frame it as articulately (though he claimed he would have left out the profanity). I reminded him that my friend was an attorney, and talking is what they do best.

The circle on my patio remained quiet for some time. Everyone needed to digest the discussion before moving on, to avoid mental swimming cramps. Eventually, however, we slowly and cautiously resumed retelling our favorite embarrassing stories about each other, and the laughter finally came back on that bizarre day.

I was relieved the following Monday when I discovered who my new judge was. He was a senior federal judge, the most experienced and independent-minded of the judges in the district, I was told. He didn't want any witness testimony either, so Richard did not need to stick his neck out by taking the stand after all. My new judge was someone who was not afraid to buck the system, if the right case called for it. He'd been appointed in 1986 by Ronald Reagan and had tons of experience, including time on federal appellate courts. He was on record as being critical of the federal child pornography sentencing guidelines for non-production cases. He would appreciate the nuances of my case—or so I hoped. I didn't know what he would give me in terms of a sentence, but I did not have a dark cloud of impending doom over my head anymore. He certainly was not going to be swayed by any outside forces, either. That was evident after reading his sentencing opinions and orders on other similar cases. He was on top of the controversies, even in the face of the mudslinging he'd received for "protecting perverts," as one blogger had written. In several stories written about his giving lighter sentences and articles highlighting his opposition to the sentencing guidelines, people had called him a pervert, accused him of not caring about children, and said that "his computer needs to be checked." It seems that only those who are safe in a lifetime appointment (not needing votes to stay in office) are the only ones who can speak up, and even they can be scorned.

Being near completion of my therapy, the knowledge about my new judge's background coupled with the discussion with Robert, made me want to take advantage of the extra time I would spend on house arrest to delve into these controversies. I was astonished by what I learned.

At any moment, it is estimated that there are over one million files of child pornography online and readily accessible. It is further estimated that at least two hundred new files are added every day, from producers and those who create new victims. The acronym PTHC (preteen hard-core) is the *most popular* search term on several *well-known* peer-to-peer networks. Computers and the Internet have made the problem of child pornography both insidious and ubiquitous on a global scale. This harrowing reality, however, also makes the quantification of harm caused by nonproduction offenders much more difficult than when child pornography as an industry required in-person association or conventional mail for sale and distribution of the analog media—back when meetings occurred in dark alleys and abandoned buildings.

Determining the appropriate punishment then was a simpler matter; the amount of damage caused by offenders could more easily be quantified since they were closer to the "source"—where the children were actually being harmed—and were actively financing it by buying, if not otherwise participating. In the Internet age, however, the harm done by nonproducers is less black and white. Certainly the criticisms highlighted by my friend at my "patio hearing," as well as the U.S. Sentencing Commission's findings issued in the fall/winter of 2012 (which I read) have merit. Numerous scholarly works have made these arguments as well, written by forensic psychologists and legal scholars such as Charles Patrick Ewing, Amy Adler, Michael Seto, Jérôme Endrass, and Lisa and Laura Zilney. While none of these researchers condone child pornography and clearly deem it unsuitable for any civilized society, it is the response toward these offenses they have serious issues with. For weeks, I immersed myself in this body of literature. As I became a newly informed citizen on all things "sex offense law," numerous points stood out, even after accounting for my obvious personal biases.

It turns out that the most vocal opponents of the Federal Sentencing Guidelines are the federal judges who are pressured to administer these punishments. Federal judges are appointed for life, in the hope that they will rule on each case based on its own merits, not be swayed by public opinion (and ultimately votes). They are appointed by the president and approved by the Senate, thus ensuring the checks and balances between the three branches of government. The role of the judicial branch, as we are taught in school, is to interpret the laws the legislative branch writes and the executive branch enforces.

In the Supreme Court case *United States v. Booker,* in 2005, the justices ruled that federal district judges do not have to strictly adhere to the Federal Sentencing Guidelines when handing out their punishments. From this outsider's perspective, the case seems like a reminder to all that federal judges do, in fact, have discretion. Not surprisingly, the word *guidelines* was also involved as a point of contention. However, despite our rule of law going back over two hundred years and the 2005 reminder, some judges' sentences in nonproduction cases have been contested as too lenient, and some of those have been reversed on appeal. Some judges have even apologized to defendants as they handed them multiyear sentences on remand, after initially sentencing them to zero to twelve months, stating that their hands had been forced. (I would later learn that the judge to whom I'd been reassigned had had his decision in a recent case overturned twice. He'd refused to send a sick, elderly man, who was the caregiver for his cancer-stricken wife, to prison—where he would certainly die during the mandatory five-year stay.)

A hypothetical case I read presented a situation where someone was caught trading, via email, a single image of a prepubescent child engaged in penetrative intercourse with an abuser. The offense enhancement score, according to the Federal Sentencing Guidelines, would automatically be a 33, and the recommended sentence would be eleven years and three months to fourteen years, with a twenty-year maximum. However, if that person had direct sexual contact with a prepubescent child (even if more than once), depending on the state in which the crime was committed, the *maximum* prison term could be capped at one to eleven years. It was further argued that this sentencing structure creates a disturbing incentive for those sexually attracted to children to carry out their urges upon them, rather than sublimate their desires with the illicit media.

To my surprise, I learned that common assumptions about sex offenders are wildly inaccurate. Peer-reviewed articles available on PubMed, which are science-driven, not agenda-driven, present an interesting contrast to popular conceptions. Recent research by Seto, Endrass, and other psychologists and criminologists have concluded that one-sixth of people whose initial offense involves online child pornography are also contact offenders. Thus using online activity is a good screening mechanism for ferreting out criminals who pose a physical danger to children. This also means, though, that 83 percent of these offenders are *not* child molesters. Several other reports also showed that viewing child pornography by itself is not a risk factor for "evolving" into a contact offender. One report even suggested that child pornography may provide an outlet for pedophiles who might otherwise act upon their impulses and physically harm children.

Interestingly, the incidence of child molestation and contact offense cases dropped by 50 percent concurrently with the massive expansion of online child pornography in the 1990s—*before* the latest set of severe laws aimed at deterrence were put in place. This is reminiscent of research done by Danish criminologist Berl Kutchinsky, who noted a drop in violent sexual offenses against women *and* children after the legalization of pornography in Denmark, Sweden, and West Germany in the late sixties and early seventies.

Further, the recidivism rate of those with only nonproduction online child pornography offenses is under 4 percent after completion of therapy and counseling. This was shown in multiple studies involving thousands of offenders. Sex criminals, in general, have the second-lowest recidivism rate, just behind murderers. The recidivism rate for nearly every other nonsex crime, except murder, is around 50 to 70 percent within three years. This flies in the face of the public perception that *all* sex offenders are hardwired to reoffend. I was shocked to learn that the recidivism rate for *contact offenders* was in the 8 to 13 percent range (depending on the specific study). In the same way that I'd assumed PTSD was only a problem of combat veterans, I'd thought that 99 percent of all child molesters are destined to be repeat offenders. That is what we are told all the time on the news and talk shows and by politicians. Sensational stories of repeat offenders fuel the fury and portray the most horrific events as the rule rather than exception, much like plane crashes.

Federal nonproduction child pornography cases have drastically increased in both number and severity of punishment over the last few decades. At one point they doubled over five years. And from 1997 to 2007, possession cases increased, from about 24 to 1,084. Similarly, over the same period, the average prison term went from 20.6 to 91.3 months. Given that it currently costs the federal government about $30,000 per year to incarcerate someone, this means, without retroactively adjusting for inflation, the cost for sentences handed out in 1997 would amount to $1.23 million (in 2007 dollars), while the 2007 price tag was $247 million for the same offenses. Therefore, the cost to punish nonviolent offenders, who exhibit a very low repeat-offense rate, increased by nearly a quarter of a *billion* dollars. And this is just the tip of the iceberg. The cost of lost income tax probably adds an opportunity cost of more than another half billion. The experience, service, and job creation of those incarcerated are removed from society as well.

Ratcheting up the severity of the punishment for these offenses certainly has not acted as a deterrent either. Nonproduction cases account for over 80 percent of the recent upsurge in federal sex offense cases, which collectively grow by 15 percent per year. This also means that 80 percent of the upsurge in those registering as sex offenders, as these offenses require, are the nonproduction child pornography offenders who pose little risk for *any* future crimes. These federally mandated state programs cost over half a billion dollars annually, have no evidence of improving public safety, and can only keep track of about half of the registrants at any given time. It has been suggested by multiple scholars that this money would be better spent going after the producers and creators of the systems that allow these files to exist, rather than the less harmful "end users" of this material.

And those are just the costs in taxpayer dollars. A huge social price is paid by the families of these offenders. Having an incarcerated parent is a well-established childhood trauma, is catastrophic to childhood development, and increases a multitude of life problems later. Relationships and families are destroyed, and suicide rates are very high. The mental health ripple effects across families and communities are incalculable. It certainly adds another layer of harm for future generations to grapple with.

According to some law enforcement agencies, there are anywhere from 50,000 to several hundreds of thousands of Internet users against whom there is sufficient evidence for federal child pornography charges to be brought, whether their actions are intentional or unintentional. So there is potential for these problems to become much worse.

How did our society paint itself into this corner? The problem, it is argued, was that policy is created in the setting of unchecked public hysteria. Sex offenses that involve children are so repugnant, and our reactions to them so visceral, that expanding the scope of these laws is extremely easy and goes unimpeded. Compare this to gun control. After every mass shooting at a school or shopping mall, there is moral outrage calling for stricter gun control. However, quick to oppose any reactive legislation is the powerful gun lobby, which effectively ensures that drastic, overnight changes never happen in the aftermath of a massacre. But standing up for gun rights is a far easier sell than questioning the expansion of sex offender laws. Those who do raise concerns are marginalized; castigated as perverts, deviants, or child molesters themselves; or portrayed as uncaring toward children. This is similar to how early critics of the War on Drugs were received—they were labeled as amoral junkies or enablers of addiction, among other things.

The authors of the material I read speculate that what keeps this going, like most poor public policy, is fear, ignorance, and misinformation. The news media, elected politicians, law enforcement, and federal prosecution offices have also realized what an easy target nonproduction child pornography cases present. It is not surprising that these comprise the overwhelming majority of new sex offenses cases (despite being the least threatening subtype with the lowest recidivism rate). The political and PR return on investment is lucrative, indeed. It takes very little effort to catch someone accessing child pornography online, the public brings its approval to the voting booth, and the headlines write themselves.

I often wondered why I was not contacted and warned when my activity was first detected, in October 2012. Since watching even a single file is enough to be prosecuted and incarcerated, I could have been called in the next day and frankly asked *Why is someone like you looking at this shit?*—and my house searched accordingly. If the current U.S.

laws are in the name of child safety, several aspects of how I was investigated run contrary to that aim. Why was I observed online for *nine* months? If law enforcement had a legitimate fear that I was a danger to children (my own or pediatric patients), why was nothing done for all that time? I can only conclude it was already known that I was not an immediate hands-on threat. It was more important to spend many months building the case, so I was allowed to watch four more times over those months. The police's inaction tacitly disclosed their position on the matter: that the harm I was generating toward children was not worth preventing sooner.

To use a War on Drugs analogy, the child pornography on a free, public peer-to-peer network is equivalent to a massive pile of cocaine sitting out in the open in a park. Rather than going after the people who produced the cocaine and/or covertly add to this pile every night, it is far easier for law enforcement to wait in the bushes and pounce on the poor schmucks, who, for whatever reason (susceptibility to addiction, curiosity, depression, etc.) can't help but walk up to the pile in broad daylight and take a scoop of the powder for themselves. A victory is then declared, as the offending "scooper" is paraded around town and pelted with rocks by the jeering crowds. Meanwhile, the Great White Mountain only grows.

The news media always get a surge in ratings and clicks when they cover sexual deviancy cases. Law enforcement, prosecutors, and politicians get to pad their stats with these nonproduction cases, as well. By looking tough on sex crimes they build their careers and get reelected. That's not callousness; it's just Job Security 101. Sex offenders, of course, are entirely unsympathetic characters and have no voice. Going after them draws no public ire. It's open season. Society overall feels safer, when in reality not much has been done to address the true problem, though a ton of money has been expended.

The conclusion of the works I read is that change will probably come from three sources, in addition to vocal federal judges: psychologists and social scientists who produce research without political pressures and hidden agendas; taxpayers who rally against expensive, ineffective government programs that lack evidence to back them up; and those who resist the Orwellian incursions against civil liberties that are carried out behind the façade of improved public safety.

The United Kingdom appears to have a better understanding of the situation than we do in the States. While sexual offenses against children are not taken lightly, nor swept under the rug, a system is employed that saves time, energy, and resources that can be used toward apprehending the more dangerous offenders. A caution program is in place, in which those with limited involvement in child pornography (simply possessing or accessing) are given a warning, referred for counseling, and then followed for five years. The repeat offense rate is nearly zero for this low-risk group. This is what happened to Who guitarist Pete Townshend (a victim of childhood sexual abuse himself), when he was snared by Operation Ore in 2003. He has since gone on to be a huge advocate for children, raising millions of dollars for a variety of causes. With a caution, there is no conviction or charge, and people emerge with their lives intact.

It was demoralizing to learn all this. I began to feel that my life has been bracketed by both ass-ends of the perplexing paradoxes that are our sex offense laws. By infrequently viewing media that made me remember that I was sexually abused as a little boy, I was exposed to a potentially longer federal prison sentence (guideline of four to fifteen years) than the people who molested me might have faced (one to eleven years) had they been caught and prosecuted under state law—despite the fact that their actions haunted me for decades, stunted my emotional growth, and ultimately contributed to the destruction of my public life and career. Given how many men were sexually abused as children (one out of six is one estimate), the way men are socialized to stifle their emotions, the availability of child pornography online, and the lucrative "cottage industry" that nonproduction cases have become for public figures and organizations, I believe that many more cases like mine are on the horizon. They will come at a massive and growing cost to society, and leave a wide swath of destruction in their wake.

Chapter Seventeen

FINALLY, MY SENTENCING HEARING ARRIVED: July 11, 2014, 360 days after the raid on my home. A similar-size crowd showed up for me again and filled the gallery. Family, friends, neighbors, residents, technicians, and students. My wife sat behind me, behind the defendant's table. After a very complimentary opening defense statement by Dickins, which entirely focused on the good I did for cancer patients and co-workers, I finally had the floor.

It had been nearly a year since it all began. The wave of adrenaline and stress response hormones that instantly flooded my bloodstream was the strongest it had been since the phone call I had with the detective who led the raid on my home. I did not have Ritalin and PowerPoint with me, two crutches that normally held my reeling mind in check whenever I spoke publicly. Instead, I had control over my dissociation. Whenever I started getting so emotional that I felt like I might either sob uncontrollably or vomit, I could let myself drift just far enough to let me say everything I wanted to say. Once I'd said it, I would drift back into myself and check off what categories I had discussed and which ones remained.

Still, afterwards, I had to ask friends and family if I mentioned certain details—because I couldn't remember *exactly* how I put things. Apparently my brain still performs well when dissociated. But I now know how to use these powers only for good. Just in case, though, I wore the two Rainbow Loom bracelets my daughter had made for me, and in the coat pocket of my suit I carried a Lego microscale Y-wing Fighter and an orca that my son had built.

Here is the court transcript of my statement, in its entirety (though with some names modified or omitted):

THE COURT: Now, Dr. Pelloski, you have the right to make a statement on your own behalf. Do you wish to do so?

THE DEFENDANT: Yes, sir.

THE COURT: You may.

THE DEFENDANT: Thank you, Your Honor. Your statements are correct in that I did harm children with my activities, and that's one of the hardest things that I'll ever have to grapple with.

And I created harm in two ways:

The first way is that, the children in that media that I viewed, I used their abuse for some therapeutic gain of my own. I didn't respect their rights. Their rights were never respected. The other way—the other way is that my presence in that world told others that were already there that there was another one among them, and I was one of those people. And, when I was on house arrest, I read books and articles on this global problem. And the more I learned, the more disgusted I was with myself for allowing myself to sink that low. There is no excuse for what I did. There just isn't. I—at any given time, there are millions of files online. And what keeps it there is people's interest or people looking, and I was part of that. And you're right. It goes against everything else that I've ever done or stood for or worked on.

And the harm—that's just the beginning of the harm that I created. My friends, family, students, residents, colleagues, patients were devastated with this. There were patients' families, with this news, on top of having a child with cancer, they're now worrying about "did our doctor look at my child in a certain way?" To take one trauma and add another to it, that's harm that I created. I brought undue attention, bad attention, to Ohio State University and Nationwide Children's Hospital. They gave me a career opportunity of a lifetime, and I destroyed it. I was expected to build programs and to teach, and that's all gone now. I betrayed the people who trained me and the people who are relying on me in the future. I had students working in my lab who my endorsement of them now is worthless. A letter, phone call, it's—it doesn't matter anymore.

My wife was humiliated. She had to corral our children when our house was being raided. She cringes when she meets people and realizes for the first time that they realize who her husband is. And her health has deteriorated by being on guard and making sure that our children make it through this time. And they have. She has done an amazing job.

And, as you mentioned before, in this time I've been on house arrest, there have been hundreds of patients that I was expected to treat, and they went somewhere else. They were the responsibility of other cancer docs. And we're already stretched thin as it is. So, I have added to the burden of an oncology physician shortage on top of it. I've taken myself out.

And, so, I've generated a lot of harm. And I've hurt those who have loved me the most. And I'm thankful for their love and support through all this. I'm surprised anyone stayed, and they did. And they—they helped get us through this. Our community, our neighbors, have ensured that our children have had a normal kindergarten year. And they've done really well.

And I know that I need to be punished with all this harm that I created. We need to send a message to others that my actions are not acceptable. I understand that. But I also understand and believe that I'm a much different person than I was a year ago. I want to thank the Court, the Judges, and the prosecution for trusting me to remain on house arrest so that I could repair relationships with my family, with my friends and my children. I took every opportunity that I could to get the psychological and psychiatric help that I've really needed forever. And I've been able to turn it around.

Professionally and publicly, my life is a mess now. But, personally, I'm better. I felt physically and mentally healthier when I turned 40, when I was on house arrest, facing a federal child pornography felony, than when I turned 30 and was a top flight resident at one of the best cancer centers in the world. And it was really simple. It was just talking. It didn't require a million dollar machine or a fancy pill. It was just addressing events that happened in my life and making meaning and sense of them.

So, when this is over, I have a moral obligation to redeem myself. And I'm going to do it in two ways. One is, I want—I desperately want to return to the oncology field. That's what I've trained for. That's what I have a lot to offer. That's been discussed. The other area, having this time to learn and research about myself and about this world of online child pornography; some part of what I want to do is to raise awareness or funding for research for the problem of online child pornography, the devastating, long-term consequences of childhood sexual abuse, and the problems with post-traumatic mental illnesses. And, so, I envision myself working with, or working for, organizations like the Center for Missing and Exploited Children or the Sidran Institute, which works with post-traumatic mental illnesses. So, I—those are the two areas that I believe that I can help in the future. I have to. And seeing what I've been able to accomplish while not healthy, now that I am, I think I can do even better. And I think my capacity for redemption is really limited only by how much society is willing to forgive me and how much they let me participate and return to working in it.

It's almost embarrassing how foolish—how simple it is to have taken care of myself. I had my wife asking me to talk to someone, to go to counseling. I had colleagues worried about my mental health. And I ignored them because I knew better, because I had this great career, and I could point to it and say, I'm doing just fine. I wasn't. It was a lie. And I'm so ashamed that it took this catastrophe—it took me, by harming other children in that media that I viewed, it took that to finally make me realize that there is a problem and I need to talk—it's almost as if I needed everything to be knocked away for my wake-up call. And I'm wide awake now, Your Honor.

That's all I have.

THE COURT: Very well. Thank you for your statement.

As I was speaking, whenever I paused, I could hear the sniffles of weeping throughout the otherwise stone-silent courtroom. The carpet, wood, and seat cushions of the courtroom seemed to snatch any extraneous sounds right out of the air, before they could finish being produced, so as not to distract from whomever was speaking. I never turned around to see the gallery, but I could sense my people right behind me, supporting me, so that I did not fall backward in retreat. I had to stop looking at the court stenographer as I spoke; her watery eyes would have made me completely lose my composure. After I spoke, and the judge acknowledged me, he quietly nodded.

Then, the prosecution had its turn:

THE COURT: Does the government have a statement?

PROSECUTION: Yes, Your Honor, and I will be brief.

As the Court mentioned at the beginning of this hearing and as—defense counsel has alluded to this—this is, obviously, a unique case.

As I'm sure we're all well aware, it is all too common that in cases that involve child pornography offenses there is a stark dichotomy when you consider two of the most pertinent sentencing factors. And that's the defendant's history and background and the nature or gravity of the offense. And I think we can all agree that this case is one that very vividly illustrates that dichotomy and the very difficult balancing that consideration of those two competing factors requires.

As I have indicated in my sentencing memorandum that the Court has received, the government does not dispute that the defendant's background, everything that he has accomplished, all of the things that we have talked about here today is a mitigating factor in considering and determining an appropriate sentence. The government does not, however, believe that all of these things that he has done, while positive, can completely mitigate the very serious crime that he has committed. We believe that a term of incarceration is warranted by the very serious nature of this offense, that it's necessary to comport with the statutory goals of sentencing.

Now, as defense counsel has discussed here today and as the Court has indicated by its review of the very positive letters that the defense has submitted to the Court, the defendant has, undoubtedly, been an asset to society, has given many positive contributions to this world, this very complex world of childhood cancer. He's been an asset to those with whom he has worked. We have all read these letters and understand that.

The government understands and respects the positions and the emotions and the feelings of the people who have written in and talked to defense counsel on behalf of the defendant. And I'm sure that it is very difficult for those who have only seen this positive side of him to understand and accept the seriousness of the crime that he has committed, that he has repeatedly downloaded, accessed and viewed images of children being raped. And that is the countervailing aspect of this case that is incumbent on the government to ensure that it is considered and at least addressed here today.

Now, we can start with Congress' view of these cases. And I've mentioned that in my sentencing memorandum. There can be no doubt that Congress believes that all offenses that involve child pornography are serious. That comes not only from the sentences that are statutorily imposed, but also by the sentencing guidelines that Congress has, itself, in some circumstances, mandated.

There has been a lot of discussion, a lot of criticism, of those guidelines. I am well aware of that, as I'm sure the Court and defense counsel are. I don't want to go into detail about the various criticisms and issues with those guidelines. What I think is important is the rationale behind them; and it is, I think, the rationale that Congress has taken into consideration when it has addressed child pornography crimes. And that is the very serious and ongoing harm that these crimes cause to countless victims.

For whatever reason that defendants have and whatever reason this defendant had for deciding to repeatedly access these videos and these images that depict the rape of children, those actions and those decisions cause very real and significant harm. It's not something that we might understand the harm as easily or as readily as we understand the harm to a hands-on victim, someone who has actually been raped. I think we can conceive of that very easily, but the—our understanding—our ability to realize the harm that is caused to these victims I think is more difficult, but it's there.

And in what I have read in other cases where there are identified victims and they have submitted victim impact statements, it becomes very clear that this is a real harm. They suffer from paranoia because they are afraid that every person that they run into on the street may be someone who has seen their image, the image of them being raped and abused as children. They are afraid to trust anyone. They are unable to get past the pain of the initial rape and abuse because men like the defendant dredge it up every time they download this image or this video again and again and again, causing the victims to re-live this pain. All of this causes them to suffer from panic attacks, insomnia, and various other mental and emotional issues.

So, Your Honor, I submit that this is a serious offense not because Congress said so, not because the sentencing guidelines provide for lengthy terms of incarceration. This is a serious offense because of the very serious damage it does to the victims.

And, again, Your Honor, I'm not going to stand here and say that the guidelines are perfect. I believe that, in the very numerous child pornography cases that I have prosecuted, I have very rarely objected to a below-guideline sentence. But, again, the rationale behind those guidelines and the rationale that underlies Congress' decision to repeatedly enhance and lengthen the terms of incarceration required for these offenses, that is—that is what I think is important here. It is the rationale that these offenses seriously harm the children who are victims and society in general.

And, Your Honor, defense counsel mentioned something that I think is also significant when considering both the dichotomy that is presented in this case and the harm, the seriousness of this offense. And that is—and I wrote it down and circled it, the word "compassion," that that is something that they have found to have come across with everyone they've talked to in regards to this defendant. And, again, I have no doubt that he has been a very compassionate doctor to everyone he has treated and a compassionate co-worker to those of his colleagues, particularly those who have written in to the Court, but I find it troubling that a person with that sort of—in this line of work who would be so compassionate in that line of work apparently did not understand this concept of the harm that I'm talking about here today. And it appears that he has grasped that at this point. But for the years—the several years that this was ongoing—and it appears to have started as early as 2007, from the evidence that was found on these computers—for this length of time, that this doctor who is caring for young children and treating young children is looking at images of children being raped and abused. Your Honor, I feel that that makes this offense that much more disturbing and dangerous.

This is an individual who should have known better. And it is actually clear that he did know better. There is forensic evidence found on his computer that showed that he repeatedly, again, over a period of years, installed peer-to-peer programs, used them to download and access and view child pornography, and then would delete the entire peer-to-peer program. Then, when he wanted to go back and look at child pornography some more, he would again reinstall the peer-to-peer program, doing this repeatedly over the course of the years. He knew what he was doing was wrong, but he chose to continue to do it over and over and over again, causing more and more harm to the victims depicted in those images and videos that he was downloading.

Your Honor, this is a serious crime, and it is one that deserves real punishment. And when I say "real punishment," Your Honor, we're not asking for a ten-year sentence, the statutory maximum. We are not actually asking even for a guideline sentence. The probation officer in this case has recommended a sentence below the guideline range, and we're not opposed to that. But we do believe that a term of incarceration is warranted in this case. We believe that is necessary to reflect the seriousness of this offense. And we believe that this defendant's history and background cannot completely mitigate his offense into oblivion with a slap-on-the-wrist sort of sentence.

So, Your Honor, we would ask that the Court impose a sentence of incarceration in this case. We believe that the sentence recommended by the probation officer is reasonable. We would ask for a sentence in line with that or slightly below it.

THE COURT: Very well.

For the next half-hour or so of my sentencing hearing, the judge expounded on his views about the societal problems that both child pornography and the response to nonproduction offenders pose. He echoed many of the concerns that I'd come across in my research on the subject. He said multiple times that I was not a pedophile, that I'd undergone lie detection, and that I posed no danger to children or any-one—and that *most* with my offense share these characteristics:

> In most of these cases, these men would—are not at all predis-posed toward committing any kind of a hands-on offense with a child. There are a few who are pedophiles, and their motiva-tion, of course, is more insidious. Often, pedophiles use these kinds of materials to facilitate breaking down the barriers that a child would otherwise have to voluntarily engaging in this kind of activity. But most of the defendants the Court sees would never ever consider touching a child improperly. And I'm con-vinced that that's true in this case. Dr. Pelloski underwent poly-graph examination to determine whether or not he had ever engaged in any hands-on offense, or even considered it. And the indications are clear that he has not. And there is just no sugges-tion that he would ever engage in improper conduct, physically, with a child. And that's true of most of the cases the Court sees.

I am sure this was somewhat of a relief to all of those who came out to support me, who filled the gallery and hung on every word the judge said. It is one thing to hear *me* say I am not "that guy," but it is another thing to hear it from a federal judge who has been privy to all the information and listened to all sides of the case.

He also mentioned that in his nearly thirty years on the bench, he had never seen so much support for a defendant before. The number of letters of support exceeded fifty by then; more had trickled in during the extra few months of house arrest.

The courtroom was full. This gave me immense comfort and vali-dation. This was a *child pornography* case, which is so taboo that nearly all offenders stand alone before the court. It was even more amazing that I had this much support in light of the best efforts of the academic medical centers' legal departments. All these people's presence was a continuation of the love that had buoyed me throughout this whole process; it was there again in that courtroom to see me through.

And despite the dire predictions made by those legal eagles, no one lost their job, student enrollment, career, reputation, clinical practice, or NIH funding for supporting me. No news articles were written vilifying those who stood by me. There was no backlash. Period.

The judge said several things during his address that really stood out and painted a grim picture of what the future of this phenomenon of child pornography holds, unless things change.

> I am afraid that, because of the nature of the offense, that social science and legal scholars and media and investigative reporters have not really engaged in the kind of public discussion and debate that would be healthy, if it were not such a sensitive and difficult area to discuss.

He looked over at the section of the gallery where the reporters sat when he made these comments.

> Based on my experience of these cases, it is my impression that this social phenomenon of the viewing of pornography, and including child pornography, is becoming—it's increasing, and it's becoming almost common. I doubt that there is a local church that does not have members who are involved in this kind of activity. I doubt that there is any business of any size which does not have employees, including executives, who are involved in this kind of activity. I doubt that there is a family in this country who does not have a male member who is involved, surreptitiously, in this kind of activity. And I think we've ignored it, and we need to address it. Social science needs to address it. The legal system needs to be adjusted to accommodate it.

He later added:

> I believe that the federal sentencing guidelines, which provide Draconian sentences for people who simply possess these images, are in need of revision as well. The guidelines, as they exist, really do not reflect the advancements of technology. They seem to harken back to an era where these images were bought and sold or

traded in back rooms somewhere surreptitiously, and they're really out of touch with the fact that one click of a computer mouse can produce hundreds of images on a person's computer and that, without any payment whatsoever and without any tit-for-tat trading, without any "You give me your images and I'll give you mine," it just happens automatically with this file-sharing technology. So, the guidelines call for, in many cases, sentences that are far out of proportion to the actual culpability of the defendants.

He then said something that made me remember what I'd observed at the very beginning of my case, something I had not thought about for quite a while.

I might also say, the law enforcement is out there. The word needs to be gotten out to men of all ages that, if you download these images on your computer, you're going to get caught. It doesn't make any difference who you are; you're going to get prosecuted. And Dr. Pelloski's a pretty good example of that. Law enforcement is out there, every night, fishing on the Internet. They have the hash tag numbers—they have the file numbers of many, many hundreds, even thousands, of known images of child pornography. And they're going to get you sooner or later if you're involved in this kind of activity. And I don't think the general public is aware of that. And, so, we need to do some more work there, too, in terms of—if the penalties and the laws that are seeking to protect children from this kind of victimization are going to work, we need to get the message out that, if you're downloading these images, you're going to get caught; you're going to appear in a federal courtroom; it's going to ruin your career; it's going to ruin your family; and you're going to go to prison.

I recalled how many times I heard, "I didn't even know *that* was illegal!" when I first explained to people what exactly it was that I did. Many assumed that only producing, buying, or selling the material was a crime—not just viewing this media, which was free and already floating around in cyberspace. These were highly educated people, who just like me, also "should have known better." Men *and women*, too. A few people told me that they had accidentally stumbled across this media themselves on peer-to-peer networks in the past. They were worried sick the police might be knocking on their doors next.

Personally, I knew it was wrong and illegal when I viewed. I didn't know just *how* illegal it was, though. I certainly didn't peruse the Federal Sentencing Guidelines and weigh the risks before I logged on either.

My judge eventually called for a five-to-ten minute recess, and went into his chambers, presumably to consider his sentence. I slowly walked away from the podium I had gripped throughout the first portion of the hearing as if I were going over a waterfall and took a seat at the defendant's table. Then I carefully turned around to scan the gallery and see who was there. A sea of red eyes greeted me, drying now from crying, along with smiles and gestures of encouragement.

My defense team showed a keen interest in what was about to happen. They were discussing it, quietly but animatedly, postulating the same way my colleagues and I would discuss the results of a new clinical trial that was to have a significant impact on the standard of cancer care. I was too dazed to take in who was saying what. I could only look down at the soft, white cotton handkerchief I had borrowed from my father-in-law, which was drenched with sweat and tears from when I gave my statement. It was fluttering in my still-trembling hands.

"What are you thinking he will give him?"

"I never thought this before, but … probation-only … maybe?"

"Nah. Six months."

"I don't know."

"This is right after *Bistline*. You have to remember that."

"I know, but, if there ever was the case for probation-only, this is it. You heard him."

"If he gets anything lower than ten months there will be an appeal, and then we will be in this shit for another year."

The words *another year* struck me and I turned toward my team, revealing my eavesdropping. I could tell they felt a little embarrassed about their disinterested, academic discussion of my fate, which was literally hanging in the balance—in real time. Charles recognized my concern and explained what the legal intrigue was about. "OK. This is the judge's first case since the *Bistline* case was reassigned. He gave that guy probation-only. He was old and sick, and the judge didn't want him to go to prison and die there. So it got appealed and was sent back to him on remand. He gave the same exact sentence, and his second decision was thrown out. And the case has been reassigned to *another* judge. The legal community around here knows that your case is where he will be drawing the line for future cases like yours. Many are curious where that line will be."

I took a deep breath and sighed, not sharing in the intellectual excitement of the moment. "I seem to be cutting-edge, even when I am committing crimes," I said dejectedly. Then I joined the discussion. "So, probation-only is not an option? You don't think?"

"I don't. If he goes too low, there will be a knee-jerk appeal that no one wants. I don't even think the prosecutor would want to appeal either. So the judge has to be delicate with how he handles this. He will not want another appeal." At this point the other two attorneys joined in.

"Yeah. I am surprised [the prosecutor] recommended eighteen to forty-eight months. She came *way* down. I was not expecting that— eighteen? Not from her," Newton added in a whisper. He looked down at me, sensitive to the pins and needles I was sitting on, having seen me like that before, when I was given my charge nearly a year before. "That was an amazing statement, Doc. I am glad you got to talk before the prosecution." He patted me on my hunched, exhausted shoulder.

"Yeah," added Dickins, "you pretty much took the sting out of what could have been said after. You owned up. You manned up. And didn't bullshit. That is what federal judges appreciate," he said nodding in a slow and wistful manner.

I was encouraged a bit. And, as I always do (one of my healthier defense mechanisms), I added some levity. "Hey, if I do get prison time and I get to self-surrender, can you ask the judge to remove the alcohol restriction on my bond? Because I could probably down a whole fifth of vodka right about now," accompanied by a defeated smile.

"Ahhh … No," Charles shot back in jest.

I looked up at the massive oil painting that hung in the courtroom: a very stately and elder judge who looked very familiar. It had caught my eye earlier during the hearing, "I have been meaning to ask," I said pointing to the painting, "Is that …?"

"Yes. He is your judge. So if you are praying right now, you may want to pray to that painting, too, while you are at it."

When my judge returned, he quickly gave his ruling: twelve months and one day of incarceration. The flood of adrenaline and stress hormones that had preceded my personal statement returned, temporarily rendering me deaf this time. I didn't hear the part about five years of supervision upon release and registering as a tier-I sex offender for fifteen years—which meant I could no longer live in my own home, since it is within a thousand feet of a park. I was never sure what a park has to do with a computer-based crime in which the offender has been thoroughly vetted, shown to not be a pedophile or contact offender, and has an expected recidivism rate near zero—but that is my city's ordinance nonetheless. However, hearing my $10,000 fine certainly brought me back into the moment. I would be allowed to self-surrender to prison, too. There would be time and opportunity to explain to the kids and say goodbye. Thank God.

I could feel the gallery stir and quietly gasp in shock, frustration, anxiety, as my sentence was announced. But for me, this sentence was actually what I'd hoped and thought I would get from the time this all started. I could live with it. If I couldn't handle twelve months in a low-security U.S. federal prison, then my grandmother's ghost would have no choice but to come back, smack me in the face, and order me to stop being such a sissy. I knew I could recover from this and that my children would not have their lives destroyed. I knew I could make it through without having to join a white-supremacist gang or get tattoos of tears on my face.

I know my supporters were expecting or hoping for probation-only, but I thought what I got was fair. It was a punishment that I actually wanted. Not just because anything less would have meant an instant appeal, but because if I walked there would have been the appearance that the "rich, perverted doctor" had hired fancy lawyers to buy his way out of prison. Even though I no longer worried about what people said about me, I still didn't want to hear that shit. I wanted to do *some* time, to show that there are no free passes. Being punished is part of redemption. In that regard, I was glad to receive *more* time than what the judge clearly wanted to give me, as evidenced by his subtext and body language. This impression was borne out by subsequent written documents about his decision (see the judge's Opinion and Order in the Addenda section). He made it very clear to everyone in the court-room and those who can read between the lines of legalese that his hands were tied by the statutes and appeals process.

Court was adjourned.

My attorneys asked that I remain at the defendant's table while they went through the follow-up discussions and paperwork with the pros-ecutor and probation officer. I didn't mind. It gave me more time to reflect on what just transpired.

I thought it unfortunate that the issue of my mental health had not been discussed in the courtroom. I *did* know better—but I commit-ted my offense anyway. Just as intelligent and educated people smoke when they know it is unhealthy, or as people with advanced degrees still speed or get DUIs when they know it creates danger on the roads, or when Ivy League–educated stockbrokers get popped for insider trad-ing when they know the rules. It has nothing to do with smarts. If that were the case, no one with a solid education would ever commit a crime. You don't need an advanced degree to know right from wrong. Kindergartners know right from wrong.

Crimes are committed because of an emotionally induced lapse of judgment, selfishness, a disregard of rules, and/or most importantly, a lack of consideration for others who are being harmed by the action. An offender's ability to split atoms or solve simultaneous linear equa-tions doesn't assure law-abiding behavior. Depression, PTSD, bipolar disorder, addiction, etc., are not illnesses of cognition or intelligence, nor are they influenced by a formal education. They are illnesses of emotions. I think it is very dangerous to confuse superior intellectual intelligence with superior emotional intelligence. That was part of the reason why no one ever suspected I had problems. The 4.0-average athlete, scientist-doctor guy must have it all together, right?

The crux of the matter *was* my mental health. I know this because after addressing my sexual abuse, exorcising my PTSD, recognizing that I have a support system and unconditional love, getting all my secrets out, and being as physically healthy as I have ever been, I have absolutely no psychological reason to ever step foot into the horrific world of child pornography again. It has nothing to do with the rules, the law, rationally "knowing better," or a Kholberg level-I fear of punishment. I have fixed my insides, irrespective of what the outside world thinks or does.

Ironically, and not to minimize my PTSD and its inciting abuse, I believe that in addition to their contributions to the horrifically negative aspects of my life (my offense, emotional problems, and difficult relationships) my mental health issues also played a significant role in my successes. They, or my response to them, enabled me to accomplish many great things in such a short period of time. There were moments along the way where my mind and body wanted to give up—whether it was staying awake for more than forty hours at a stretch to scrub in for another emergent surgery as an intern, or memorizing the Krebs Cycle, or writing a grant proposal at 2 a.m. when everyone else was asleep. When all I wanted to do was something else—something easier—my mental *illness* helped push me through those moments with hypervigilance, tolerance to psychological pain, and a refusal to surrender to fatigue or uncertainty. It also provided me an amazing sense of empathy, which my patients and their families appreciated. I could relate to their fear because I knew how it felt to be powerless and different from others. I could talk and walk them through a very terrifying phase of their lives, when they were confronted with their own mortality, while supporting and promoting their own inner confidence and dignity.

The difference in me now, though, is that I can control this intensity. I can shut it off when it is not needed. High-alert is no longer the default setting for my mind's operating system, being on at *all* times. So I no longer have a need to escape from it, either. But I do take comfort in knowing that when I need to dig deep for that little something extra, when I must be impervious to the effects of hours, toil, and fear,

I have this power in reserve to draw upon. Intellectually *and emotionally* (finally) I can now throw a ninety-nine mile an hour fastball with devastating, explosive movement when my back is against a wall.

Eventually, after my spell of introspection and a brief housekeeping discussion with my attorneys, I walked out the double doors of the courtroom. My supporters had all waited for me, and were spontaneously arranged in a twenty-foot semicircle around the doorway. They wore forced, sympathetic smiles, and some began a new round of tears, still primed from the reading of the sentence. My wife. My mom. My dad. My in-laws. My residents. My lab techs. My students. My friends and neighbors. I stopped in the center, still bearing the weight of the sentencing and my reflections, and just looked around at their faces, thanking them silently with a nod at each. All those people, whom I'd hurt the most but who unconditionally loved and supported me, were there, yet again, in my moment of defeat and despair. They stood steadfastly, unswayed and undeterred. I couldn't get closer. There were reporters all over the place, and I did not want to "out them" to the press.

That was when my wife completely breached protocol. Abandoning all plans to remain out of the public spotlight, she met me in the center of the circle, kissed me on the lips for several seconds, and then wrapped her arms around my broken body in a way she had not done in a long time. She whispered in my ear, "Don't worry. We will make it work."

"I love you."

Judge Graham's Opinion and Order

Fortunately, my mental health issues were not lost on the judge who ultimately presided over my case. He put his opinion and order into a formal written document, in the anticipation that it may be used in future cases and discussions about these offenses and how they are handled. It came out ten days after my hearing. It addressed *everything*—including my mental health and abuse history. My judge understood. I am very lucky to have crossed paths with him. I certainly hope this can help others in my situation—and for those not in it—to better understand.

Here is his opinion in its entirety, with some names modified or omitted.

IN THE UNITED STATES DISTRICT COURT
SOUTHERN DISTRICT OF OHIO
EASTERN DIVISION

United States of America,	Case No.: 2:13-cr-230
v.	Judge Graham
Christopher E. Pelloski	Magistrate Judge King

OPINION AND ORDER

This matter is before the Court for the sentencing of the Defendant, Christopher E. Pelloski. On July 11, 2014, the Court sentenced the Defendant to 12 months and one day imprisonment, a $10,000 fine, and a term of five years of supervised release for knowingly accessing with intent to view digital files that contained child pornography in violation of 18 U.S.C. § 2252(a)(5)(B). This Opinion and Order explains the basis for the Court's sentence.

This case highlights a growing social phenomenon that Internet technology has given birth to and which is an increasingly troublesome phenomenon in our society. As a result of federal laws punishing the possession of child pornography, federal courts have become increasingly involved in sentencing child pornography offenders. As the Court has previously noted:

> Child pornography possession cases on the docket of a United States district judge will include men of all ages ranging from late adolescence to old age. They will include students, teachers, administrators, physicians, lawyers, executives, church leaders, and others from all walks of life. Most lead otherwise normal and productive lives. They are good husbands, good fathers, good employees, good students, good friends. Few if any have prior criminal records. When they are caught, the consequences are enormous. Reputations are shattered, careers are ended, and families are destroyed. Suicides are not uncommon. The human costs are staggering, certainly equal to those in the most serious cases of drug addiction and in a population that is usually otherwise healthy.

Hon. James L. Graham, The Sixth Circuit Broke New Ground in Post-Booker Guideline Sentencing with a Pair of Important Decisions, 26 Fed. Sent. R. 102, 112 (December 2013) (hereinafter "Bistline Article").

In sentencing child pornography offenders, the Court focuses on the characteristics of each offender based on the sentencing factors outlined in 18 U.S.C. § 3553(a). Defendants convicted of the production of child pornography are the most culpable of the child pornography offenders sentenced by the Court. They are, without question, deserving of lengthy sentences of imprisonment given the direct and lasting harm they inflict upon children. In the tier below producers of child pornography are those defendants who distribute images of child pornography. These defendants create the potential for continued viewing of horrible images of child pornography throughout a child's lifetime. Because these defendants introduce these images into circulation, they bear a large share of culpability and should be punished accordingly.

Most individuals before the Court, however, are charged with the possession and viewing of child pornography. These individuals use the images of child pornography for sexual stimulation. But in the vast majority of these cases, there is no indication that the offenders have or will ever commit a contact offense with a child. The Defendant in this case is a distinguished physician who devoted his life and career to the research and treatment of pediatric cancer. It is a tragic irony of this case that the Defendant engaged in the downloading and viewing of child pornography. In so doing, he harmed the same group he had dedicated his career to helping.

I.Background

In October 2012, the Franklin County Internet Crimes Against Children Task Force (the Task Force) conducted an online investigation to detect child pornography offenses. PSR at ¶ 9–10. Through their investigation, members of the Task Force determined that the Defendant was using peer-to-peer sharing programs to download child pornography. Id. at ¶ 10. From March 29 through July 8, 2013, the Defendant possessed 59 files containing child pornography. Id. at ¶ 11.

Law enforcement agents executed a search warrant at the Defendant's residence on July16,2013, and seized numerous computer and digital media storage devices from his residence. Id. at ¶ 13. At the time of the search, the Defendant was not at home. Id. Law enforcement agents contacted the Defendant by telephone at which time he admitted to using file sharing programs to download pornography. Id. at ¶ 15. The Defendant admitted that he had searched for and viewed images of minors that were sexual in nature. Id. A forensic analysis of the Defendant's computers revealed multiple images of child pornography and files indicating past viewing of child pornography. PSR at ¶ 16.

On July 24,2013, the Government filed a single-count Complaint (doc. I) charging the Defendant with receiving visual depictions of minors engaged in explicit sexual activity via the Internet in violation of 18 U.S.C. § 2252. On September 25, the Defendant underwent a Computer Voice Stress Analysis, a form of polygraph testing, at the request of the Government. PSR at ¶ 17. The Defendant denied ever sexually abusing children. Id. Two different examiners assessed the results of that test and concluded that the Defendant's denial was truthful. Id.

On October 4, the Government filed a single-count Information (doc. 16) charging the Defendant with knowingly accessing with intent to view digital files that contained child pornography in violation of 18 U.S.C. § 2252(a)(5)(B). That same day, the Defendant entered into a plea agreement (doc. 17) with the Government in which he agreed to plead guilty to the sole count charged in the information.

II. The Defendant's Guideline Range

Pursuant to U.S.S.G. § 2G2.2, the base offense level for 18 U.S.C. § 2252(a)(5)(B) is 18. The specific offense characteristics include: (1) material involving a prepubescent minor or a minor who has not attained the age of 12, which requires a two level increase pursuant to U.S.S.G. § 2G2.2(b)(2); (2) material that portrays sadistic or masochistic conduct or other depictions of violence, which requires a four level increase pursuant to U.S.S.G. § 2G2.2(b)(4); (3) the use of a computer for the possession and receipt of the material, which requires a two level increase pursuant to U.S.S.G. § 2G2.2(b)(6); and (4) between 10 and 150 images, which requires a two level increase pursuant to U.S.S.G. § 2G2.2(b)(7)(A). The Defendant's adjusted offense level is therefore 28. In light of the Defendant's acceptance of responsibility, he is entitled to a three level reduction to his adjusted offense level for a total offense level of 25. With no criminal history to speak of, the Defendant's criminal history score is zero, placing him in criminal history category I. The Defendant's guideline imprisonment range is therefore 57 to 71 months. The Probation Office recommended a below guidelines sentence of 48 months imprisonment and five years of supervised release. At the sentencing hearing, the Government recommended a sentence between 18 and 48 months. (Sentencing Tr. at 25).

III. Discussion

The Court's concerns regarding the child pornography sentencing guidelines are well documented. See generally United States v. Childs, 976 F. Supp. 2d 981 (S.D. Ohio 2013); Bistline Article, 26 Fed. Sent. R. 102. "There is widespread agreement among judges, lawyers and legal scholars that the guidelines for child pornography offenses are seriously flawed." Childs, 976 F. Supp. 2d at 982. Indeed, the belief that the child pornography sentencing guidelines are flawed is shared by the Sentencing Commission and the United States Department of Justice. See United States Sentencing Commission, Report to Congress: Federal Child Pornography Offenses, at ii (Dec. 2012), www.ussc. gov/Legislative_and_Public_Affairs/Congressional_Testimony_ and_Reports/Sex_Offense_Topics/201212_Federal_Child_ Pornography_Offenses/ (last visited July 2, 2014) (hereinafter "Child Pornography Report") ("as a result of recent changes in the computer and Internet technology that typical non-production offenders use, the existing sentence scheme in non-production cases no longer adequately distinguishes among offenders based on their degrees of culpability"); Letter from Anne Gannon, Nat'l Coordinator for Child Exploitation Prevention and Interdiction, Office of the Deputy Attorney General, U.S. Dep't of Justice, to Honorable Patti B. Saris, Chair, U.S. Sentencing Commission, at 1 (Mar. 5, 2013), available at http://sentencing.type-pad.comlfiles/doj-letter-to-ussc-on-cp-report.pdf (last visited July 2, 2014) ("the Department agrees with the Commission's conclusion that advancement in technology and the evolution of the child pornography 'Market" have led to a significantly changed landscape—one that is no longer adequately represented by the existing sentencing guidelines") (hereinafter "DOJ Letter").

A. *Booker. Kimbrough. and the Sixth Circuit's Decisions in Bistline I and Bistline II*

In the Court's view, United States v. Booker, 543 U.S. 220 (2005) and its progeny support the conclusion that the child pornography sentencing guidelines are entitled to limited deference. In Booker, the Supreme Court held the Sentencing Reform Act of 1984's mandatory guidelines unconstitutional, rendering the guidelines "effectively advisory." 543 U.S. at 245. The Booker Court's holding "requires a sentencing court to consider Guidelines ranges, but it permits the court to tailor the sentence in light of other statutory concerns as well," such as the individual characteristics of the defendant or the circumstances of the offense. Id. (internal citations omitted). To promote the goals of "honesty, uniformity, and proportionality in sentencing," the Booker Court recognized that the Sentencing Commission would remain in place, "writing Guidelines, collecting information about actual district court sentencing decisions, undertaking research, and revising the Guidelines accordingly." Id. at 264 (citation omitted).

Post-Booker, the Supreme Court repeatedly emphasized the importance of the Sentencing Commission in formulating the sentencing guidelines in light of its institutional expertise and its focus on empirical analysis:

> While rendering the sentencing guidelines advisory . . . we have nevertheless preserved a key role for the Sentencing Commission. . . . Congress established the Commission to formulate and constantly refine national sentencing standards. . . . Carrying out its charge, the Commission fills an important institutional role: It has the capacity courts lack to base its determinations on empirical data and national experience, guided by a professional staff with appropriate expertise.

Kimbrough v. United States, 552 U.S. 85, 108--09 (2007) (internal quotations and citations omitted). See also Rita v. United States, 551 U.S. 338, 349 (2007) ("The Guidelines as written reflect the fact that the Sentencing Commission examined tens of thousands of sentences and worked with the help of many others in the law enforcement community over a long period of time in an effort to fulfill this statutory mandate. They also reflect the fact that different judges (and others) can differ as to how best to reconcile the disparate ends of punishment."). In Kimbrough. the Court recognized a district court's authority to vary from the sentencing guidelines solely on policy grounds. 552 U.S. at 108–110. In so holding, the Court noted that the crack cocaine guidelines at issue in Kimbrough "d[id] not exemplify the Commission's exercise of its characteristic institutional role" because the Commission "did not take account of 'empirical data and national experience'" when formulating them. Id. at 109–10 (internal citations omitted). Thus, the district court did not abuse its discretion in imposing a below guidelines sentence despite it being a "mine-run case." Id. at 110–11.

Although Kimbrough concerned the crack cocaine guidelines, numerous courts have applied its rationale to reject the guidelines for a variety of offenses on policy grounds. See United States Sentencing Commission, Report on the Continuing Impact of United States v. Booker on Federal Sentencing, 37–43 (Dec. 2012), available at http://www.ussc.gov/sites/default/files/pdf/news/congressional-testimony-and-reports/booker-reports/2012-booker/Part_A.pdf. (last visited July 2, 2014). Indeed, many courts have rejected the child pornography guidelines on policy grounds relying on Kimbrough. Id. As with the crack cocaine guidelines at issue in Kimbrough, "the Commission did not use [an] empirical approach when formulating the Guidelines for child pornography," United States v. Dorvee, 616 F.3d 174, 184 (2d Cir. 2010), and the Commission itself has reported that the child pornography guidelines produce disproportionately severe sentences in light of the purposes of sentencing set forth in §3553(a), United States Sentencing Commission, Child Pornography Report, at xviii. Contrary to its historical institutional role and empirical practices, "at the direction of Congress, the Sentencing Commission has amended the Guidelines under § 2G2.2 several times since their introduction in 1987, each time recommending harsher penalties." Dorvee, 616 F.3d at 184 (citation omitted).

Despite the parallels to the crack cocaine guidelines at issue in Kimbrough, the circuit courts are split as to whether judges may depart from the child pornography guidelines based on a policy disagreement. In United States v. Bistline, the Sixth Circuit Court of Appeals held that district courts are required to give compelling deference to the congressionally-mandated child pornography guidelines. 665 F.3d 758 (6th Cir. 2012) (hereinafter, Bistline I); 720 F. 3d 631 (6th Cir. 2013) (hereinafter, Bistline II). Given that "defining crimes and fixing penalties are legislative . . . functions," Bistline I, 665 F.3d at 761, and that Congress delegated to the Commission only "a limited measure of its power to set sentencing policy," Id. at 762, the Bistline I court concluded that "a district court cannot reasonably reject § 2G2.2—or any other guidelines provision--merely on the ground that Congress exercised, rather than delegated, its power to set the policies reflected therein," Id. Subjecting the district court's sentencing decision to "close scrutiny," the Sixth Circuit found that the defendant's sentence of one day in prison combined with significant terms of home confinement and supervised release was substantively unreasonable. Bistline I, 665 F.3d at 764–68; Bistline II, 720 F.3d at 633–34.

The Fifth and Eleventh Circuits have joined the Sixth Circuit in holding that district courts are limited in their authority to reject the child pornography guidelines on policy grounds. See United States v. Miller, 665 F.3d 114, 120–21 (5th Cir. 2011) (2012) ("we will not reject a Guidelines provision as 'unreasonable' or 'irrational' simply because it is not based on empirical data and even if it leads to some disparities in sentencing"); United States v. Pugh, 515 F.3d 1179, 1201 n.15 (11th Cir. 2008) (recognizing that Kimbrough authorizes district court to deviate from the Guidelines based on policy reasons but holding that the child pornography guidelines "do not exhibit the deficiencies the Supreme Court identified in Kimbrough"). Conversely, the Second, Third, and Ninth Circuits have approved of below guidelines sentences for child pornography offenders based on a district court's policy disagreement with § 2G2.2. See United States v. Henderson, 649 F.3d 955, 963 (9th Cir. 2011) ("similar to the crack cocaine Guidelines, district courts may vary from the child pornography Guidelines, § 2G2.2, based on policy disagreement with them, and not simply based on an individualized determination that they yield an excessive sentence in a particular case"); Dorvee, 616 F.3d at 184 (holding that district courts may vary from the child pornography guidelines based solely on a policy disagreement with § 2G2.2); United States v. Grober, 624 F.3d 592, 602–10 (3d Cir. 2010) (citing Dorvee and affirming the district court's categorical rejection of child pornography guidelines on policy grounds); see also United States v. Stone, 575 F.3d 83 (1st Cir. 2009) (implying that district court could have categorically rejected § 2G2.2 and stating in dicta "[w]ere we collectively sitting as the district court, we would have used our <u>Kimbrough</u> power to impose a somewhat lower sentence").[1]

Although correlation does not imply causation, it is worth noting the disparity in average sentences for nonproduction child pornography offenders between circuits that permit categorical rejection of the child pornography guidelines on policy grounds (the Pro-Rejection circuits) and those circuits that do not (the Anti-Rejection circuits). The mean sentence in the Pro-Rejection circuits for a nonproduction child pornography offense was 75.53 months imprisonment. Hamilton, <u>Sentencing Adjudication</u> at 450. In contrast, the mean sentence in the Anti-Rejection circuits was 109.51 months, an increase of almost three years. <u>Id.</u> Despite numerous opportunities to do so,[2] the Supreme Court has yet to address this circuit split. Such a ruling would clarify the scope of <u>Kimbrough</u> and potentially ameliorate sentencing disparities between the circuits. Absent further guidance from the Supreme Court, this Court is precluded by <u>Bistline I</u> and <u>Bistline II</u> from sentencing the Defendant to a below guidelines sentence based on a policy disagreement with the child pornography guidelines. The Court recognizes that it is bound by the Sixth Circuit's decision in <u>Bistline</u>.

B. *18 U.S.C. § 3553(a)*

In imposing a sentence, a district court is obligated to consider the factors set forth in 18 U.S.C. § 3553(a). After considering these factors, a district court must impose a sentence that is sufficient, but not greater than necessary, to satisfy the purposes of sentencing: just punishment, respect for the law, deterrence, protection of the public, and rehabilitation of the defendant. In making this determination, a district court may not presume that the guideline sentence is the correct one. <u>Nelson v. United States</u>, 555 U.S. 350, 352 (2009); <u>Rita v. United States</u>, 551 U.S. 338, 351 (2007).

1. Nature and Circumstances of the Offense

There is no disputing that "child pornography is ... a serious crime," <u>United States v. Robinson</u>, 669 F.3d 767, 776 (6th Cir. 2012), because "[it] harms and debases the most defenseless of our citizens," <u>United</u>

States v. Williams, 553 U.S. 285, 307 (2008). Child pornography offenses "result in perpetual harm to victims and validate and normalize the sexual exploitation of children." United States Sentencing Commission, Child Pornography Report, at vi. In the instant case, the Defendant downloaded and viewed a number of images of child pornography on his personal and work computers. PSR at ¶¶ 9–16. The images depicted the sexual exploitation of minors, including prepubescent children, and also portrayed sadistic or masochistic conduct. Id. at ¶¶ 24–27.

Based on the Court's experience in sentencing defendants for non-production child pornography offenses, the nature and circumstances of the Defendant's offense here are, sadly, routine. The Court evaluates the seriousness of the Defendant's conduct in light of the Sentencing Commission's conclusion that "the current sentencing scheme results in overly severe guideline ranges for some offenders based on outdated and disproportionate enhancements related to their collecting behavior." United States Sentencing Commission, Child Pornography Report, at 321. Significantly, the Department of Justice agrees with the Sentencing Commission's general conclusion:

> [T]he Department agrees with the Commission's conclusion that advancements in technologies and the evolution of the child pornography "market" have led to a significantly changed landscape--one that is no longer adequately represented by the existing sentencing guidelines. Specifically, we agree with the Report's conclusion that the existing Specific Offense Characteristics ("SOCs") in USSG § 2G2.2 may not accurately reflect the seriousness of an offender's conduct, nor fairly account for differing degrees of offender dangerousness. The current guidelines can at times under-represent and at times over-represent the seriousness of an offender's conduct and the danger an offender possesses.

DOJ Letter at 1.

In 2010, in cases in which U.S.S.G. § 2G2.2 enhancements were applicable, the enhancements for possessing materials depicting prepubescent minors (§ 2G2.2(b)(2)), use of a computer (§ 2G2.2(b)(6)), and number of images (§ 2G2.2(b)(7)) applied in over 95% of cases. United States Sentencing Commission, Child Pornography Report at 209. The enhancement for possession of material portraying violence or sadomasochistic conduct (§ 2G2.2(b)(4)) applied in 74% of all § 2G2.2 cases. Id. These four enhancements apply to the Defendant's conduct in this case and do not accurately depict the severity of the Defendant's offense.

> Innovations in digital cameras and videography as well as in computers and Internet-related technology, such as peer-to-peer ("P2P") file-sharing programs, have been used by offenders in the production, mass distribution (both commercial and non-commercial distribution), and acquisition of child pornography. These technological changes have resulted in exponential increases in the volume and ready accessibility of child pornography, including many graphic sexual images involving very young victims, a genre that previously was not as widely circulated as it is today. As a result of such changes, entry-level offenders now easily can acquire and distribute large quantities of child pornography at little or no financial cost and often in an anonymous, indiscriminate manner.
>
> Several provisions in the current sentencing guidelines for non-production offenses—in particular, the existing enhancements for the nature and volume of the images possessed, an offender's use of a computer, and distribution of images— originally were promulgated in an earlier technological era. Indeed, most of the enhancements, in their current or antecedent versions, were promulgated when offenders typically received and distributed child pornography in printed form using the United States mail. As a result, enhancements that were intended to apply to only certain offenders who committed aggravated child pornography offenses are now being applied routinely to most offenders.

Id. at 312–313.

In evaluating the seriousness of the Defendant's offense, the Court looks to the factors recommended by the DOJ itself, including:

How an offender obtains child pornography; the volume and type of child pornography an offender collects; how long an offender has been collecting child pornography; the attention and care an offender gives to his collection; how an offenders uses his collection once obtained; how an offender protects himself and his collection from detection; and whether an offender creates, facilitates, or participates in a community centered on child exploitation.

DOJ Letter at 2.

Here, the Defendant collected child pornography through the use of a peer-to-peer sharing network. Although he began viewing child pornography as early as 2007, there is no suggestion that the Defendant paid money to obtain these images or that he was a member of an online community centered on child exploitation. The Defendant did not protect his collection from detection. When confronted by law enforcement agents, the Defendant admitted responsibility for downloading and viewing the images of child pornography on his computers. The size of the Defendant's collection, 59 images, is unremarkable in light of the fact that 67.6% of cases involving § 2G2.2 enhancements involve 600 or more images. United States Sentencing Commission, Child Pornography Report at 209. Further, the type of images at issue in this case is, like the case as a whole, sadly routine.

In summary, while the offense in question is serious, the enhancements applied to the Defendant in this case yield a sentence that is greater than necessary to achieve § 3553(a)'s purposes.

2. History and Characteristics of the Defendant

Prior to his arrest in this case, the Defendant was a productive member of the community with no criminal history. From January 1, 2010 to July 24,2013, the Defendant was a highly successful physician at the Ohio State University Medical Center. PSR at ¶ 76. During this time, the Defendant worked as a full-time clinician, an associate professor in radiation oncology at the James Cancer Hospital, and the Residency Program Director for the OSU Medical Center. Id. Before his employment with the OSU Medical Center, the Defendant worked as a resident and then full-time assistant professor at the M.D. Anderson Cancer Center in Houston, Texas from 2001 to 2009. Id.

Although successful in his academic and professional endeavors, the Defendant experienced a turbulent, and, at times, traumatic childhood. Id. at ¶ 38. The Defendant also reported being sexually abused on three separate instances as a child. Id. First, when he was three or four years, an adult in the home fondled the Defendant. Id. Several years later, when he was six, after swimming at a neighbor's pool, the neighbor sexually assaulted the Defendant while he was changing. Id. A year later, the Defendant's paternal aunt fondled him and tried to force him to kiss her. Id. The Defendant attempted to inform his grandparents of the molestation, but their response was unsupportive and they reprimanded the Defendant for "talk[ing] dirty." Id.

Throughout his adult life, the Defendant received intermittent mental health counseling. PSR at ¶¶ 51–53. In 1997, the Defendant was diagnosed with Attention Deficit Disorder and Generalized Anxiety Disorder in 2003. Id. at ¶ 51. Following his arrest, the Defendant began to attend outpatient mental health therapy with Rachel Beauchamp. Id. at ¶ 54. Beauchamp summarized her treatment of the Defendant, noting that he presented with symptoms of depression and alcohol abuse. Id. She assessed the Defendant for Post-Traumatic Stress Disorder (PTSD) and sexual abuse issues. Id. The Defendant's PTSD symptoms included traumatic memories, flashbacks and dissociative symptoms resulting from his childhood sexual abuse. Id. Based on the Defendant's description of symptoms, Beauchamp treated him for PTSD with dissociative symptoms and alcohol use disorder, early full remission. Id. Beauchamp reported that she is working with the Defendant to address the link between his traumatic memories and the viewing of child pornography as a way to make sense of intrusive mental images of his own abuse. Id. at ¶ 55. The Defendant has attended sessions on a weekly basis and fully complied with Beauchamp's treatment program. Id. at ¶ 54.

On November 14, 2013, the Defendant underwent a psychological evaluation with Dr. Myron Kimmel. Id. at ¶ 56. Kimmel interviewed the Defendant and his wife, tested the Defendant, and reviewed Beauchamp's reports. Id. In his interview, the Defendant reported that he began to use peer-to-peer programs to download pornography more than ten years ago. Id. at ¶I 59. In 2005, he reported downloading child pornography "accidentally." Id. As he began to search for and view images of child pornography, he remembered his past molestation as a child. Id. Psychological testing indicated that the Defendant suffered from PTSD, generalized anxiety disorder, and alcohol abuse. Id. at ¶¶ 60–62. Kimmel concluded that there was no indication that the Defendant attempted, or considered attempting, a contact offense, and therefore he was at the "lowest level of risk." PSR at 'If 63. In conclusion, Kimmel recommended that the Defendant continue treatment with Beauchamp and to continue his regimen of psychiatric medications. Id.

In the Court's view, the Defendant's childhood experiences as a victim of sexual abuse act as a significant mitigating factor in this case. See United States v. Janosko, 355 F. App'x 892, 894 (6th Cir. 2009) (treating defendant's sexual abuse as a child as a mitigating factor when sentencing child pornography offender); United States v. Prisel, 316 F. App'x 377, 382 (6th Cir. 2008) (same); United States v. Grober, 595 F. Supp. 2d 382, 410 (D.N.J. 2008) (same); United States v. Hanson, 561 F. Supp. 2d 1004, 1007 (E.D. Wis. 2008) (same). The Defendant's lack of criminal history also weighs in favor of a lesser sentence of incarceration. See United States v. Qualls, 373 F. Supp. 2d 873 (E.D. Wis. 2005) ("It is appropriate for a court, when considering the type of sentence necessary to protect the public and deter future misconduct, to note the length of any previous sentences imposed. Generally, a lesser period of imprisonment is required to deter a defendant not previously subject to lengthy incarceration than is necessary to deter a defendant who has already served serious time yet continues to re-offend."). Further, the Defendant's age, education, minimal criminal history, and acceptance of responsibility are indicative of a low-risk offender, amenable to rehabilitation. Melissa Hamilton, The Child Pornography Crusade and Its Net-Widening Effect, 33 Cardozo L. Rev. 1679, 1726 (2012). Finally, the Court considers the Defendant's struggles with PTSD resulting from his childhood sexual abuse to be an additional mitigating factor in his favor.

3. Deterrence and Protection of the Public from Future Crimes of the Defendant

The Government submits that "a significant term of incarceration is a necessary and appropriate specific deterrence measure in this case." Govt.'s Sentencing Mem. at 6. In its view, a sentence of incarceration "will serve as an example to other potential offenders who may not appreciate the gravity of this conduct, and that the possibility of lengthy terms of incarceration will deter those individuals from committing similar offenses." Id. The Sixth Circuit has recognized that "[g]eneral deterrence is crucial in the child pornography context" because "the logic of deterrence suggests that the lighter the punishment for downloading and uploading child pornography, the greater the customer demand for it and so the more will be produced." United States v. Robinson, 669 F.3d 767, 777 (6th Cir. 2012) (internal citations and quotations omitted). "Affording adequate deterrence is also closely linked to reflecting the seriousness of the offense." United States v. Rothwell, 847 F. Supp. 2d 1048, 1069 (E.D. Tenn. 2012) (citing Robinson, 669 F.3d at 777). The Court considers the need for general deterrence in this case accordingly.

In this case, the Court finds the need for general deterrence more compelling than the need to protect the public from future crimes of the Defendant. On supervised release, the Defendant "will be at low risk of recidivating because of the restrictions on access to online material that the conditions of supervised release . . . [will] impose." United States v. Robinson, 714 F.3d 466, 468 (7th Cir. 2013). Moreover, following his conviction, the Defendant will be subject to the Sex Offender Registration and Notification Act, which will impose additional restrictions on the Defendant. 42 U.S.C. §§ 16901 et seq. Further, as the Court previously noted, the Defendant's individual characteristics indicate that he is a good candidate for rehabilitation, further reducing the likelihood of him committing future crimes. Polygraph testing confirmed that the Defendant has never abused children, PSR at ¶ 17, and additional psychological examination indicated that the Defendant was at the "lowest level of risk" for committing a contact offense, Id. at ¶ 63.

4. Sentencing Disparities

Subsection 3553(a)(6) is concerned with national disparities among the many defendants with similar criminal backgrounds convicted of similar criminal conduct. <u>United States v. Greco</u>, 734 F. 3d 441, 451 (6th Cir. 2013). In 2012, less than 33% of child pornography offenders were sentenced to within-guideline sentences. United States Sentencing Commission, 2012 Sourcebook of Fed. Sentencing Statistics, Table 28 (2012), available at http://www.ussc.gov/sites/default/files/pdf/research-and-publications/annual-reports-and-sourcebooks/2012/Table28.pdf (last visited July 2, 2014). In 2011, for nonproduction child pornography offenses, 28% of defendants received sentences of less than five year imprisonment, 5% of defendants received sentences of one year or less, and 2% of defendants received sentences of probation-only. Hamilton, <u>Sentencing Adjudication</u> at 447–48 (citing United States Sentencing Commission, <u>Commission Datafiles</u>, http://www.ussc.gov/research-and-publications/commission-datafiles). The Court sentences the Defendant with these statistics in mind.

C. *Sentence*

At sentencing, after calculating the Defendant's guideline range, the Court questioned the parties regarding what they believed would constitute a reasonable sentence in this case. (Sentencing Tr. at 25). The Government stated its belief "that a sentence between 18 and 48 months would be appropriate." (<u>Id.</u>). In response to the Court's enquiry, the Defendant asserted that a sentence of 12 months would be a reasonable punishment under the circumstances. (<u>Id.</u> at 25–26). The Court considered the parties' representations in fashioning its sentence in this case.

The Defendant's actions and their consequences in this case will deprive the community of a highly-gifted and renowned pediatric oncologist. In letters to the Court, the Defendant's colleagues have testified to his skill and expertise as a physician and scientist. Moreover, the Defendant's patients and colleagues described him as a caring and tireless advocate for children suffering from cancer. Undoubtedly, the Defendant's skills and expertise as a pediatric oncologist would be put to better use outside of prison. While his conviction will likely end his career as a practicing physician, the Defendant's medical research knowledge, and skill are of unique value to the community. The Court believes this is a unique mitigating factor which supports a sentence below the guideline range.

In determining the Defendant's sentence, the Court has weighed the relevant 3553(a) factors. A sentence of incarceration is consistent with Congress's retributive judgment that child pornography offenses are reprehensible. Further, a term of imprisonment will serve Congress's established interest in the general deterrence of child pornography offenses. Nonetheless, the Court will limit the Defendant's term of incarceration in light of the Defendant's lack of criminal history, childhood sexual abuse, struggles with PTSD and depression, his amenability to rehabilitation, and his potential contribution to society in the fight against childhood cancer. For the foregoing reasons, the Court finds that a sentence of 12 months and one day imprisonment, a $10,000 fine, and a term of five years of supervised release is sufficient to reflect the seriousness of the offense, to promote respect for the law, and to provide just punishment for the offense. See 18 U.S.C. § 3553(a)(2)(A). The Court appreciates that the Defendant's sentence is a significant variance below his guideline range. The Government's recommendation that the Defendant serve a sentence as low as 18 months imprisonment supports the Court's conclusion that a variance of this magnitude is justified in this case.

Absent the restrictions of the Sixth Circuit's Bistline decisions, the Court would find that a further downward variance would be appropriate in this case based upon the Court's policy disagreement with the child pornography guidelines. This Court's policy disagreement with the child pornography guidelines are based on the very same criticisms expressed by the sentencing commission as discussed in <u>Bistline</u>.

At sentencing, the Government requested the opportunity to file specific objections to the Court's written Opinion and Order. (Sentencing Tr. at 44–45). The Government's request is GRANTED. Either party may file objections within seven days of the Court's Opinion and Order being issued.

IT IS SO ORDERED.
s/ James L. Graham
JAMES L. GRAHAM
United States District Judge
DATE: JULY 21,2014

---

[1] The Seventh, Eighth, and Tenth Circuits appear to recognize district courts' broad authority to reject guidelines on policy grounds under Kimbrough while remaining skeptical of district courts that reject § 2G2.2 for policy reasons. See Melissa Hamilton, Sentencing Adjudication: Lessons from Child Pornography Nullification, 30 Ga. St. U. L. Rev. 375, 428–432 (2014) (hereinafter "Hamilton, Sentencing Adjudication").

[2] Bistline v. United States, 134 S. Ct. 1514 (2014) (denying certiorari); Bistline v. United States, 133 S. Ct. 423 (2012) (same); Miller v. United States, 132 S. Ct. 2773 (2012) (same).

FDA Advisory Statement on PTSD

By *Esther Giller and Elizabeth Vermilyea*

Thank you for the opportunity to attend this meeting and to present to the FDA information about posttraumatic stress conditions and the need for increased understanding and treatment. The Sidran Institute is a national nonprofit organization exclusively dedicated to educating professionals and the public about traumatic stress conditions, including PTSD.

PREVALENCE

Kessler et al. (1995) found that 60% of men and 51% of women in the general population reported at least one traumatic event at some time in their lives. Almost 17% of men and 13% of women who had some trauma exposure had actually experienced more than three such events. These data are consistent with several prevalence studies on PTSD.

The NIH National Comorbidity Survey found that childhood sexual abuse was a very strong predictor of the lifetime likelihood of PTSD. The trauma most likely to produce PTSD was found to be rape, with 65% of men and 45.9% of women who had been raped developing PTSD (Kessler, et al, 1999). This study shows that PTSD is associated with nearly the highest rate of service use and possibly the highest per-capita cost of any mental illness.

CHRONICITY

Epidemiologic studies demonstrate that PTSD is a chronic problem for many people. Studies of chronicity demonstrate 33-47% of PTSD patients reporting experiencing symptoms more than a year after the traumatic event (Davidson, 1991 & Helzer, 1987).

In a focused study of severe PTSD, Ford (1999) demonstrated exceptionally high levels of service use among patients meeting criteria for DESNOS (Disorders of extreme stress not otherwise specified). Switzer et al. (1999) studied service use among clients with

PTSD at an urban mental health center and found 94% of clients had a history of trauma and 42% had PTSD. Switzer documented especially high levels of service use among those with PTSD as compared to others.

Leserman et al. (1998) and Freidman and Schnurr (1995) showed that PTSD is also associated with high levels of use of non-mental health services. An HMO study (Walker et. al., 1999) reported substantially increased healthcare costs among patients who reported childhood trauma. (Hidden costs include medical costs for suicidal and parasuicidal behaviors as well as other somatoform and psychophysiological disorders commonly reported by trauma survivors.)

Child sexual and physical abuse may not only produce PTSD in some, but may increase PTSD susceptibility in response to later, adult stressors (Briere, Woo, McRae, Foltz, & Sitzman, 1997, Journal of Nervous and Mental Disease). People who have experienced assaultive violence (interpersonal victimization) at home or in the community, have also been shown to be at very high PTSD risk (21%) (Breslau, et. al., 1998, Archives of General Psychiatry).

COMORBIDITY

The moderating effects of PTSD can significantly complicate any other co-occurring disorder including developmental disorders. Persons with PTSD are likely to have at least one other mental health disorder. Even in the most conservative studies, people with PTSD were two to four times more likely than those without PTSD to have almost any other psychiatric diagnosis (Kessler et. al., 1995). Somatization was found to be 90 times more likely in those with PTSD than in those without PTSD. This shows an important but frequently overlooked connection between PTSD and physical complaints.

Many people with PTSD turn to alcohol or drugs in an attempt to escape their symptoms. Clients who are dually diagnosed with substance abuse and PTSD may benefit from trauma treatment instead of or in addition to traditional model substance abuse programs.

THE COST OF TRAUMA

Early outcome studies showed that early diagnosis and appropriate treatment of trauma-related disorders are cost effective, especially when compared with the cost of incorrect or inadequate treatment occurring prior to a correct diagnosis (Loewenstein, 1994).

Ross and Dua (1993) studied women with trauma related dissociative disorders who were admitted to an inpatient service over four years. Prior to correct diagnosis, the patients had averaged 98.77 months in treatment. Following a correct diagnosis, they averaged 31.53 months in the system. Before diagnosis, about 2.8 million dollars (Canadian) had been spent on treatment for this group. If the 98.77 months prior to correct diagnosis were reduced to 12 months, the estimated savings would be $250,000 per patient.

In a study of rape victims, Koss et. al. (1990) found that severely victimized female members in an HMO had outpatient medical expenses double those of control HMO members.

Findings suggest that from 3.1 to 4.7 million crime victims received mental health treatment in 1991, for an estimated total cost of $8.3 to $9.7 billion (Cohen & Miller, 1994). These recipients represent only a small portion of trauma victims in need of treatment, since those with PTSD are typically reluctant to seek professional help.

Recent outcome data has largely focused on veteran populations. Fontana & Rosenheck (1997) found that short-term specialized programs to treat PTSD were more cost effective and beneficial than either long-term specialized units or non-specialized programs. Although this study does not address those who suffer with chronic PTSD from childhood trauma, it does demonstrate the efficacy of specialized treatment delivered in an accessible, cost effective manner.

MARGINALIZED POPULATIONS

There has been increasing attention paid to PTSD resulting from high-profile "single blow" traumas, such as school shootings, transportation disasters, etc. But PTSD resulting from chronic trauma (such as experiencing or witnessing childhood abuse, domestic violence, and interpersonal victimization in the community) is not well known in the general population, among primary health care providers, or even among mental health care providers in many settings. Also, male survivors of abuse (perhaps the most marginalized subgroup of all) are frequently overlooked, even within the trauma-focussed survivor empowerment movements and specialized trauma treatment units.

MISDIAGNOSIS

Misdiagnosis and incorrect or inadequate treatment is not unusual for adults and children with PTSD. For example, refractory depression, substance abuse, and eating disorders, among others, often mask underlying but undiagnosed PTSD. Flashbacks and other dissociative episodes can frequently be mistaken for psychosis (especially schizophrenia), and unnecessary anti-psychotic medication can undermine treatment progress. Schools increasingly report disciplinary problems with no understanding that some children may be suffering from violence-related trauma disorders rather than ADHD or ADD. Consequently, they are improperly treated with Ritalin, while their real problems remain unaddressed.

EDUCATION

There is a dearth of treatment providers properly trained to recognize and treat PTSD, especially complex chronic types, and the topic is rarely addressed in universities and professional schools. Public education about PTSD is lacking as well, with lay people commonly associating PTSD with combat and little else.

CONCLUSION

These data clearly indicate the critical need for recognition of and appropriate treatment for survivors of traumatic experiences who develop traumatic stress-related mental health conditions. In addition to research and development of pharmaceutical and psychotherapeutic treatment approaches, successful intervention depends on a two-fold approach to education: in professional and treatment settings, as well as in the patient population and general public. Since primary care physicians and community mental health staffs are most likely to see people with PTSD, they must learn to ask about trauma exposure, recognize symptoms of PTSD, and refer patients appropriately.

Educating professionals first is paramount to managing the influx of clients that will certainly follow public awareness programming. The Sidran Foundation is actively involved in a variety of trauma education initiatives.

REFERENCES

Cohen, M.A. & Miller, T.R. (1994). Mental health care for crime victims. Nashville, TN: Vanderbilt University.

Davidson, J.R.T., Hughes, D., & Blazer, D. et. al. (1991) Posttraumatic stress disorder in the community: An epidemiological study. Psychological Medicine, 21, 713-721.

Fontana, A., & Rosenheck, R.A. (1997). Effectiveness and cost of the inpatient treatment of posttraumatic stress disorder: Comparison of three models of treatment. American Journal of Psychiatry, 154, 758-765.

Ford, J.D. (1999). Disorders of extreme stress following war-zone military trauma: Associated features of posttraumatic stress disorder or comorbid but distinct syndromes? Journal of Consulting and Clinical Psychology, 67, 3-12.

Freidman, M.J. & Schnurr, P.P. (1995). The relationship between trauma, post-traumatic stress disorder and physical health. In M.J. Freidman, D.S. Charney & A.Y. Deutch (Eds.), Neurobiological and clinical consequences of stress: From normal adaptation to post-traumatic stress disorder (pp. 507-524).

Helzer, J.E., Robins, L.N., & McEvoy, L. (1987) Posttraumatic stress disorder in the general population. New England Journal of Medicine, 317, 1630-1634.

Kessler, R.C., Sonnega, A., Bromet, E. (1995). Posttraumatic stress disorder in the national comorbidity survey. Archives of General Psychiatry, 52, 1048-1060.

Kessler, R.C., Zhao, S., Katz, S.J., Kouzis, A.C., Frank, R.G., Edlund, M.J., & Leaf, P. (1999). Past-year use of outpatient services for psychiatric problems in the National Comorbidity Survey. American Journal of Psychiatry, 156, 115-123.

Leserman, J., Li, Z., Drossman, D.A., & Hu, Y.J.B. (1998). Selected symptoms associated with sexual and physical abuse history among female patients with gastrointestinal disorders: The impact on subsequent health care visits. Psychological Medicine, 28, 417-425.

Loewenstein, R.J. (1994). Diagnosis, epidemiology, clinical course and cost effectiveness of treatment for dissociative disorders and MPD: Report submitted to the Clinton administration task force on health care financing reform. Dissociation, Vol. VII, No. 1, March 1994.

Ross, C.A. & Dua, V. (1993). Psychiatric health care costs of multiple personality disorder. American Journal of Psychotherapy, 47, 103-112.

Switzer, G.E., Dew, M.A., Thompson, K., Goycoolea, J.M., Derricott, T., & Mullins, S.D. (1999). Posttraumatic stress disorder and service utilization among urban mental health center clients. Journal of Traumatic Stress, 12, 25-39.

Walker, E.A., Unutzer, J., Rutter, C., Gelfand, A., Saunders, K., Vonkorff, M., Koss, M.P., & Katon, W. (1999). Costs of health care used by women HMO members with a history of childhood abuse and neglect. Archives of General Psychiatry, 56, 609-613.

Description of Traumatic Amnesia
From: *Diagnostic and Statistical Manual of Mental Disorders*

Fifth Edition. American Psychiatric Association, 2013

The individual afflicted with dissociative amnesia reports gaps in recall for aspects of their personal history. There are chunks of time in their past which they are unable to recall. Some traumatic or stressful event or events are associated with the loss of memory … the following criteria must be met in order for a diagnosis of dissociative amnesia to be arrived at:

CRITERION A: an inability to recall information of a very personal nature. The inability may be the outcome of an underlying trauma or stress. The inability to recollect cannot be attributed to normal forgetfulness.

CRITERION B: memory is reversibly impaired. Memories of personal nature cannot be recalled in verbal form. Even if it is temporarily retrieved, the memory cannot be retained wholly in one's consciousness. The impairment does not occur exclusively during the course of other dissociative disorders (such as dissociative identity disorder, dissociative fugue, etc), PTSD, acute stress disorder, or somatization disorder. The impairment is also not a result of substance abuse, and it is not due to any neurological or general medical condition.

CRITERION C: the symptoms of the disorder are such as to cause clinical stress which is significant in nature, and which can impair the subject's social, occupational, or other areas of functioning.

SELECTIVE AMNESIA: Here, the individual is not able to recall all that happened in an event, just a select few tidbits. For instance, a rape victim might be able to recall just parts of the event of rape and not the full event in its entirety… Individuals suffering from dissociative amnesia also tend to report symptoms of depression, anxiety, depersonalization, trance states, analgesia, and spontaneous age regression. The disorder usually also co-occurs with sexual dysfunction, impairment in relationships, self-harm and suicidal impulse, as also aggressive impulse.

DNA Methylation Mechanisms in Trauma and PTSD

From: "Epigenetic Risk Factors in PTSD and Depression,"
by *Florian Joachim Raabe* and *Dietmar Spengler.*

Frontiers in Psychiatry, 4:80 (Aug. 7, 2013; PMID: 23966957).

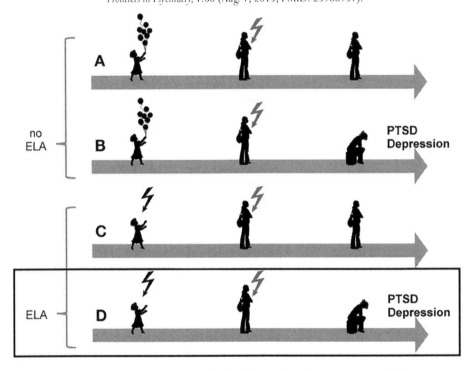

Model for the role of early-life adversity for PTSD and depression. In the absence of a history of early life adversity (ELA), adults can be resilient to disease upon exposure to severe trauma and stress (A) while others will develop PTSD or depression (B). Similarly, not all children exposed to early life adversity will develop disease upon a new exposure to trauma and stress (C). On the other hand, exposure to early life adversity in childhood can give rise to a vulnerable phenotype predisposing to disease upon anew exposure to trauma and stress (D).

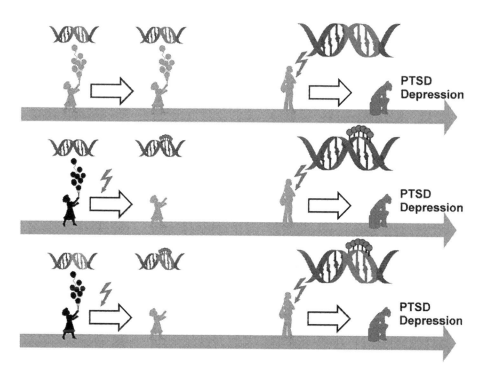

Model for epigenetic risk factors in PTSD and depression.
Genetic mutations can confer an increased vulnerability to PTSD and
depression which manifest following a new exposure to stressful life
events (flash symbol). Although carrying a predisposition to disease,
such individuals can stay healthy in the absence of trauma and stress
(upper panel). Early life adversity (flash symbol) can elicit epigenetic programming of stress genes via DNA (de-)methylation (symbolized by lollipops on DNA double helix) leading to altered expression.
These alterations confer an increased vulnerability to later on trauma
and stress and ultimately result in manifestation of PTSD and depression (middle panel). Genetic mutations (lightest segment of the DNA
double helix) can serve as a substrate for epigenetic programming in
response to early trauma and stress (flash symbol) via DNA (de-)meth-
ylation (symbolized by lollipops on segment of DNA double helix).
This pre-activation can result in PTSD and depression following a new
exposure to trauma and stress (lower panel).

Supporting Bibliography

Child Pornography Law and Psychology

Justice Perverted: Sex Offense Law, Psychology, and Public Policy. Charles Patrick Ewing. Oxford, UK: Oxford University Press, 2011.

Reconsidering Sex Crimes and Offenders: Prosecution or Persecution? Lisa Anne Zilney and Laura J. Zilney. Westport, CT: ABC-Clio, 2009.

"Contact Sexual Offending by Men with Online Sexual Offenses." M.C. Seto, R.K. Hanson, and K.M. Babchishin. *Sexual Abuse,* 23(1):124–145 (2011).

"The Consumption of Internet Child Pornography and Violent and Sex Offending." J. Endrass, F. Urbaniok, L.C. Hammermeister, C. Benz, T. Elbert, A. Laubacher, and A. Rossegger. *BMC Psychiatry,* 9:43 (2009).

"Pornography and Rape: Theory and Practice? Evidence from Crime Data in Four Countries Where Pornography Is Easily Available." B. Kutchinsky. *International Journal of Law and Psychiatry,* 4(1–2):47–64 (1991).

Post-Traumatic Stress Disorder and Sexual Abuse

"Influences of Maternal and Paternal PTSD on Epigenetic Regulation of the Glucocorticoid Receptor Gene in Holocaust Survivor Offspring." R. Yehuda, N.P. Daskalakis, A. Lehrner, F. Desarnaud, H.N. Bader, I. Makotkine, J.D. Flory, L.M. Bierer, and M.J. Meaney. *American Journal of Psychiatry,* 171(8):872–880 (2014).

"Epigenetic Risk Factors in PTSD and Depression." F.J. Raabe and D. Spengler. *Frontiers in Psychiatry,* 4:80 (2013).

"Childhood Maltreatment Is Associated with Distinct Genomic and Epigenetic Profiles in Posttraumatic Stress Disorder." D. Mehta, T.

Klengel, K.N. Conneely, A.K. Smith, A. Altmann, T.W. Pace, M. Rex-Haffner, A. Loeschner, M. Gonik, K.B. Mercer, B. Bradley, B. Müller-Myhsok, K.J. Ressler, and E.B. Binder. *Proceedings of the National Academy of Sciences,* 110(20):8302–8307 (2013).

"Childhood Trauma and Risk for PTSD: Relationship to Intergenerational Effects of Trauma, Parental PTSD, and Cortisol Excretion." R.Yehuda, S.L. Halligan, and R. Grossman. *Development and Psychopathology,* 13(3):733–753 (2001).

The Courage to Heal:A Guide forWomen Survivors of Child Sexual Abuse. Ellen Bass and Laura Davis. NewYork, NY: Collins Living, 2008.

Miscellaneous Referenced Medical Articles

"FANCD2 Is a Potential Therapeutic Target and Biomarker in Alveolar Rhabdomyosarcoma Harboring the PAX3-FOXO1 Fusion Gene." M. Singh, J.M. Leasure, C. Chronowski, B. Geier, K. Bondra, W. Duan, L.A. Hensley, M. Villalona-Calero, N. Li, A.M. Vergis, R.T. Kurmasheva, C. Shen, G. Woods, N. Sebastian, D. Fabian, R. Kaplon, S. Hammond, K. Palanichamy, A. Chakravarti, and P.J. Houghton. *Clinical Cancer Research,* 20(14):3884–3895 (2014). Note: Acknowledgements list C.E. Pelloski, N. Beeler, and I. Snyder.

"Mental Health and Stigma in the Medical Profession." J.E. Wallace. *Health* (London), 16(1):3–18 (2012).

"The Future of Radiation Oncology in the United States from 2010 to 2020: Will Supply Keep Pace with Demand?" B.D. Smith, B.G. Haffty, L.D. Wilson, G.L. Smith, A.N. Patel, and T.A Buchholz. *Journal of Clinical Oncology,* 28(35):5160–5165 (2010).

Pertinent Online Resources

"First comprehensive report on U.S. cancer care finds patient access threatened by growing demand, physician shortages, struggling small physician practices." American Society of Clinical Oncology press release on the anticipated cancer specialist shortage: http://www.asco.org/first-comprehensive-report-us-cancer-care-finds-patient-access-threatened-growing-demand-physician (Accessed Oct. 9, 2014)

National Center for Missing and Exploited Children. http://www.missingkids.com/home

Sidran Institute—Traumatic Stress Education and Advocacy: http://www.sidran.org/

United States Sentencing Commission, Report to the Congress: Federal Child Pornography Offenses: http://www.ussc.gov/news/congressional-testimony-and-reports/sex-offense-topics/report-congress-federal-child-pornography-offenses (Accessed Oct. 9, 2014)

Made in the USA
Middletown, DE
09 February 2021